Social Security for Future Generations

Sustainability, Equity, Simplification

John A. Turner
Serena E. McCarthy

To my wife and daughter, Kathy and Sarah,
and my parents, Henry and Mary.
JAT

To my parents, David and Ellen McCarthy,
who always encouraged me as a writer.
SEM

Social Security for Future Generations: Sustainability, Equity, Simplification
Copyright © 2026 by John A. Turner and Serena E. McCarthy

All rights reserved. Please respect the intellectual property rights of authors and publishers. No part of this book may be used or reproduced in any manner whatsoever without written permission from the publisher, except in cases of cited quotations and references in articles, reviews, and academic journals in accordance with US Fair Use laws.

Published by Upriver Press
P.O. Box 51455
Colorado Springs, CO 80949
upriverpress.com

ISBN Print Version: 9798991284721
ISBN Ebook: 9798991284738

Library of Congress Control Number: 2025933953

Cover Design: James Clarke (jclarke.net)

Printed in the United States of America

Upriver Press publishes books by leading scholars and experts who bring well-researched, evidence-based ideas to public discourse. The views of our authors do not necessarily represent the opinions of the staff at Upriver Press.

Social Security for Future Generations

Sustainability, Equity, Simplification

John A. Turner
Serena E. McCarthy

Contents

1. Social Security Is in Dire Need of Reform — *9*
2. Fairness — *33*
3. What Reforms Do Americans Want? — *39*
4. Improving the Reform Process — *53*
5. Social Security Contributions and the Tax Code — *69*
6. Ideas from Financial Literacy Research — *85*
7. Simplifying Social Security — *107*
8. Improving Information and Assistance — *129*
9. Social Justice and Equity Proposals — *137*
10. Supporting Low-Wage Workers — *151*
11. Proposals Relating to Changes in Actuarial Factors — *157*
12. Proposals Inspired by the US Pension System — *167*
13. Lessons from Other Countries — *177*
14. Reforming Government Programs That Affect Social Security — *191*
15. New Revenue Sources for the Short-Run Shortfall — *197*

Epilogue: Social Security for Future Generations	*213*
Appendices	**217**
1. Summary of Proposals	*217*
2. Why Population Aging Makes Social Security Reform More Difficult	*235*
Acknowledgements	*241*
About the Authors	*243*
Works Cited	*245*
Index	*311*

CHAPTER 1

Social Security Is in Dire Need of Reform

Social Security celebrated its ninetieth anniversary on August 14, 2025. When President Franklin D. Roosevelt signed the Social Security Act in 1935, he spoke of *negative* liberty, which is freedom from government interference in personal affairs—an idea founded on the Bill of Rights. Roosevelt also emphasized the importance of *positive* liberty, which is financial freedom achieved through government programs, including Social Security. He called this the *new* Bill of Rights (Goodwin 1995).

Franklin and Eleanor Roosevelt's lives reflect the demographic changes that have affected Social Security since its inception. Even though President Franklin had access to the best medical care available at the time, he died of a stroke in 1945 at age sixty-three (Goodwin 1995). He thus did not survive long enough to be eligible to receive Social Security benefits. Eleanor Roosevelt died from tuberculosis in 1962 at age seventy-eight (Green 2025). In that year, tuberculosis killed 9,506 people (US Centers for Disease Control and Prevention 2024). As bad as that situation was, it was far better than the roughly sixty-one thousand tuberculosis deaths in 1940 (Communicable Disease Center 1951).

Over the years, the number of tuberculosis deaths continued to drop; in 2022, the disease killed 565 people (US Centers for Disease Control and Prevention 2024). Eleanor Roosevelt died from a disease that now affects annually only 0.8 people out of one hundred thousand US-born residents of the United States (US Centers for Disease Control and Prevention 2025). These tremendous improvements in medicine serve as one measure of America's overall public health progress since the start of Social Security.

Today, demographic changes are making Social Security more expensive to finance than in the past. The program's future is being impacted by the ratio of retirees to workers, which is called the *old-age dependency ratio*. Demographic changes affect this ratio in three ways: the birth rate, life expectancy (mortality), and immigration. Changes in mortality and life expectancy have been dramatic, but analysis shows that changes in the birth rate have been the most important factor affecting the old-age dependency ratio (Huston and Isaacs 2025).

Roughly ten thousand baby boomers will turn sixty-five every day until 2030. This population group is growing at one of the fastest rates in American history (West Health Institute 2017). In 2000, thirty-five million Americans were at least sixty-five. By 2030, with the retirement of the baby boom generation, the number of people in that age group is projected to reach seventy-four million (Antonelli 2018).

When younger generations think about the future of Social Security, they see storm clouds on the horizon. A National Opinion Research Center survey found that 70 percent of Americans age thirty and older believed the country is not well-prepared to address the needs of the rapidly growing older population (West Health Institute 2017).

This book addresses a situation that will affect the lives of future generations of Americans. Some books about Social Security reform focus primarily on restoring solvency, which is the most important issue. Our book also devotes considerable thought to broader issues related to the program, including other government programs that affect it.

Changes Since Social Security Began

The Social Security Administration began monthly benefit payments in 1940 when the average worker earned less than $1,000 a year (Goodwin 1995). A lot has changed since Congress enacted this legislation. For example, the ratio of beneficiaries to workers in 1960 was one to five; in other words, there were five workers for every beneficiary. By comparison, this ratio in 2025 was roughly one to three. Social Security actuaries project it to be one to two by 2030 (Durante 2024b). The cost of funding the program, therefore, is being borne by fewer workers relative to retirees.

What does this mean in terms of costs per worker? Social Security is a pay-as-you-go system. In 1960, it cost each worker $200 in payroll taxes (on average) to pay each beneficiary $1,000 in benefits. By 2030, each worker will need to pay $500 on average to pay each beneficiary $1,000 in benefits. These numbers indicate the magnitude of the effect of population aging on the cost per worker of providing Social Security benefits.

In addition to the increase in the ratio of beneficiaries to workers, other economic and demographic changes have increased the need for Social Security reform. Inequality in wage earnings and income has worsened. Changes in pension law have increased the inequality in assets held in pension plans. Americans have relied more on defined contribution plans, such as 401(k) plans, and less on defined benefit plans, such as the employer-funded plans that previous generations of workers received. Average life expectancy has increased, but primarily for Americans with higher incomes and education levels. Other factors include falling marriage rates and the increasing labor force participation of women.

Favreault, Samartino, and Steuerle (2002a) wrote, "Since Social Security's inception, sweeping social and demographic shifts have radically altered the structure of the American family." These changes include increased divorce rates and higher rates of single-parent households. Families may include two parents, same-sex parents, only one parent, grandparents, and other relatives. These changes have made some aspects of Social Security outdated. In this book, we examine changes that have occurred in America over the past ninety years that heighten the need for Social Security reform.

Why Social Security Is the "Third Rail" of American Politics

We have known about these warning signs for a long time; nevertheless, it has been more than forty years since the last major reform of Social Security (1983). In this respect, the United States is a remarkable exception among wealthy countries. Most have reformed their social security programs during those decades (Borsch-Supan and Coile 2020).

In the US, the primary reason for a reluctance to reform the system is political. In some ways, political hesitation to implement reforms seems to be at odds with broad awareness of the program's looming shortfalls. According to a survey by the Nationwide Retirement Institute (2024), "Americans are increasingly alarmed about Social Security's solvency and more than three in four (79 percent) US adults believe the Social Security system needs to change." Everyone sees the need, but politicians are hesitant to do anything to help.

In fact, to even talk about reforms today is viewed as dangerous for politicians. As House Speaker Thomas "Tip" O'Neil, a Democrat, stated in the 1980s, Social Security is the "third rail" of American politics, which was a reference to the electrified third rail of the Washington, DC Metrorail system. He implied that Social Security is "murderous to touch" (Shenkman 2005). Policy analysts sometimes call the topic of Social Security reform "the elephant in the room" (Fortune 360 Group 2024). Some people call it "political kryptonite" (Grassley 2024), a reference to the radioactive material that debilitated Superman. Still, lawmakers understand that delaying reforms will make matters worse. Republican Senator Charles Grassley, age ninety-two in 2025, wrote, "The longer Washington kicks the can down the road, the tougher it will be to secure solvency."

Continuing to do nothing is a bad choice. In 2014, the Committee for a Responsible Federal Budget (2014) wrote, "If Congress waits until the 2030s to act, the needed changes to keep the program solvent would be significantly larger and more difficult." However, it appears that Congress is adopting the traditional strategy of waiting until a crisis occurs to provide cover for making unpopular but necessary decisions. The hesitancy to implement reforms showed up again during the 2024 election. Presidential candidates from both major parties offered to cut income taxes to attract votes, but neither proposed the idea of reforming Social Security.

For decades, policy analysts have been advocating for Social Security reform. Steuerle and Bakija (1994) wrote, "Because of the imbalance between promised benefits and available taxes, some reform of Social Security is inevitable." And according to Arnold (1998), "The one position that virtually everyone who studies Social Security shares is that reforming Social Security expeditiously is preferable to waiting until the problem becomes more severe."

Mitchell, Myers, and Young (1999) edited a book titled *Prospects for Social Security Reform*. In the introduction, they wrote the following: "There is no immediate crisis, since projected system revenues are projected to be adequate to pay promised benefits for about twenty years. But ideally, well before the crisis arrives, reforms must be implemented for the Social Security system to continue to play a key role in Americans' retirement."

Early in this century, some policy experts were optimistic that reform of Social Security was imminent. Aaron and Reischauer (2001) wrote a book titled *Countdown to Reform*, with a clock on the cover showing the time of 11:53, indicating that reform would soon occur at midnight. Favreault, Sammartino, and Steuerle (2002a) wrote, "Social Security, the largest of all federal programs, is likely to undergo many legislative changes early in this century." Diamond and Orszag (2004) noted that twenty years had passed since a major reform and that aspects of Social Security had become outdated.

Despite these predictions, more than forty years have passed without any major reforms. Congress and presidents have procrastinated, resulting in uncertainty as to the timing and nature of Social Security reforms. Delays have increased the likelihood that solutions will be implemented at the last minute, as happened in 1983. The past thirty-five annual reports of the Social Security Trustees (including 2025) have projected trust fund depletion, but Congress has not addressed the problem (Goss 2024). Nevertheless, the program has paid scheduled benefits consistently and in full for more than eighty-five years (starting in 1940).

Without reforms, Social Security will eventually become insolvent. In 2025, Social Security's actuaries projected that the Old-Age and Survivors Insurance (OASI) trust fund, which finances Social Security, would be depleted in 2033. They projected the same thing in 2024. The insolvency date was moved to late 2032 when Congress passed President Trump's One Big Beautiful Bill Act in mid-2025. That law, which will expire in 2028 unless Congress extends it, reduced income taxes on Social Security benefits for most older Americans (Committee for a Responsible Federal Budget 2025). According to the Social Security Administration (2025j), the law eliminated federal income taxes for nearly 90 percent of Social Security beneficiaries. Social Security actuaries have projected that, at the time of trust fund depletion, the program will be able to pay only 77 percent of scheduled benefits.

Social Security reform is already harder to accomplish than it was in 1983. The American Academy of Actuaries (2023) provided an excellent explanation for why that is the case.

> The last time the trust funds were close to depletion was in 1983. The cash shortfall that year was 1 percent of taxable payroll. In contrast, the expected cash shortfall in 2034 will be three times as large (3.12 percent of taxable earnings), so paying all benefits that year will require much larger tax increases and/or benefit reductions

than in 1983. If Congress cannot agree on Social Security reform until 2034, enacting benefit reductions for only those who become eligible for benefits in 2034 or later will not help, so delay could force them to increase Social Security taxes by 25 percent in 2034 (unless Congress is willing to break its tradition of not cutting benefits already being paid or is willing to use general revenue). That may be difficult, as Congress may also need to enact tax increases to keep Medicare's Hospital Insurance Trust Fund from being depleted around 2031.

Delays increase the severity of the reforms required. In 1983, Social Security was fully funded over the seventy-five-year projection period. By 2007, the deficit was 2 percent of taxable payroll (Gokhale 2010, p. 173). By 2024, the deficit had risen to 3.5 percent of taxable payroll. With one additional year of delay, to 2025, the deficit had risen to 3.82 percent of taxable payroll (Van Bramer 2025). Ongoing procrastination will likely lead to substantial benefit cuts and/or tax rate increases.

If policymakers acted in the best interests of Social Security participants, Social Security would be reformed as quickly as possible (Committee for a Responsible Federal Budget 2016b). Because the problem worsens with delay, the process is one of accumulating errors, which are errors that get worse over time. By acting sooner, the difficult effects of reforms would be dispersed across more years and more workers. In the mid-1990s, Steuerle and Bakija (1994) wrote, "That future reform is inevitable, and not simply a political intention, is crucial for policymakers and the American public to comprehend." In 2010, the Urban Institute (2010) wrote that, "modest adjustments can restore solvency."

Sadly, that is no longer the case. Necessary reforms will have a stronger impact on Americans than if Congress had made changes sooner. Americans seem to understand this reality. A Bankrate survey in 2025 found that 72 percent of American workers are worried that Social Security's promise of future benefit payments will not be kept (Gillespie 2025).

The Committee for a Responsible Federal Budget (2016b) argued that it is important to overcome policy inertia and reform Social Security as soon as possible. They argued that it is a myth that Congress can postpone Social Security reform without serious consequences. To make a point, the organization showed that benefit cuts (including for current beneficiaries) in 2016 would have been 16 percent. By postponing those cuts to 2026, current beneficiaries would see benefits drop by 20 percent. If the benefit cuts *excluded* current beneficiaries, the cuts would need to be 20 percent in 2016 and 33 percent in 2026. Steuerle and Kramon (2024) stated the situation this way: "Politicians tend to avoid discussing this hard reality, recognizing how unpopular the solutions are. But something has to give. It's time for us all to grow up."

Policy inertia is related to the unpopularity of common solutions. A 2024 survey indicated that only 20 percent of Americans wanted to better fund Social Security by increasing taxes on workers. By comparison, 34 percent favored the idea of making employers pay higher taxes, and 47 percent wanted to increase taxes on people with higher incomes. As Margenau (2022) argued, Americans' resistance to increased taxes explains why Congress struggles to reform Social Security. "The fault, dear Americans, is not in our politicians but ourselves."

In other words, Social Security is seen as a "the third rail" because responsible politicians who propose reasonable reforms often lose elections to opponents who say those solutions will lead to benefits cuts. Arnold (1998, p. 391) wrote, "Legislators are extraordinarily attentive to what they hear from constituents, careful about how they deal with organized interests, and cautious when they cast major votes, calculating how specific votes might look in the middle of the next campaign if challengers decide to focus attention on them."

Passing legislation to reform Social Security is further complicated by the fact the Senate would need at least sixty votes (Primus, Watson, and Smalligan 2025). For example, the Social Security Fairness Act, signed into law in 2025, required sixty votes in the Senate (Pecorin 2024). Other types of legislation can be passed with a simple majority of fifty-one votes, such as with an expedited reconciliation process. However, those approaches cannot be used to change Social Security benefits or the payroll tax.

In addition to the barriers described above, broader economic and cultural trends also stymie those who wish to implement Social Security reforms.

The Inequality Factor

It is important to recognize that Social Security functions within a broader US retirement income system. Policy analysts have described this system as a "three-legged stool." One leg is Social Security. The other two are pensions and private savings. Social Security's role and effectiveness are affected by the other two legs. And all three are affected by the growing inequality in wealth among Americans.

Traditional solutions to Social Security's problems focus on payroll tax rate increases and benefit cuts. These solutions are politically difficult to implement because both proposals, if they are applied to *everyone,* are particularly onerous for lower-income workers.

Moreover, changes to US pension law have strongly benefitted the wealthiest Americans. Turner (2025) examined nine features of pension law (ERISA) that particularly benefit high-income workers. Seven of the nine features were enacted since 2000, suggesting that the pension system has become more inequitable since then. For example, between 2000 and 2024, the maximum annual contribution to a 401(k) plan for individuals age fifty or older, including catch-up contributions, rose from $30,000 to $76,500. Because most workers with 401(k) accounts contribute less than $30,000 a year, this change only benefited upper-income workers who can afford to contribute substantially more each year. In 2024, the average total of employer and employee contributions for participants in 401(k) plans was $13,570 (Brumley 2025).

In addition to pension and retirement savings plans, people also try to prepare for retirement by building equity in an owner-occupied home and by investing in stocks and bonds. The laws around this system allow the top income quintile to receive 84 percent of the tax expenditures that result from the deduction of mortgage interest on owner-occupied homes. This population also receives 95 percent of the tax expenditures that result from the net preferential tax rates on capital gains and dividends (Congressional Budget Office 2021). Both factors make the US tax system less progressive; that is, less beneficial to people with less wealth and lower incomes. For these reasons, we argue that Social Security reforms should shift more of the cost to workers in the top income quintile. Doing so would offset the large tax subsidies they receive for other forms of retirement savings.

When the Social Security Act took effect, and for several decades afterward, economists generally assumed that most citizens would be rational about their financial affairs. They believed that most people were well-informed about the economic issues that affected their lives and that they would make well-considered decisions. That is no longer the case. Drawing insights from psychology, sociology, and finance, economists came to recognize that most Americans lack time to obtain quality information, or that they simply lack interest in economic issues. Complex systems can be challenging for many people to understand, and people may not be able to devote the necessary effort to make thoughtful choices. And many people lack basic financial literacy.

There is no question that most Americans find Social Security to be a complex and confusing program. And because average Americans are working hard to pay bills and feed their families, they typically do not have the time or energy to learn more.

Disinformation, Polemical Viewpoints, and Polarization

Addressing Social Security reform has also been hindered by disinformation, polemical viewpoints, and ideological differences. Discussions among economists and business leaders about Social Security reform frequently become controversial and heated, which makes it harder to address the "third rail." Reforms in the current era of retrenchment are difficult because they require benefit cuts, payroll tax increases, or both. Also, political polarization is increasing, making Social Security reform even more challenging (Gallup 2024a).

Disinformation has caused widespread confusion about Social Security. For example, prominent people have falsely claimed that Social Security is a Ponzi scheme. Milton Friedman (1999), a conservative Nobel Prize-winning economist from the University of Chicago, who was a graduate professor for one of this book's authors, claimed that Social Security is "the biggest Ponzi scheme on Earth." More recently, Elon Musk, the wealthiest person in the world, and presumably someone knowledgeable about finance, also called Social Security a Ponzi scheme (West 2025). Thankfully, leading economists have debunked this view. McDade (2014) at the Urban Institute argued that, "Social Security is not a Ponzi scheme," and West (2025) at the Brookings Institution, stated that Musk's claim was an example of "why Social Security disinformation is dangerous."

A Ponzi scheme is a fraudulent investment ploy that fools people into believing they are making high-return investments when in fact their money is being used to pay the "investment returns" of earlier investors. Eventually, these schemes fall apart when investors discover the fraud and new investors stop depositing money. Bernie Madoff operated the largest Ponzi scheme in history. He defrauded investors out of an estimated $65 billion over seventeen years (Hayes 2024).

Social Security does share a minor similarity with a Ponzi scheme: Both are both pay-as-you-go systems, meaning that those who pay into the system fund other people. In the case of Social Security, the money contributed by current workers pays the benefits of current retirees. However, some critics of Social Security have used this minor similarity to distort the truth.

Social Security is fundamentally different than a Ponzi scheme. A key difference has to do with intergenerational transfers of wealth, which occur from parents to children when the children are young, and from adult children to their older parents when the parents are retired. Historically, working-age family members have supported older family members who are no longer able to work. This income transfer is done partly in recognition of the transfers they received when they were young, and partly due to the knowledge that when they are older and unable to work, the younger working-age family members will support them. This same principle of intergenerational transfers underlies Social Security. Current workers have the assurance that a new generation of workers will support them when they retire. The motivation for Social Security is to provide retirement benefits for millions of Americans. By contrast, a Ponzi scheme is run by a criminal whose sole motivation is personal profit.

In short, Social Security is not a fraudulent Ponzi scheme. The implied claim that participants will eventually be big losers because Social Security will not pay their benefits is false. Social Security is a government program that has paid promised benefits for decades. With the proper reforms, the program can continue to help millions of Americans for generations to come.

Principles for Reform

In this section, we discuss basic principles for Social Security reform, including principles that address issues arising from the complexity of Social Security and the low level of financial literacy in American society.

Solvency and Adequacy

Solvency refers to "the ability of the Trust Funds to pay 100 percent of currently scheduled benefits" (Social Security Administration 2023d, p. 1). Social Security's actuarial balance, "often measured over seventy-five years, summarizes Social Security's current trust fund balance and annual future streams of revenues and outlays as a single number" (Congressional Budget Office 2023).

A major goal of Social Security reform proposals is to restore solvency. The Committee for a Responsible Federal Budget (2023a) stated, "Any Social Security reform plan should, first and foremost, extend the solvency of the program to avoid the automatic cuts scheduled under current law." The projected trust fund depletion date would be delayed, but only slightly, if Congress passed legislation combining the Old-Age and Survivors Insurance (OASI) and Disability Insurance (DI) Trust Funds into a single OASDI Trust Fund.

Related to solvency is the *adequacy of benefits,* including the effect of benefits on alleviating poverty. According to AARP (2023), "Solvency proposals must ensure meaningful benefits for future generations." Social Security benefit reductions would likely increase poverty rates among older adults. Those reductions would disproportionately harm Black and Hispanic beneficiaries who, on average, rely more heavily on Social Security benefits as a source of retirement income (Johnson and Smith 2024).

Sustainability

As the Committee for a Responsible Federal Budget (2023a) argued, "Comprehensive reform should achieve *sustainable solvency* to ensure benefits can be paid in full for the next seventy-five years and beyond." According to the Government Accountability Office (2023c, p. 2), "Sustainable solvency means the actuaries project that the difference between Social Security's assets and costs will be positive throughout a seventy-five-year period and stable or rising at the end of that period."

The OASDI Trustees (2024) explained the concept of sustainable solvency as follows: "If lawmakers design legislative solutions only to eliminate the overall actuarial deficit without consideration of year-by-year financing, then a substantial financial imbalance could remain for 2098, the end of the seventy-five-year valuation period. In that case, the long-range sustainability of program financing could still be in doubt."

Sustainability, therefore, may require reductions in scheduled benefits, but those reductions do not need to be across the board. Reforms could cut benefits for higher-income Americans who would remain well-off despite this change. When evaluating proposals that reduce Social Security benefits, the sustainability of Social Security is not the only issue to consider. Another important criterion is equity.

Equity

In this context, *equity* refers to fair treatment of people in relation to age, birth year, gender, race and ethnicity, income, education, marital status, and life expectancy.

First, we need to consider *earnings inequality*; specifically, the changes over time in Americans' real wages. Over the three decades following World War II, average real wages (corrected for inflation) for nonsupervisory workers grew 91 percent. By comparison, between 1979 and 2013, average real wages of nonsupervisory workers grew by only 9 percent. Between 1979 and 2013, the wages of the top 1 percent of wage earners grew 138 percent, while the average wages of the bottom 90 percent grew only 15 percent. Over that period, wages of the median worker grew only 6 percent, less than 0.2 percent per year, compared to a decline of 0.2 percent per year for the bottom 10 percent of wage earners. For workers in the ninety-fifth percentile, the average annual wage growth was 1 percent per year (Mishel, Gould, and Bivens 2015). Thus, there have been large differences in the wage growth of the top earners compared to the falling wages of the lowest earners.

Some researchers say those numbers are too simplistic. Biggs (2025) argued that real wages have declined for many workers because health insurance costs have risen. Real compensation, which is gross earnings before subtracting the cost of health insurance, has increased. That might be the case, but our point stands: The percentage of earnings that is not subject to the Social Security payroll tax because it is above the payroll tax ceiling has increased. This is arguably a major cause of the decline in Social Security's finances compared to the expectations following the 1983 reform (Walker 2025).

Another issue related to equity is *intergenerational equity*. Congressional procrastination may allow baby boomers to be unaffected by Social Security benefit reductions and payroll tax increases. However, inevitable reforms in the 2030s could disproportionately affect millennials and younger generations. "The generation likely to feel the biggest financial burden of fixing Social Security will be millennials" (Hannon 2024). It would be more equitable to pass reforms as soon as possible so that more generations would share the burden of the reforms.

The next equity concern is *income inequality by race*. Social Security reforms could address the systemic disadvantages linked to the racial wealth gap between most minorities and Whites. Kenney and Boyens (2023) noted that if Social Security is not changed, "Black beneficiaries will receive an estimated 26 percent less in median lifetime benefits than White beneficiaries, a difference of about $140,000 over a lifetime." This racial gap in Social Security benefits stems from multiple disadvantages, but lower earnings account for the largest portion of the gap (Johnson and Smith 2023).

People of color, people without a college degree, and people who never marry are more likely to have inadequate retirement income (Kenney and Boyens 2023). Benefit cuts for all beneficiaries would therefore be most harmful to those who rely most heavily on Social Security benefits as a source of income, such as those with low lifetime earnings and inadequate retirement savings, widows, and very old people (Committee for a Responsible Federal Budget 2023a).

Equity concerns also include *life expectancy and education*. The life expectancy gap between people without a bachelor's degree and those with one has greatly expanded over time. This has had important implications for Social Security reform. In 2021, with life expectancy slightly decreased by the Covid-19 pandemic, people without a bachelor's degree had a life expectancy of age seventy-five whereas people with a degree had a life expectancy of age eighty-three, a gap of eight years. Twenty years earlier, the gap was only two years (Rubin 2023).

Other countries have raised the retirement ages for their social security programs (Chen and Turner 2007). Raising Social Security retirement ages may appear equitable if we only consider the average life expectancies for men and women, but life expectancies in the United States vary greatly by income and education. Data show that lifespan inequality has been increasing over time, in conjunction with rising income inequality (Burtless, 2016). Given the widening gap in life expectancy between the wealthy and those with low incomes, proposals to raise retirement ages would disproportionately affect low-income workers with shorter life expectancies (Burtless 2016).

The last major Social Security reform, in 1983, gradually raised the full retirement age by a total of two years over two six-year periods, 2000 to 2005 and 2017 to 2022. Congress legislated this increase in anticipation of increases in life expectancy (Diamond and Orszag 2004, p. 58). That increase resulted in a monthly benefit cut that was expected to be offset in terms of lifetime benefits by greater life expectancy. However, Case and Deaton (2021) found that between 2010 and 2018 (the end of their study period), life expectancy declined for people without a bachelor's degree. For people with a bachelor's degree, life expectancy rose during this period. The people in the bottom half of the life expectancy distribution depend the most on Social Security benefits; thus, they should receive special consideration.

Simplification

Steuerle and Bakija (1994) wrote, "Reform is most likely to succeed if it returns to basic principles such as progressivity, equity, and efficiency." To that list, we add *simplicity*. Social Security is unnecessarily complex with inconsistent rules and confusing terminology. Kotlikoff (2012) argued that Social Security is so complex that few people completely understand its rules. "I hate to admit this, but I may be one of the twenty top experts in the country on Social Security provisions. But even I am learning new Social Security provisions over time."

Sherri Goss (2009), who is a certified financial planner, explained that Social Security is so challenging that even she has made mistakes. "Unfortunately, sometimes I make mistakes when explaining the benefits. Why? For the same reason that some people at Social Security sometimes make mistakes. Social Security is very complicated and technical. Add to that the fact that personal situations differ, and it's pretty easy to inadvertently make an error."

Simplification of Social Security could improve participants' decisions. If they better understand the consequences of choosing one option or another (such as claiming benefits earlier rather than later), they will at least be making thoughtful choices. Simplification could also reduce the frequency of Social Security Administration payment errors and related issues.

In its criteria for evaluating reform proposals, the Government Accountability Office (2023c) stated, "How readily a proposal could be implemented, administered, and explained to the public" must be considered (GAO 2023c, p. 1). Social Security's retirement earnings test is a widely misunderstood aspect of the program (GAO 2023c).

A simplified Social Security program would significantly help workers. First, reducing complexity would make it easier for workers to understand the program. As it is now, many workers do not understand basic Social Security issues that affect them, such as how large their benefits will be. Turner, Zhang, Hughes, and Rajnes (2019) found that some workers either considerably overestimate or underestimate their likely future Social Security benefits. Relatively few have an accurate estimate. With advances in technology, such as artificial intelligence (AI) and robo advisors, Social Security could do more to help individuals understand the program's benefits and options.

Turner and Muir (2014) examined ways to help workers learn more about financial literacy and how to find financial advice, which can help them better understand Social Security. Hadass, Labouré, Shen, and Turner (2020) discussed new approaches to communicating with workers that could improve workers' understanding of Social Security. Good communication can increase workers' trust in Social Security and alleviate fears that they might not receive their scheduled benefits.

The complexity of Social Security can lead workers to retire sooner than they should. A simplified program, combined with better efforts to educate workers, can help people see the financial benefits of staying in the labor force longer. We have designed proposals to encourage people to continue working, particularly at early retirement ages.

Simplification of the program can also occur by using automatic adjustments to benefits or contributions. This approach is used in some other countries. Automatic adjustments typically "become effective once a trigger indicates a need for an adjustment, and they periodically adjust the program without the need for legislation" (American Academy of Actuaries 2018, p. 1). Munnell (2023a) argued that any Social Security reform package should "include a mechanism that automatically adjusts revenues or benefits if shortfalls emerge" to avoid recurrent future funding problems. Such measures can support the goals of sustainable solvency and intergenerational equity. Earlier reforms would more equitably share the costs of reform across generations. These adjustments could also apply to economic and demographic changes, such as declines in marriage rates and increases in the inequality in life expectancy between low-income and high-income workers.

A simplified Social Security program should improve workers' ability to predict their future benefits with some accuracy. In her survey of criteria for social security reform, Bielawska (2021) included the importance of predictability. For workers, predictability should stem from helping them better understand how their Social Security benefits are determined and Social Security's stability in providing those benefits. Workers generally cannot predict the outcome of last-minute reforms. This lack of predictability is especially a problem for workers who are nearing retirement or who are unsure of the possible outcomes.

An Overview of This Book

Those are the key issues relating to Social Security reform. The remainder of the book focuses on proposals for Social Security reform, examining the program from different perspectives. We do not attempt to create a full set of proposals to restore solvency for seventy-five years. Instead, we focus primarily on new proposals that we think should be included in a reform package.

We address issues of fairness in Social Security reform, and we present survey data on how Americans would like Social Security to be reformed and what they know (and do not know) about Social Security. Some of our proposals apply to the Social Security reform *process*. Some proposals derive from the history of Social Security. Others apply to the federal income tax system or the importance of financial literacy. We raise the importance of simplification, in part because more than half of adults read at less than a sixth-grade level (Gaehde 2022). And we give attention to issues of social justice along with the unique needs of low-wage workers. Some of our solutions pertain to actuarial adjustments, the US pension system, and ideas from other countries. We present proposals that will provide an immediate influx of revenue.

We do not consider proposals for privatizing Social Security, such as mandating that all citizens have a retirement account. We do not favor privatization because of the financial market risks for Social Security beneficiaries; however, we do encourage people to have good voluntary savings habits. Two of our proposals involve the novel use of private sector investments to help fund Social Security.

We propose changes that are justified on grounds of equity. Low-income workers need higher Social Security benefits. By comparison, high-income workers receive most of the tax subsidies in the private pension system. The changes to Social Security that we propose, on net, will reduce the need for across-the-board payroll tax hikes and benefit cuts.

CHAPTER 2

Fairness

Before President Franklin Roosevelt established Social Security, families traditionally took financial responsibility for their parents during old age. They did this, in part, out of gratitude for the help they had received from their parents when they were young, and in recognition that their older parents were not able to support themselves by working. Also, the younger generation recognized that they would one day need help when they were older. Social Security has provided some support for older family members. Levin (2023) referred to Social Security as a system of organized gratitude of the younger generation toward their parents.

An important issue in Social Security reform is fairness between older and younger generations. Social security reforms worldwide, in the last three decades, have systematically imposed an increased burden on those who have not yet retired while generally sparing those who have already retired.

Social Security reforms typically protect the benefits of current beneficiaries because those people are usually unable to work or make other changes to offset benefit cuts. Thus, current workers must bear the full costs of reforms. Many believe that benefits for future retirees are a promise that should be honored for those near retirement.

A common belief is that Social Security reforms in the era of population aging always involve winners and losers, with some individuals ending up worse off than they would otherwise be. However, these conclusions are often based on a misleading comparison. If the comparison is whether people are better or worse off than their current status quo, that is a misleading standard. It ignores the reality that, without a reform, beneficiaries would face a substantial cut in benefits. The appropriate comparison is whether a given reform leads to better or worse conditions for people compared to no reforms and the resulting automatic benefit cut.

Current workers might be chagrined to pay increased taxes for older generations; however, it is helpful for them to remember that good Social Security reforms will enable *them* to have protections when they are beneficiaries. The equity standard could be that current workers—the future beneficiaries—will be protected from Social Security reforms when they retire.

That said, today's workers will need to pay higher costs than current beneficiaries had to pay when they were working. With population aging and the associated increase in the old-age dependency ratio (the ratio of beneficiaries to workers), it will not be possible for future participants to have the same payroll tax rate as current participants without benefit cuts. It will be impossible to base the standard of intergenerational equity on equal treatment of different generations. The burden on younger generations will inevitably be higher because, as Fagin (2024) noted, "Over the past eighty years, the ratio of workers to beneficiaries has shrunk from forty-one to three." Thus, the financial approaches that worked well in the past will not remain viable.

A Spectrum of Inequities

In an opinion piece in *The New York Times*, Steuerle and Kramon (2024) argued that "the social safety net in the United States is increasingly favoring the old over the young." The authors specified how changes could be made to promote intergenerational equity. They also cited examples of the economic headwinds facing younger generations: student debt, lower net worth, and an inability to buy a home. The article argued that Congress should address the inequities between older and younger generations, in part by raising Social Security retirement ages and reducing the increase in lifetime benefits. The authors also argued that cuts in Social Security benefits could target people with high incomes. "Because many lower-income older Americans depend heavily on these programs, benefits for the wealthy could be the first target. And some of those savings could go to the neediest retirees, as well as programs for the young." As Hertel-Fernandez (2009, p. 6) stated, "A framework for true intergenerational equity would call for measures that maintain and strengthen social insurance safety nets for the elderly, particularly in ways that would reinforce existing positive cross-generational effects and reduce intragenerational disparities."

In addition to disparities *between* generations, the US also struggles with disparities *within* generations. Wealthy retirees can maintain a high quality of life regardless of Social Security income. However, despite improvements over time, poverty rates among people ages sixty-five and older are a concern. This is especially true for people who are eighty and older.

As Kuttner (2023) concluded, "Social Security is more essential than ever, given the collapse of decent pension plans engineered by corporations and Wall Street, to transfer all the risk to workers and retirees." For those with only a 401(k) plan, a financial market downturn early in retirement can cause serious financial problems. Older generations, during their working years, often had access to defined benefit plans, which are employer-sponsored pensions that provide retired employees with a series of retirement payments during the remainder of their lives. These plans are protected by the ERISA pension law, passed in 1974. So, people who worked in that era, before the advent of 401(k) plans, did not have to worry as much about financial market downturns during retirement or living longer than expected. By contrast, a study found that 60 percent of 401(k) participants worry that they will run out of money from their plan if they live sufficiently long in retirement (Godbout 2025).

Fairness between men and women is another key issue. Women are more likely than men to struggle financially during retirement. They usually have lower income levels during their working years and they typically have longer life expectancy. In recent decades, more women have developed well-paying careers, but on average they still "receive lower Social Security benefits, have lower retirement account ownership rates and lower estimated retirement account balances, and own fewer assets than men" (Fritzberg and Shadrina 2024). The gender gap in retirement security is larger for women of color than for White women (Fritzberg and Shadrina 2024). Social Security benefit cuts could be a problem for many older women, who may be widowed or lack other sources of retirement income.

Women are also more likely than men to be caregivers to family members and, thus, to be out of the paid workforce. Sixty-one percent of eldercare providers are employed (US Bureau of Labor

Statistics 2023b). Fourteen percent of the population, 37.1 million people, provide unpaid eldercare. Most of those people (59 percent) are women. Female caregivers often reduce their work hours, decline promotions, take leaves of absence from work, or even quit their jobs to care for others. The Family Caregiver Alliance (2015) explained how these work-related decisions can have long-term consequences for women's financial security later in life.

> Caregiving places a further strain on the precarious nature of many women's retirement income, particularly since time out of the workforce does not only have short-term financial consequences. For most women, fewer contributions to pensions, Social Security and other retirement savings vehicles are the result of reduced hours on the job or fewer years in the workforce.

Some caregivers experience health problems related to being or having been caregivers (Family Caregiver Alliance 2015). Health issues can interfere with their ability to work even after caregiving responsibilities have ended. Time out of the workforce can erode a person's job skills.

Caregivers can benefit from the Social Security Caregiver Credit Act of 2023, which amended "the Social Security Act to credit individuals serving as caregivers of dependent relatives with deemed wages for up to five years of such service" (Congress.gov 2023b). This Act, which recognizes the needs of vulnerable groups, was passed without any increase in Social Security funding to pay for it. It specifies how deemed wages are determined for caregivers. Caregivers can take care of spouses or older or younger relatives. This law can also help "sandwich generation" caregivers who care for an older and younger relative, such as their parents and a grandchild.

Despite these challenges, it is possible to make changes to Social Security that provide equity and improve the solvency outlook. Before we present our proposals for reform, it is helpful to understand the types of changes that Americans want. Lawmakers and policymakers, in a democratic society, will benefit from that knowledge. That is the topic of the next chapter.

CHAPTER 3

What Reforms Do Americans Want?

Republicans and Democrats, perhaps unsurprisingly, have disagreed about how to approach Social Security reform. In 2024, Republicans in the House of Representatives proposed raising the full retirement age, which is currently sixty-seven, for those who reached age sixty-two in 2024 or later (Konish 2024). However, raising the full retirement age would be a nontransparent way of cutting Social Security benefits. This option is "functionally equivalent to reducing benefits" (American Academy of Actuaries 2017, p. 8). The 2024 Republican proposal for Social Security reform also included further reducing Social Security benefits for Americans with high earnings (Konish 2024).

Democrats, by comparison, would like to protect Social Security benefits. This can be done, for example, by imposing the payroll tax on individual earnings over $400,000 per year (Konish 2024). The Social Security 2100 Act, proposed in 2023 by Representative John Larson, a Democrat, involved a "doughnut hole." The hole referred to a "tax-free zone" between the Social Security payroll tax cap of $176,100 (in 2025) and $400,000. Earnings over $400,000 would be taxable (Fabino 2023). In response to this idea, Social Security actuaries estimated that the proposed payroll taxation of annual earnings above $400,000 "would push back insolvency by ten years." It would also reduce the long-term funding shortfall by about 60 to

63 percent (McIsaac 2024; Social Security Administration 2024bb).

We need to consider what politicians think and plan, but as a democratic nation that is supposed to rely on self-governance, it is also important to discuss what surveys have revealed about Americans' views regarding Social Security's long-term future and possible options for reform. We start by looking at what Americans think about the program's importance and future.

Perspectives on Social Security's Value and Future

Americans are deeply concerned about the future of Social Security. The 2024 Nationwide Retirement Institute (NRI) Social Security Survey found that more than three out of four respondents (79 percent) strongly agreed (30 percent) or somewhat agreed (49 percent) with the following statement: "The Social Security system needs to change" (Nationwide Retirement Institute 2024, p. 6). In this survey, 72 percent of respondents strongly agreed (34 percent) or somewhat agreed (38 percent) with this statement: "I worry about the Social Security program running out of funding in my lifetime" (Nationwide 2024, p. 5). Men (69 percent) were less likely to agree with that statement than women (75 percent). However, most men and women expressed concern about Social Security's future. Surveys show that women tend to worry more than men about Social Security's future.

In retirement, women are more likely than men to be single, divorced, or widowed, and they may struggle due to a lack of financial support from a spouse (American Academy of Actuaries 2017). Between 2025 and 2095, the Social Security Administration projected that an increasing proportion of women will receive Social Security benefits based on their work, rather than their spouse's work (Social Security Administration, 2024b).

Americans also want to learn more about Social Security. Studies show that many men and women, including those near retirement age, have limited knowledge of Social Security. Only two in ten participants in the Financial Literacy Center's telephone survey reported feeling "very knowledgeable" about how Social Security works. By contrast, 57 percent described themselves as "somewhat knowledgeable" (Schneider and others, 2010, p. 2). Most of these respondents overestimated their knowledge. Only 22 percent received a grade of A or B on a seven-question Social Security Literacy Quiz. Half received a D or F. Those with higher education and higher income scored higher. The Financial Literacy Center's survey showed that most respondents (89 percent) expressed a desire for the Social Security Administration to play a more significant role in educating the public, as they felt it was "very important" for the Agency to inform them about how Social Security works (Schneider and others, 2010, p. 5).

A similar survey by Massachusetts Mutual Life Insurance Company gave respondents a thirteen-question Social Security quiz (MassMutual 2024). In this online poll of near-retirees (ages fifty-five to sixty-five) who had yet to claim Social Security benefits, less than 1 percent of respondents got a perfect score on the quiz, while 78 percent received a grade of D (37 percent) or F (41 percent). Clearly, workers need and want more education to improve their knowledge about Social Security. We also believe that simplifying Social Security, particularly by reducing complicated terminology, will address Americans' desire for a better understanding of the program. Social Security is an overly complex system that demands participants to have an unrealistically high level of financial knowledge (Bauer 2021).

Americans are eager to see Congress act on Social security reforms that protect its long-term future. Most older adults receive or will receive Social Security OASI benefits. As the Center on Budget and Policy Priorities (2024b) noted, "97 percent of older adults (ages sixty to eighty-nine) either receive Social Security or will receive it." A recent survey showed that an overwhelming 96 percent of respondents agreed that it is important to "reform Social Security so it is available for current retirees and younger generations" (Peter G. Peterson Foundation 2023a).

In addition, most Americans would like Congress to reform Social Security as soon as possible. A 2023 survey found that 87 percent of Americans wanted Congress to act immediately instead of waiting another decade to address Social Security's funding shortfall (National Institute on Retirement Security 2024).

In an AARP (2020) survey, 39 percent of respondents indicated that they rely on or plan to rely on Social Security "in a substantial way." Another 43 percent responded that they rely on or plan to rely on it "somewhat." The National Institute on Retirement Security (2020) estimated that Social Security is the sole source of retirement income for 40 percent of older Americans, despite the original designers of Social Security intention for it to be supplemented by other sources of retirement income.

Despite their strong desire to see the long-term success of Social Security, many Americans are not confident that it will be there for them in the future. Gallup polls conducted over many years (2005 to 2024) have consistently shown that most Americans worry about Social Security "a great deal" or "a fair amount" (Gallup 2024b). These polls show a surprising level of distrust in a federal program that has paid scheduled benefits on time for decades. A 2023 Gallup poll asked people this question: "Do you think the Social Security system will be able to pay you a benefit when you retire?" Fifty percent of non-retirees said yes and 47 percent said no (Gallup 2024b). These results align with Gallup's historical data. In Gallup's 1989 survey, the results were nearly identical (Gallup 2024b). Thus, even though Social Security's finances were in good shape for more than four decades, a sizable proportion of Americans distrusted the program's future. Confidence in the future of Social Security declined seven percentage points between 2020 and 2025, from 43 percent to 36 percent, according to surveys conducted by AARP (2025). Levels of distrust in Social Security are not aligned with its past reliability.

Americans' Views on Proposed Reforms

This section discusses survey data on what changes Americans would and would not like Congress to include in future Social Security reforms.

Reducing Benefits. The most important survey result, in our view, relates to Social Security benefit cuts. A 2023 poll by The Associated Press-NORC Center for Public Affairs Research found that 79 percent of Americans are opposed to Social Security benefit cuts (Seitz and Fingerhut 2023). A Gallup poll found that Americans tend to prefer increased Social Security payroll taxes (61 percent) as an alternative to reduced benefits (31 percent) (Jones 2023).

Some policy analysts have argued that a combination of benefit cuts and payroll tax rate increases would constitute a balanced approach to Social Security reform (e.g., Diamond and Orszag 2004). That approach is balanced in a mathematical sense, but polling data indicate that most workers prefer payroll tax increases more than benefit cuts. That poll might explain why the Bowles-Simpson National Commission on Fiscal Responsibility and Reform, created by President Barack Obama in 2010, failed. Leaders of that effort recommended the highly unpopular measure of significant benefit cuts to reduce Social Security's seventy-five-year budget deficit (Ruffing and Van Der Water 2011).

A poll for *Newsweek,* however, found that support for benefit cuts varies by age. As people grow older, their support for reducing Social Security benefits declines (Carbonaro 2024). In this poll, 30 percent of Gen Z respondents (born between 1997 and 2012) favored cutting Social Security benefits. By comparison, 20 percent of millennials (born between 1981 and 1996) wanted to reduce benefits. Only 11 percent of Gen X respondents (born between 1965 and 1980) liked that type of reform. And a mere 3 percent of baby boomers (born between 1946 and 1964) wanted Congress to cut benefits (Carbonaro 2024). Similarly, The Associated Press-NORC survey (2023) found that opposition to cutting Social Security benefits was more common among adults who were forty-five and older (88 percent) compared to people younger than forty-five (70 percent). However, most adults in both age categories opposed cutting benefits.

There is much greater support for only cutting the Social Security benefits of the highest earners. The University of Maryland's Program for Public Consultation (2024) found that 92 percent of voters in six swing states favored reducing the benefits of the upper 20 percent of earners. Social Security's actuaries projected this reform could eliminate 11 percent of the funding shortfall (Program for Public Consultation 2024).

Increasing the Full Retirement Age. Raising the full retirement age (FRA) is another idea with limited public support, presumably because it is a benefit cut. Three out of four Americans oppose increasing the FRA from sixty-seven to seventy (Seitz and Fingerhut 2023). A Data for Progress poll of voters found that only 8 percent of respondents (5 percent of Democrats, 9 percent of Independents, and 9 percent of Republicans) thought that the FRA should be increased above its current level of sixty-seven (Jacobs 2023). In this poll, voters were more likely to favor *lowering* the FRA to below sixty-seven (45 percent) or keeping it the same (43 percent) (Jacobs 2023).

Some proposals have suggested raising both the FRA and the earliest eligibility age (EEA), which is sixty-two (Social Security Administration 2024u). However, this raises a concern about a lack of equity, because those with more education and higher incomes have longer life expectancies. Raising either the FRA or EEA, or both, would mostly hurt those with less education and lower incomes.

Despite these concerns, most Americans think that postponing retirement will be inevitable. One survey asked participants to respond to the following statement: "By 2050, most Americans will work into their seventies to have enough resources to retire." An overwhelming majority (83 percent) said probably or definitely (Pew Research Center 2019). People in their seventies in 2050 would have been born in 1980 or earlier. The Young Adults and

Workplace Wellness Survey found that only 52 percent of adults between twenty-four and thirty-five expressed confidence in being able to retire when they wanted to. Only 21 percent stated that they were "very confident" that they would be able to do so (Georgetown University 2023). This survey found that "68 percent of young adults indicate they would like to retire before age sixty-five, [but] fewer than one-half (44 percent) expect that it will be possible" (Georgetown University 2023, p. 3).

Reduce the Cost-of-Living Adjustment. The annual cost-of-living adjustment (COLA) is designed to ensure that the purchasing power of Social Security benefits remains stable against inflation. The value of the COLA is computed each year based on data from the Consumer Price Index for Urban Wage Earners and Clerical Workers (Social Security Administration 2024l). This index "tracks monthly changes in goods and services for urban wage earners and clerical workers, representing about 32 percent of the US population" (Cagnassola 2023). In 2024, the COLA was 3.2 percent. In 2025, it was reduced to 2.5 percent due to decreased inflation.

Some policy analysts have argued for raising the COLA since older adults have greater out-of-pocket healthcare expenses than do younger adults. Those expenses increase more rapidly than the average rate of inflation (AARP 2012). The Consumer Price Index for the Elderly (CPI-E) is an experimental measure for Americans age sixty-two and older, which might more accurately reflect the actual expenses of older adults (Anderson 2024).

However, there are also proponents of a decreased COLA. They have argued that the current method for calculating the COLA overstates inflation because it fails to account for the substitution effect in consumer purchases. That effect occurs when consumers switch to lower-priced goods as a way of dealing with inflation. The chained consumer price index estimates the effects of inflation more accurately because it accounts for the effects of consumers switching to alternative goods with smaller price increases (AARP 2012, p. 3).

The Office of the Chief Actuary of the Social Security Administration (2023) evaluated the effect of using the CPI-E to calculate the COLA. It found that doing so would increase the annual COLA by about 0.2 percentage points, on average. By contrast, the actuaries have estimated that using the chained CPI-W to calculate the COLA would reduce it by about 0.3 percentage points, on average. Munnell (2024d) noted that the impacts of switching to the other indices roughly offset one another and argued that the current method for calculating the COLA is best. "In view of the offsetting effects—a 0.3 percent overstatement of inflation due to not accounting for the substitution effect and the projected 0.2 percent understatement due to not reflecting the spending patterns of the elderly—the current method of adjusting benefits seems just about right."

We agree with Munnell's argument that the unchained version of the CPI-W should continue to be used to calculate the COLA, as it is a reasonably accurate measure of inflation experienced by older individuals.

Increase the Payroll Tax Rate. Social Security OASI's primary funding source is payroll taxation of employers, employees, and self-employed workers. That source accounts for 90 percent of its funding (Congressional Budget Office 2020). Other income sources include interest on the government bonds held by the Social Security Trust Fund and personal income tax payments on Social Security benefits.

Surveys indicate that most Americans are open to increased payroll taxes as an alternative to cutting Social Security benefits. One study asked people to respond to the following statement: "It is critical to preserve Social Security even if it means increasing Social Security taxes paid by working Americans." Eighty-two percent of respondents agreed and half of those people strongly agreed (Tucker, Reno, and Bethell 2013, pp. 10-11). One option could be to gradually increase the OASDI payroll tax rate, for both workers and employers, from 6.2 percent to 7.2 percent over twenty years (Tucker, Reno, and Bethell 2013). Gallup's historical data from 2005 to 2023 indicate that, over time, an increasing proportion of Americans expressed a willingness to pay higher payroll taxes if the alternative were reduced benefits (Gallup 2024b). In a 2023 YouGov poll, 57 percent of respondents stated that Social Security should receive more funding. Those favoring the increase included 66 percent of Democrats and 54 percent of Republicans (Sanders, L 2023).

Raise Benefits. Raising benefits is something few countries have done in recent years. As stated earlier, population aging increases the old-age dependency ratio, which is the ratio of retirees to workers. That means a smaller number of workers must bear a heavier financial cost for a larger population of older beneficiaries. That makes it more difficult to increase their social security benefits in a pay-as-you-go system.

Mandatory Enrollment of Newly Hired State and Local Government Workers. As stated by the Congressional Research Service, "The largest and most high-profile group of noncovered workers is the segment of state and local government employees who participate in alternative public retirement systems that do not have a Social Security component" (Li 2024). Because these workers have alternative retirement arrangements, they do not contribute to the Social Security system. As of 2024, 27 percent of state and local government employees (5.9 million people) lacked Social Security coverage (Li 2024). These uncovered workers include police officers, firefighters, and public school teachers (Li 2024). In the Joint Center's poll, more than half of all Americans supported "enrolling all new state and local government employees in Social Security to foster solvency of the system" (Leigh and Wells 2013, p. 7).

Reduce the Old-Age Dependency Ratio. The old-age dependency ratio plays a key role in Social Security financing (Turner 1984). Because Social Security is essentially financed on a pay-as-you-go basis, this ratio acts like a shadow price; that is, it affects how much each worker must pay to fund Social Security benefits for the beneficiaries. A shadow price is the cost of something that people do not purchase in the market. For example, if there are ten workers for every Social Security beneficiary, it will cost each worker on average ten cents to raise the level of benefits per beneficiary by one dollar. By comparison, if there are five workers for every beneficiary, it will cost each worker twenty cents to raise each beneficiary's benefits by one dollar.

In 1950, there were sixteen workers per beneficiary. In 2021, the ratio was roughly three to one (The National Commission on Fiscal Responsibility and Reform 2010, Peter G. Peterson Foundation 2025b). The Simpson-Bowles Commission (2010) wrote, "Unless we act, these immense demographic changes will bring the Social Security program to its knees. Without action, the benefits currently promised under Social Security are a promise we cannot keep."

Various policies and cultural trends could affect the old-age dependency ratio. If more women and men were working, that would lower the ratio. If birth rates decreased, the country would see a higher old-age dependency ratio when those babies grew up and entered the workforce. A reduction in immigration would raise the ratio, in part because most immigrants are of working age. We could improve the ratio of workers to beneficiaries by reducing death rates related to drug addiction and suicide.

With these surveys of Americans' preferences for reforming Social Security in mind, we turn next to our solutions for reform. Our ideas are based on research and economic principles. Some will be favored by Democrats and some will be favored by Republicans. Each solution can be adjusted to accommodate policy preferences. And they are designed to avoid the "third rail" effect that lawmakers fear.

In general, we recommend incremental adjustments to the current system, while considering variations at different levels of effect. We use a multi-perspective approach to analyzing Social Security reform. Our proposals are categorized according to subject areas such as financial literacy, the US pension system, and social security programs in other countries.

Reforms that incorporate research about human behavior can help Social Security better serve participants who are not always rational or well-informed. The study of behavioral economics suggests several ways that Social Security could be reformed to improve participant outcomes.

The following quote gives emphasis to the importance of working together on policy reforms. "To save Social Security for the long haul, all of us must do our part. The most fortunate will have to contribute the most, by taking lower benefits than scheduled and paying more in payroll taxes. Middle-income earners who are able to work will need to do so a little longer. At the same time, Social Security must do more to reduce poverty among the very poor and very old who need help the most" (National Commission on Fiscal Responsibility and Reform 2010).

Hopefully, our proposals will inspire bipartisan reforms so that Social Security can serve millions of Americans for generations to come.

CHAPTER 4

Improving the Reform Process

In this chapter, we focus on ways to improve the *process* of reforming Social Security. Lawmakers, even when they want to make changes to Social Security, often run into procedural barriers that make it difficult to pass legislation. However, as we described in previous chapters, delaying reforms leads to worse outcomes for average Americans. By implementing change sooner, the reforms can be smaller and more gradual.

Our first proposal is to use automatic adjustment mechanisms for future Social Security reforms, which would compensate for the lack of timely legislative action. Munnell (2023a) stated that any Social Security reform package should include an automatic adjustment mechanism. This tool would involve predefined reforms that adjust program parameters—benefit amounts, contribution rates, and benefit eligibility ages—in response to a trigger that signals the need for changes. The resulting periodic adjustments can help keep the program on track financially, eliminating the need for policymakers to enact new reforms.

Saxegaard and others (2016) noted the main structural features of automatic adjustment mechanisms (AAMs): "There are four main structural features characterizing AAMs which are typically elevated into formalized legislation: (1) the trigger variables (i.e., the indicators used in determining when and how an adjustment should be made); (2) the adjusting parameters that are linked to the trigger indicators; (3) the frequency of adjustment; and (4) the boundaries of adjustments."

Automatic adjustments to Social Security can result in small, frequent changes. De Tavernier and Boulhol (2021, p. 85) explained that automatic adjustment mechanisms may be a way to "generate changes that are less erratic, more transparent and more equitable across generations." For example, automatic adjustments could result in modest, recurring changes in payroll tax contributions or future benefit payments.

Automatic adjustments would occur without congressional action. Policymakers can establish automatic adjustments that trigger predefined changes if they cannot agree on alternative reforms (De Tavernier and Boulhol, 2021). Thus, automatic adjustments can ensure that reforms will occur.

Automatic adjustments are a type of default. They have been used successfully in other aspects of pensions, such as automatic enrollment in 401(k) plans. They can be powerful tools for overcoming policy inertia, which often serves as a barrier to reform. "With an automatic adjustment mechanism, the default action is to change the system either by increasing taxes, reducing benefits, or both, and legislation would need to be enacted to prevent that change" (American Academy of Actuaries 2018, p. 6).

Saxegaard and others (2016, p. 4) also explained the advantages of automatic adjustments. "Automatic adjustments can theoretically make the reform process politically less painful and more likely to succeed." Similarly, Rajnes and Turner (2014, p. 16) noted that "automatic adjustment mechanisms reduce the political risk that no action will be taken until a crisis—rather, actions will be taken automatically, without the intervention of politicians." Policymakers could decide to override them. In that case, the predefined changes would not be implemented (Turner 2010).

The experience of other countries shows that politicians' ability to override automatic adjustments can be problematic. Rajnes and Turner (2014) noted that, in multiple countries, policymakers have chosen to override automatic adjustments. "One issue with these mechanisms has been how automatic they actually were in practice, with Sweden, Germany, and Italy making changes to the adjustment mechanism when unpopular adjustments were required. In 2009, Germany passed a law that, for the second consecutive year, overrode the automatic adjustment mechanism."

Two-thirds of the countries in the Organization for Economic Cooperation and Development (OECD) use at least one automatic adjustment mechanism in their social security programs (De Tavernier and Boulhol 2021). In Sweden, an automatic balancing mechanism adjusts social security benefits. It is triggered by changes in national life expectancy and the condition of the Swedish economy (Bosworth and Weaver 2011). Capretta (2006) clarified why this mechanism includes the performance of the Swedish economy to maintain the solvency of the system. "Although correcting for longer life spans helps stabilize costs, it is not sufficient to assure solvency at a fixed contribution rate, as fertility and population growth, labor force participation patterns, and productivity growth all play important roles in long-term pay-as-you-go financing."

Germany bases social security benefit calculations in part on a sustainability factor. This factor adjusts for demographic changes. Germany's sustainability factor decreases social security benefits in response to increases in the old-age dependency ratio

(Capretta 2006). Bosworth and Weaver (2011, p. 6) noted that the sustainability factor accounts for more than life expectancy changes because "by being based on the ratio of contributors to beneficiaries, it incorporates developments in fertility, migration, and changes in labor force participation."

Italy has linked its standard retirement age to its national life expectancy. This automatic adjustment mechanism promotes the financial stabilization of its social security system, which is important in a country where demographic factors have created serious financial issues for the program. In Italy, where the life expectancy is relatively high and the birth rate is low, the automatic adjustment reduces social security expenditures for the system to remain viable for the long term (Bosworth and Weaver 2011).

Canada has added a default procedure for ensuring the long-term financial viability of the Canada Pension Plan (Bosworth and Weaver 2011, p. 15). The Canada Pension Plan is the country's primary social security plan for all provinces except Quebec. Every three years, the chief actuary provides an estimate of the seventy-five-year financial sustainability of the Canada Pension Plan. If the actuaries project an actuarial deficit, policymakers must agree on reforms that year, otherwise the predefined automatic adjustments take place.

If legislators are unable to reach an agreement in time, two things will happen. Contribution rates will increase to meet half of the anticipated deficit (phased in over three years), and price indexation of benefits will be frozen for three years (Bosworth and Weaver 2011, p. 15). Policymakers would need to act to override these automatic reforms. Bosworth and Weaver (2011) noted that workers (whose contribution rates are increased) and current beneficiaries (whose benefit amounts are frozen in nominal dollars—no price-indexation) share the burden of these reforms.

Japan's social security system uses an automatic adjustment mechanism known as *macroeconomic indexing*. Demographic factors, such as the size of the workforce and the national average life expectancy, are used to adjust social security benefit amounts (Chen, Hughes, and Turner 2016). This mechanism promotes the system's long-term financial sustainability.

We propose that the US adopt a system of automatic adjustments for Social Security. The automatic adjustment mechanism could involve a trigger, such as the projected date of trust fund depletion being less than or equal to ten years from the present. The resulting adjustment could be an increase in the payroll tax rate of 0.25 percent for both employers and employees. If the projected trust fund depletion date were less than five years away, the cost-of-living adjustment could be reduced, and the payroll tax rate could be increased.

The Social Security system already includes some program amounts determined by automatic adjustment provisions. An example is the annual cost-of-living adjustment of benefits for inflation. The automatic adjustments we propose would occur if Congress failed to act, protecting the system's solvency and encouraging Congress to act. Policymakers could choose to override automatic adjustments, but having default reforms in place could be a backup plan if Congress takes no action.

The date at which the automatic reform occurred could be more or fewer years from the projected date of trust fund depletion. Alternatively, the trigger mechanism could be based on the increase in payroll tax rates or the cut in benefits needed to restore solvency.

We do not favor automatic adjustments based on changes in national life expectancy. The US faces large inequality gaps in life expectancy across different groups. College graduates live on average nearly eleven years longer than people who have not graduated from high school. That gap increased from eight years in 2000 to nearly eleven years in 2019. If US college graduates were a country, the country's life expectancy would rank fourth in the world. If those who did not graduate from high school were a country, the country's life expectancy would rank 137 in the world (Institute for Health Metrics and Evaluation 2025).

Social Security benefits can be claimed as early as age sixty-two. Because Americans with lower education levels do not usually live as long, any automatic adjustments that, for example, raise either the early retirement age or full retirement age would be unfair to those people.

Reforming the Evaluation Period

Our second proposal for improving the Social Security reform process is to use a shorter evaluation period than seventy-five years. We propose a forty-year period, with the requirement of the Social Security Trust Fund's financial stability or improvement in the fortieth year.

Payroll tax revenues are the primary source of Social Security funding. In 2022, OASI received 90 percent of its revenue from payroll taxes (GAO 2023b). Current payroll tax revenues are inadequate, however, given the benefit payments scheduled to be distributed. Because the projected trust fund depletion date is rapidly approaching, the need to reform Social Security is urgent. Policymakers and others have proposed a wide variety of approaches. The Social Security Administration's Office of the Chief Actuary has provided estimates of the projected financial effects of individual policy changes and proposed reform packages (Social Security Administration 2024o; Social Security Administration 2024p).

Policymakers and policy analysts usually evaluate Social Security reform proposals in terms of their effects on solvency over seventy-five years. For example, the Social Security Expansion Act introduced by Senators Bernie Sanders and Elizabeth Warren, both Democrats, would lead to solvency for seventy-five years (Miller 2022). A comparison of five other Democratic proposals for Social Security reform found that only two of the proposals would "eliminate Social Security's seventy-five-year financial shortfall" and that "the other plans would not raise enough revenue to cover all scheduled benefits over seventy-five years" (Smith and others 2020, p. vii).

We believe that it would be helpful to consider reforms that address the financial shortfall during a shorter period. Proposals that close a portion of the gap "would significantly improve Social Security's finances and delay the date when the program trust funds are expected to run out" (Smith and others 2020, p. viii). The merits of those proposals tend to be overlooked because policymakers emphasize the seventy-five-year evaluation tradition.

One proposal is the Social Security 2100 Act. Introduced in 2023 by Representative John Larson, a Democrat, this proposal does not fully address the Social Security Trust Fund depletion problem, but it could become a valuable part of the solution (Konish 2024). Postponing the projected date of trust fund depletion by a decade would be better than taking no action to address the financial shortfall.

Some type of financial forecasting for Social Security is legally required because it is a self-financed federal government program. In the early days of the program, the original goal was to achieve actuarial balance in perpetuity. However, it is unrealistic to expect projections in perpetuity to be reasonably accurate (Robinson 2023). Thus, the 1965 Social Security Advisory Council recommended seventy-five years as the period for long-range projections (Huston 2021). That projection period is not a legal requirement, but it is traditional. As former Social Security Administration Chief Actuary Stephen Goss explained, "The seventy-five-year period encompasses essentially the entire future life span of all current workers and beneficiaries, even the youngest current workers, at the beginning of the seventy-five-year period. It also provides a projection period long enough to illustrate the complete and mature effects of past amendments and potential future changes to the Social Security Act" (cited by Huston 2021).

Social Security's actuaries also make shorter-term projections, but whenever Congress debates proposed reforms and whenever the media discusses these issues, the seventy-five-year projections are the focus. This tradition makes proposed reforms difficult to pass.

There are diverse opinions about the need for the seventy-five-year evaluation period. Altman viewed the seventy-five-year test as an extreme goal, longer than the planning period of private pensions and other countries' public retirement programs. Biggs argued for indefinite solvency, as a lower standard ignores the problems ahead. Steuerle recommended automatic triggers—modest revenue or benefit adjustments that kick in if Social Security goes out of balance—to ensure long-run solvency. Robert Greenstein, founder and executive director of the Center on Budget and Policy Priorities, cautioned not to "let the perfect be the enemy of the good or you may end up . . . with deadlock and no progress" (The Urban Institute 2010, p. 3).

Peter Coy (2023), writing for *The New York Times*, said that experts' opinions on the traditional period vary. Long-term solutions seek to "ease the strain on future generations" by implementing financially burdensome reforms in the present. However, choosing shorter-term solutions to the Social Security funding shortfall "can make sense if you think the distant future is so unknowable that it's not something to base current decisions on."

Other analysts have also raised concerns about the usefulness of seventy-five-year projections because they rely on assumptions that are likely to be inaccurate over such a long period. According to Robinson (2023, p. 11), "The actuarial balance calculation relies on assumptions and methods that limit its usefulness as a guide to public policy decisions." According to the American Academy of Actuaries (2020, p. 2), "The actuaries typically use year-by-year assumptions about a number of critical economic and demographic parameters for the first ten to twenty-five years of the projection period and then apply 'ultimate' rates."

All projections are uncertain, but long-range estimates come with higher levels of uncertainty. "In general, uncertainty increases for projections further in the future." Thus, "the projections reflect a best guess at a specific date" (Huston 2023, pp. 12-13). Long-term projections tend to be less accurate than short-term projections because it is more challenging to predict the possible variations in economic and demographic factors over the longer time frame. The

Social Security Trustees' solvency projections made between 2003 and 2023 have offered diverse views about the projected year of Social Security and Disability Insurance insolvency, ranging from 2034 to 2042 (Romig 2023b). The 2025 projection is down to 2032 (Committee for a Responsible Federal Budget 2025).

By reducing the evaluation period to forty years, it would be easier to enact Social Security reforms. That shorter period would emphasize the immediate impacts on current generations. Shorter-term projections would reduce complexity and uncertainty, and help to guide incremental policy changes. "Reforms for shorter time periods can be incremental, and thus presumably would be easier to pass, but would require more frequent legislative action. A shorter projection period would presumably facilitate reform because reforms could be made in smaller increments, and the more timely nature of such reforms would also facilitate smaller changes (Turner 2017, p. 8).

According to Penner (2016, p. 46), "For a time horizon of twenty years, the aging of the population is quite predictable, even though there are minor uncertainties surrounding mortality rates and immigration." Experience since then with Covid-19 mortality rates and immigration policy in 2025 shows that there can be substantial variations in those factors.

Given the potential inaccuracy of long-range projections, the judicious use of short-term projections could support sustainable solvency, with small, frequent (possibly automatic) adjustments to the system made in response to changing demographic and economic conditions.

In this respect, the United States is an outlier. It is uncommon for countries to use projection periods of seventy-five years or longer for their social security systems. Hoskins (2010, p. 83) examined the variation among countries in the length of the long-range actuarial projection period. "Our neighbor, Canada, with a comparable public pension program, makes sixty-year projections while several European countries, including France, use a thirty- to forty-year period. Surprisingly, the country with the oldest public pension program, Germany, is legally obliged to issue an annual report using only fifteen-year projections." Shorter-term actuarial projections in most other countries may help these countries to be more open to effective short-term solutions, reducing policy inertia.

We propose that solvency proposals be evaluated over a forty-year period. Each proposal should require the trust fund to be financially stable or show signs of improvement in the fortieth year. The new policy goal would be to maintain solvency for more than forty years. This proposal is consistent with the practice in some other countries.

Mitchell, Myers, and Young (1999, p. 7, 8) did not argue for shorter evaluation periods, but they wrote, "Current policymakers may not be able to fully anticipate the needs and priorities of future generations, making periodic revisions in social security probably inevitable." They went on to write, "Reasonable people disagree about economic and demographic projections seventy-five years or more into the future."

Using a shorter-term solvency projection period is a policy choice. We believe that our recommendation for a forty-year period is reasonable, but policymakers could choose shorter or longer periods.

Facilitate Legislative Reform

Our next proposal focuses on helping lawmakers pass Social Security reforms by reducing the number of required votes in the Senate from sixty to fifty-seven. The Senate would retain the sixty-vote requirement *for structural changes* to Social Security, such as adding individual accounts or enacting means testing.

This proposed change is used in other legislative situations. Congress often uses special "budget reconciliation" procedures to expedite the passage of budget-related legislation. A reconciliation process allows Congress to change spending, revenue, and the federal debt limit with a simple majority, circumventing the usual sixty-vote threshold needed to overcome a Senate filibuster.

The Senate has made some procedural changes affecting the Social Security reform process. For example, the Byrd Rule is a procedural restriction on budget reconciliation bills. It prohibits direct changes to Social Security benefits or funding in those bills. This rule is designed to prevent reconciliation from being used to bypass regular legislative procedures for addressing Social Security reform.

Since 1983, the Senate has needed sixty votes to enact Social Security reforms (Primus, Watson, and Smalligan 2025). That change occurred in response to amendments to the Congressional Budget Act. No major Social Security reforms to improve funding have been passed since the enactment of that legislation. Executive orders of the president can affect the administration and enforcement of Social Security laws, but major reforms require legislation passed by Congress. The intent of this rule is to require bipartisan participation in Social Security reforms. The downside, however, is that it is difficult to pass needed Social Security reforms.

To facilitate the passage of Social Security reforms, we propose that Congress should reduce the number of required Senate votes from sixty to fifty-seven. The existing sixty-vote requirement for *structural* changes to Social Security should be retained. This proposal would still encourage bipartisan participation in the reform process while making it easier to pass needed changes.

Establish a Bipartisan Commission

Our fourth proposal is to require Congress to appoint a bipartisan commission to recommend reform options for Social Security if the projected Trust Fund depletion date is ten or fewer years away.

Congress has been aware of the need for reform for decades, but as of 2025 it has passed no legislation to restore solvency. The Peter G. Peterson Foundation (2025a), noting the inaction of policymakers, stated that, "The warning bells have been chiming for years as Social Security's finances have continued to deteriorate." In 2023, Representative Tom Cole, a Republican, introduced a bill to establish a commission to consider Social Security reform options, but the legislation did not pass (Congress.gov 2023).

By establishing a commission, Congress can potentially provide a highly visible forum for important issues and assemble greater expertise than may be readily available within the legislature. Commissions can examine complex policy issues over a longer period and in greater depth than may be practical for legislators. The nonpartisan or bipartisan character of most congressional commissions may also make their findings and recommendations more politically acceptable, both in Congress and to the public (Shanton and Straus 2025, writing for the Library of Congress).

We propose that Congress be required to appoint a bipartisan commission to recommend reform options and propose legislation for Social Security if the projected trust fund depletion date is ten or fewer years away. The commission could be a technical commission composed of economists, actuaries, and other Social Security policy experts. A technical commission would provide political cover for politicians, who would not be responsible for generating policy recommendations. The commission would hold public hearings and produce a report in one year.

Establishing a bipartisan commission is a step forward to achieving reform, but it is not a guaranteed solution. The 1983 commission, for example, ended in deadlock, unable to agree on a set of proposals until President Reagan intervened. It ended up with a reform that focused on cutting benefits to restore solvency (Walker 2025).

An alternative policy would require Congress to hold Social Security reform hearings when specific triggers are met. Additional alternatives could include calling bipartisan commissions every ten years.

Paying for Legislated Benefit Increases

The Social Security Fairness Act was signed into law by President Biden in early 2025. It raised benefits for some current and future beneficiaries, and it added new spousal benefits. However, the act did not raise revenues to pay for the changes. It provides extra benefits to retirees who worked in government jobs not covered by Social Security but who also qualify for Social Security benefits from covered jobs. This legislation is projected to move Social Security's trust fund depletion date up by six months, but still in 2033 (Gibson, K. 2025). President Trump's One Big Beautiful Bill Act in 2025 is projected to move the trust fund's depletion date up from early 2033 to late 2032, in part because the law temporarily reduces the taxes that many older Americans pay on Social Security benefits (Committee for a Responsible Federal Budget 2025). However, that law will have no effect on the taxes paid on Social Security benefits for people younger than age sixty-five (Taylor 2025).

We propose to amend the Congressional Budget Act, which governs the enactment of Social Security amendments. We would require that any benefit increases be matched by increases in revenue or cuts in other benefits. This would ensure that the overall package has a neutral or positive effect on Social Security solvency.

This proposal's budget neutrality requirement would help maintain Social Security's long-term solvency, and it would force Congress to be more fiscally responsible when expanding benefits. Mandating that any benefit increase be offset by new revenue or cost-cutting measures would prevent ad hoc expansions from worsening the program's financial outlook.

Medicare has already adopted the principle of budget neutrality; however, its method is controversial. The American Medical Association has published an article titled "How Medicare's Budget Neutrality Rule Is Slanted Against Doctors" (Robeznicks 2023). Physicians had their inflation-adjusted payments drop 26 percent between 2001 and 2023.

In the next chapter, we present ideas for adjusting Social Security's revenue sources.

CHAPTER 5

Social Security Contributions and the Tax Code

In this chapter, we look at ways to improve the financial health of Social Security by changing the contribution rules and the federal tax code. We first address reforms to the policies that set workers' contributions to Social Security.

Make-Up Contributions

Under Social Security regulations, people need to work for a certain number of years to receive benefits. Not all types of work (e.g., raising children) count toward meeting that minimum requirement. However, most types of work earnings are "covered," which means that those earnings count toward the worker's eventual eligibility for Social Security benefits. Workers are required to have at least ten years of covered earnings to qualify for Social Security retirement benefits.

For most people, working ten years under Social Security is not a problem; however, meeting this minimum requirement can be difficult for some workers who face family responsibilities, physical or mental health issues, or recent immigration to the United States. A 2011 study found that recently arriving immigrants and infrequent workers comprised the largest group of people who could not qualify for Social Security benefits (Whitman, Reznik, and Shoffner 2011).

In today's dynamic economy—in which people frequently face job losses, pursue higher education, or choose to raise children—Americans often have gaps in their employment history. Other nations have addressed this question. For example, in the UK, workers can make voluntary contributions if they have gaps in their social security coverage (UK Government, 2025c). In Ireland, individuals who are no longer employed can make voluntary contributions. If they are receiving a social welfare payment, they may receive credited contributions (Citizens Information Board, 2025). In Germany, voluntary pension contributions are an option for the self-employed and freelancers, employees with low incomes, workers with gaps in their pension insurance history, and people living abroad (Fundsback 2025).

We propose that Congress allow workers with at least nine years of covered earnings at age sixty or older to make voluntary Social Security contributions. This would allow them to "buy" additional years of covered earnings and therefore meet the requirement of ten years of covered earnings.

The Required Number of Contribution Years

The Social Security Act of 1950 gradually raised the required number of quarters (per year) of coverage from six in 1954 to forty in 1971 (Cohen and Myers 1950). Despite substantial increases in life expectancy, current policy still requires that workers have forty quarters (ten years) of covered earnings—the same number of years as in 1971—before they are eligible for benefits.

The Social Security Administration (2025c) has explained how Social Security work credits are earned.

Since 1978, you can earn up to a maximum of four credits per year. Credits are based on your total wages and self-employment income for the year. You might work all year to earn four credits, or you might earn enough for all four in less time. The amount of earnings it takes to earn a credit may change each year. In 2025, you earn one Social Security and Medicare credit for every $1,810 in covered earnings each year. You must earn $7,240 to get the maximum four credits for the year.

It is helpful to compare the US situation with programs in other nations. OECD countries require on average at least thirteen years of covered earnings for a person to be eligible to receive social security benefits. Belgium, France, and Italy require people to have more years of covered earnings years, if they want to claim benefits early (Börsch-Supan and Coile 2020). In Germany, people must work for forty-five years if they want to claim benefits at age sixty-four.

We propose that the US should gradually raise the minimum number of contribution years for Social Security eligibility from ten to twelve years—for people who want to start receiving benefits between age sixty-two and sixty-four. The law could stipulate that this change would begin ten years after the law is passed. For people who prefer to receive benefits at age sixty-five or older, the law would not change; they would still be required to have ten years of covered work to be eligible for benefits.

Raising the Payroll Tax Ceiling

Wages have grown more rapidly for high earners than for the rest of the workforce; therefore, the *percentage* of total wages in the economy subject to the Social Security payroll tax has decreased. Before the 1983 Social Security reform, 90 percent of wages were covered. By 2024, this percentage had fallen to 82 percent (Munnell 2024c). This has resulted in lower revenues for the Social Security program.

We propose, in alignment with the National Commission on Fiscal Responsibility and Reform (2010), Munnell (2024c), and others, raising the payroll tax ceiling to cover a higher percentage of wages. This change should occur gradually, during a transition period. We propose that at least 85 percent of wages be covered. This change would raise revenues and the future benefits of those affected.

Usually, wages tend to rise over a worker's career. That is especially true for wealthy Americans. That means that most people would not have earnings above the current taxable maximum for Social Security until later in life. As a result, most people would not be affected by the higher payroll tax ceiling until the end of their working years, if ever.

Simplify Rules for Young Workers and Students

Current policies create complicated and inconsistent rules for young workers and college students. For example, if parents pay their teenage son or daughter to do domestic work, that money is taxable under current income tax laws. However, those earnings would not be taxable for Social Security until he or she reaches age twenty-one. These rules would be the same if the teenage son or daughter is employed in the parent's sole proprietorship or a partnership. As long as the parents' son or daughter is under age eighteen, their child's earnings are not subject to Social Security taxes.

However, with some exceptions, the rules change if the parents' business is a corporation, a partnership, or an estate. In these cases, the parents' son or daughter would be required to pay income tax and Social Security taxes, regardless of age (IRS 2024b). And, if teenagers provide nondomestic services (e.g., babysitting) for someone other than their parents, they must pay the Social Security tax.

Another unnecessarily complicated rule pertains to college and university students. Under current law, the IRS exempts students from paying Social Security and Medicare taxes on the money they make by working for the university or college where they study (IRS 2024j). Those students need to keep in mind that, despite this exemption, "their earnings remain subject to federal and state income taxes" (Rutgers University 2025).

We propose that all workers under age twenty-one pay both income tax and Social Security tax, and to apply that rule to all work arrangements. We also propose that Congress treat the earnings of students and nonstudents of the same age consistently; specifically, we propose ending the student exemption from the Social Security payroll tax.

Taxation of Fringe Benefits

According to the IRS (2024k), "Fringe benefits received in connection with the performance of your services are included in your income as compensation unless you pay FMV (free market value) for them or they're specifically excluded by law."

The growth in fringe benefits that are excluded from taxable income has eroded the Social Security tax base. Fringe benefits comprised 7 percent of total compensation in 1950, with wages being 93 percent (Durante 2024a). Chen (1981) projected that covered wages as a percentage of total compensation would fall from 84 percent in 1980 to 62 percent in 2055. He wrote, "Fringes accepted in lieu of taxable pay reduce this base, and boost the percentage of taxable payroll required for paying benefits."

Recent data confirms Chen's projection that wages would continue to decline as a percentage of compensation. According to the US Bureau of Labor Statistics (2024b), "Total employer compensation costs for private industry workers averaged $44.40 per hour worked in September 2024. Wages and salaries averaged $31.25 per hour worked and accounted for 70.4 percent of employer costs, while benefit costs averaged $13.15 per hour worked and accounted for the remaining 29.6 percent."

Some fringe benefits, such as adoption benefits provided by an employer, are exempt from federal income tax but they are still subject to Social Security tax (IRS 2024b). And the IRS (2024j) has a long list of fringe benefits that are not subject to federal income tax *or* Social Security tax. We will not list them all here, but a few examples are helpful to know. In most cases, the value of accident or health plan coverage provided by employers is not included in a worker's income. The same is true when employers provide workers with coverage for long-term care services. Flexible spending accounts (FSAs) and health savings accounts (HSAs) are usually not counted as income, or they can be listed as a deduction. Other non-taxable fringe benefits include qualified employer-provided educational assistance, use of an employer-operated gym, group term life insurance coverages provided by employers, and some qualified tuition benefits. Further complicating the picture, employer matching and nonelective contributions to 401(k) plans are not subject to the Social Security payroll tax on workers (IRS 2024f).

The growth of employer-provided health insurance has been the single largest cause of the decline in Social Security covered wages. This exclusion disproportionately benefits higher-income workers. The Congressional Budget Office determined that 28 percent of the benefit from the payroll tax exclusion of health care plans went to the top income quintile (20 percent), while 4 percent went to the bottom quintile. This imbalance reflects the lack of access to employer-provided health insurance for lower-income workers (Haltzel 2023).

Other countries do not use the US model. In Canada, for example, most fringe benefits are taxable under Canada's primary social security plan. These fringe benefits include educational assistance, premiums for life insurance plans, and premiums for health insurance plans (Government of Canada 2025a).

We propose that Congress increase the percentage of fringe benefit compensation that is subject to Social Security payroll taxes. This proposal is in line with the current treatment of adoption costs and employee contributions to 401(k) plans. We also propose a gradual increase in the *types of fringe benefits* that are subject to the Social Security payroll tax. For example, lawmakers could first count the employer's cost of group term life insurance as income subject to the Social Security payroll tax. Later, employer-subsidized transportation to work could be included.

As noted earlier, employer contributions to health insurance plans are the costliest fringe benefit. We propose making health insurance benefits subject to the Social Security payroll tax but not to federal income tax. By increasing payroll taxes on health insurance alone, Congress could *cover 31 percent* of Social Security's long-term financial shortfall (Haltzel 2023).

Taxation of Cafeteria Plans

Since 1978, employers have been able to establish tax-exempt cafeteria plans for their employees. Establishing these plans reduces the payroll tax base because these plans are not subject to the Social Security payroll tax. Thus, for the first forty-three years of Social Security, from 1935 to 1977, this was not an option.

Cafeteria plans are also called flexible benefit plans and (IRS) Section 125 plans. They allow workers to receive fringe benefits on a pretax basis, including being exempt from the Social Security payroll tax. This exemption differs from contributions to 401(k) plans, which are exempt from the income tax but not the Social Security payroll tax.

Cafeteria plans can be used for a variety of purposes, such as helping workers pay for supplemental health insurance coverage, the employees share of their premiums, medical expenses through flexible spending accounts and health savings accounts, and dependent care costs such as daycare. Some types of fringe benefits, such as group life insurance benefits that exceed $50,000 or adoption assistance benefits, require employers to withhold both Social Security and Medicare taxes.

We propose, in alignment with ideas from the Peter G. Peterson Foundation (2022), making contributions to cafeteria plans subject to the Social Security payroll tax, which would be consistent with the treatment of 401(k) contributions. Yates (1985, p. 632), decades earlier, also made this proposal.

Excluding some compensation from payroll taxation can create inequities. Workers with access to cafeteria plans receive tax-advantaged benefits that others may not, a situation that generally favors higher-earning employees. Self-employed workers cannot establish cafeteria plans for themselves.

Taxation of Retirement Savings Plans

For Social Security payroll tax purposes, employee and employer contributions to 401(k) plans are treated differently. Employee contributions to 401(k) plans, both traditional and Roth plans, are included in a worker's wages, and they are subject to the Social Security payroll tax paid by both employees and the employer. Stated differently, they are not subtracted when computing taxable wages. However, *employer* contributions are not subject to the payroll tax by either employees or the employer (IRS 2025a).

By including employer contributions—both matching and

nonelective contributions—as part of employees' wages subject to the payroll tax, we could expand Social Security's revenue base. This adjustment would also provide equal treatment for employer and employee contributions. It would eliminate a regressive aspect of the tax system, as higher-paid employees are more likely to receive those contributions.

Other pension arrangements create similar problems. For example, some types of defined contribution plans do not subject the employer's contributions to the Social Security payroll tax even though the employee's contributions are subject to the tax (IRS 2025a, IRS 2025d). Two examples of a defined contribution plan with these problems are the Simplified Employee Pension (SEP), which is generally used by small businesses, and the 403(b) plan—for public schools and 501(c)(3) nonprofit organizations.

We propose that Congress subject employer contributions to 401(k) plans and similar retirement savings plans to the Social Security payroll tax paid by employers and employees—up to the payroll tax ceiling. This proposal would raise revenue and treat employee and employer contributions the same way.

Full-Time Independent Contract Workers

In 1950, Congress extended Social Security coverage to the self-employed. The Social Security Administration (2018b) explained, "You're self-employed if you operate a trade, business, or profession, either by yourself or as a partner." Independent contract workers are a type of self-employed worker, if they earn at least part of their income by selling their labor through their business. The

US Bureau of Labor Statistics (2023c) estimated that in July 2023 11.9 million workers, or 7.4 percent of the employed workforce, were independent contractors on their sole or main job. This figure compared to 6.9 percent of the employed workforce in 2017. In 2023, 71 percent of independent contractors worked full-time. In 2023, nearly two-thirds of the self-employed were independent contractors.

In many ways, long-term independent contract workers, such as many Uber and Lyft drivers and taxi drivers, are more like regular employees than self-employed workers. They have a long-term, full-time relationship working for a company that pays them. Presumably, one of the reasons these companies categorize these workers as independent contractors is to avoid paying the employer's share of the Social Security payroll tax. The employer also does not withhold the contract worker's Social Security taxes. The contract worker is treated as a self-employed worker who must pay both the employer and employee parts of Social Security taxes (Schreur and Veghte 2018).

According to the US Department of Labor (2025), "Misclassification occurs when an employer treats a worker who is an employee under the [Fair Labor Standards Act] as an independent contractor. Misclassifying employees as independent contractors is a serious problem because misclassified employees may not receive the minimum wage and overtime pay to which they are entitled under the FLSA or other benefits and protections to which they are entitled under the law."

Independent contractors must make Social Security payments when reporting their earnings for Social Security on their federal income tax return. Thus, the worker must save money to make future Social Security tax payments. Independent contractors often can reduce their Social Security tax payments by understating their income or overstating their business expenses (Schreur and Veghte 2018).

Other countries often offer more assistance to self-employed workers. In 2022, in Canada, Uber reached an agreement with Canada's largest services-sector union to offer employee-like benefits to contractors who work as ride-hail and food delivery drivers. This agreement does not address whether the Uber workers are employees or self-employed but does provide those workers with employee-like benefits as self-employed workers (Bellon 2022). In the UK and France, Uber drivers are classified as employees (Green 2021, Männis 2020).

We propose that, in situations where a large employer has long-term relationships with many full-time independent contract workers, the employer be required to make equivalent payments of the employer share of the contract worker's Social Security taxes. Also, the employer must withhold the employee's share of Social Security tax payments from the employee's earnings and submit that money to the Internal Revenue Service. This rule could apply to employers with at least one hundred long-term independent contract workers.

This proposal is similar to a proposal made by Schreur and Veghte (2018). They recognized that it could be difficult to determine the proportion of the independent contractor's earnings that would be considered compensation for labor. This amount would have to be distinguished from business expenses, such as car mileage. To address this complexity, our proposal would retain the designation of "independent contractor," but it would apply our recommended Social Security tax rules, as described above.

By comparison, social media influencers largely provide their services as independent contractors (Newkirk and Webber 2024). They are examples of independent contractors who would not be affected by this proposal because they usually have no long-term relationship with a company that pays them.

Pass-Through Business Owners

Congress has gradually extended coverage to more self-employed workers and to more of their compensation. Nelson (1985) provided an early history.

> The 1950 amendments extended coverage to most nonfarm self-employment except that of professional groups. Specifically excluded were accountants, architects, chiropractors, Christian Scientist practitioners, dentists, physicians, funeral directors, lawyers, ministers, naturopaths, optometrists, osteopaths, professional engineers, and veterinarians. The 1950 law also required that the self-employed worker have net earnings of at least $400 during the taxable year. Despite these exclusions, nearly 4.5 million self-employed workers became covered in 1951. The 1954 Act extended coverage further by bringing in 2.5 million self-employed farmers and one hundred thousand accountants, architects, engineers, and funeral directors. The law also established an optional method of reporting for farmers. Those with a gross income of $1,800 or less could report and pay social security taxes on 50 percent of their gross. Those with gross earnings of more than $1,800 and net

earnings of less than $900 could report and pay social security taxes on $900. The 1956 Act extended coverage to an additional two hundred thousand farm operators by liberalizing the optional reporting provision and to about four hundred thousand farm landlords who were materially participating in operating the rental farm. Physicians became covered under the program in 1966.

As of 2025, self-employed individuals, including owners of S corporations, are required to pay Social Security taxes on their net earnings. S corporations can pass corporate income, losses, deductions, and credits through to their shareholders for federal income tax purposes. They are the most popular corporate structure in America. There are more than five million of them in the United States, three times the number of C corporations (S Corp 2025). Whereas a C corporation is taxed as a separate entity, an S corporation pays no corporate income tax. The self-employed, including S corporation owners, pay the Self-Employed Contributions Act (SECA) tax on their net earnings. They pay both the employee and the employer share of the tax, but the law permits them to deduct half of the self-employment tax as a business expense.

Sammartino (2017) wrote, "S corporation owners do not pay SECA tax on their profits, but they are required to pay themselves 'reasonable compensation,' which is subject to the regular Social Security and Medicare payroll tax." However, self-employed business owners can reduce their SECA taxes by underreporting their net earnings. "Without clear guidance or legal requirements, S corporations tend to underpay shareholder wages, resulting in underpaid employment taxes for funding programs like Medicare and Social Security," according to the Government Accountability Office (2009, p. 36).

Koba (2014) described how a high-income individual could use this legal loophole to largely avoid paying the Social Security SECA tax.

> So, let's say someone has set up their own S corporation, in this case a consulting firm, and makes $1 million for the year advising . . . clients. To use the loophole, that person will treat only $100,000 of that $1 million as wages. The other $900,000 is treated as company profits—not salary—even though the person, as owner, will get the money. (The $900,000 is not tax-free. It is subject to distribution taxes.) That allows the business owner to avoid paying payroll taxes into Social Security and Medicare by some $26,000. By using the loophole, the person is declaring that he or she is more of an investor than an active employee of their own company.

TurboTax (2024b) discussed the potential misuse of S corporations to avoid paying adequate taxes. "The IRS tends to take a closer look at S corporation returns since the potential for abuse is so large. For example, if you make $500,000 in one year but only designate $20,000 of that as salary income, you might trigger an IRS inquiry, since you are avoiding so much self-employment tax. The guiding principle is that you must designate a 'reasonable' amount of your income as wages, rather than a distribution."

Potential legislation developed by Representative Steny Hoyer, a Democrat, and former policy advisor Wendell Primus (Social Security Administration, Office of the Chief Actuary 2025d) includes the following proposal.

Make all distributions to all pass-through business owners up to the earnings cap subject to the SECA tax, provided those owners meet the material participation standard. Under current law, the definition of self-employment income for the purposes of SECA tax varies depending on the form of the business. This provision would ensure that all workers who materially participate in a business are subject to payroll taxes on their earnings. The earnings cap will equal the taxable maximum in that year. For example, if the owner earned $100,000 in wages and $500,000 in distributions, and the earnings cap was set to $300,000, the owner would pay payroll tax on the first $200,000 of those distributions.

The *material participation standard* refers to criteria the IRS uses to determine whether an individual is sufficiently involved with business activities for tax purposes. According to the IRS (2025f), "You materially participate in an activity if you're involved in the operation of the activity on a regular, continuous, and substantial basis." The Social Security Administration's Office of the Chief Actuary (2025a, p. 2) added this: "This provision would ensure that all workers who materially participate in a business are subject to payroll taxes on their earnings."

We propose that the Social Security Self-Employment Contributions Act (SECA) payroll tax apply to all earnings and distributions to pass-through business owners up to the taxable maximum. We endorse the Hoyer and Primus proposal.

The next chapter focuses on what we can learn about Social Security reforms from financial literacy research.

CHAPTER 6

Ideas from Financial Literacy Research

The proposals in this chapter are inspired by the research on financial literacy, including ideas that are designed to improve the financial decisions of average workers and families.

The Retirement Earnings Test and "Clawbacks"

The Social Security retirement earnings test (RET) temporarily reduces a person's Social Security benefits if the person is below their full retirement age (age sixty-seven for most workers) but older than age sixty-two, continues to work, and earns above a minimum amount. We first consider a common misperception relating to the earnings test, which can be stated as follows: The retirement earnings test results in a permanent loss of benefits and thus functions as a tax on earnings. Because the earnings test is widely misunderstood in that way, ending it would simplify the decisions of workers who are trying to decide when to retire and when to claim benefits.

The Social Security Administration (2024i), in a publication titled "How Work Affects Your Benefits," explained that the earnings test redistributes benefits to a later year without a permanent loss of benefits. However, Biggs (2008) stated that people often misperceive the earnings test as a tax.

Munnell (2019) described the earnings test as "complicated and often misunderstood." The Bipartisan Policy Center (2023) stated that "the RET (retirement earnings test) can confuse Americans who are planning their retirement, as most people are unaware that the benefit reduction is temporary and that withheld benefits are restored later in retirement."

Liebman and Luttmer (2012) conducted a survey that found that a minority of the respondents correctly understood that the earnings test leads to a temporary benefit reduction followed by a compensatory benefit increase starting at the beneficiary's full retirement age.

> As a follow-up, we asked those who believe that an earnings threshold exists (namely, those who stated that earnings at age sixty-four above some limit will cause Social Security benefits to be reduced) whether future benefits would increase if current benefits were reduced as a result of the earnings test. Only 40 percent believed this to be the case, with 52 percent answering that future benefits would be unaffected and the remaining 8 percent answering that future benefits would also be cut (pp. 25-26).

The erroneous belief that the earnings test results in a permanent loss of benefits leads to the bunching of eligible worker-beneficiaries' earnings right below the earnings test thresholds. Also, Burkhauser and Turner (1978) argued that it causes workers to redistribute work across time so that they worked slightly more hours in the years before the earnings test takes effect.

Li (2023) explained that "for earnings at or just above the annual RET threshold, the RET may encourage workers to work fewer hours and keep earnings just under the RET threshold." Emerson Sprick, a senior economic analyst at the Bipartisan Policy Center, has expressed the same concern about the earnings test. "Instead of calling the rule a retirement earnings test, the language could be changed to 'temporary benefit withholding' to better convey the benefit consequences, Sprick said" (Konish 2023a).

Because the increase in benefits at the full retirement age is permanent, it will be more generous for beneficiaries who live a long time and less generous for those who die relatively young. Thus, the earnings test may act as a tax for lower-income people because of their shorter life expectancy. Also, the logic of withholding benefits and repaying them a few years later may not be clear to many people. Among other informative resources, the Social Security Administration website includes a Retirement Earnings Test Calculator (Social Security Administration 2024x).

The retirement earnings test is too complex, making it difficult for Americans to make wise financial decisions. For example, the retirement earnings test has two thresholds: a lower exempt amount for those under the full retirement age who will not reach the full retirement age that year, and a higher exempt amount for those who will reach the full retirement age that year (Social Security Administration 2024a). These thresholds are wage-indexed (Slavov and Viard 2021a). This feature adds to the complexity of the retirement earnings test, especially given that the two threshold amounts generally increase from one year to the next.

The retirement earnings test brings about a temporary reduction of benefits. By comparison, claiming benefits *before* the full retirement age leads to a *permanent* benefit reduction. A common point of confusion among workers, however, is which of these benefit reductions is temporary and which is permanent. For example, almost half (49 percent) of the respondents in the Nationwide Retirement Institute's Survey wrongly believed that "if they file early their benefit will automatically go up once they reach their full retirement age" (Nationwide Retirement Institute 2022).

Another complication is that beneficiaries who are younger than the full retirement age, and who are unaware of the retirement earnings test, do not realize they need to report their earnings to the Social Security Administration if they continue to work. This lack of knowledge results in benefit overpayments if their earnings exceed the earnings test exempt amount. This added complexity often leads people to make mistakes. "Determining income under the retirement earnings test is more complicated for self-employed earners and certain categories of earnings, such as royalties" (Flanagan 2024). Some beneficiaries may under-report their earnings by accident if they do not know which types of income should be counted versus excluded for the retirement earnings test.

For fiscal years 2020 through 2023, the Social Security Administration estimates it made *$3.1 billion in overpayments* to people who were subject to the retirement earnings test (Social Security Administration, Office of the Inspector General 2025). To prevent overpayments, it is best for beneficiaries to report to the Social Security Administration all earnings to which the retirement earnings test potentially applies as soon as possible. "Each year your employer and the Internal Revenue Service report earnings to the SSA" (Edleson 2021). Thus, the Social Security Administration will be able to detect overpayments related to the retirement earnings test, and mandatory repayments will be demanded. Repealing the retirement earnings test would end such complications both for workers and the Social Security Administration.

The earnings test reduces benefits before the full retirement age, but that is compensated by benefit increases starting at full retirement age. This arrangement is complicated and confusing for beneficiaries and the Social Security Administration. The Social Security Administration has failed to provide all the earnings test-related monthly benefit increases scheduled to begin at the full retirement age in a timely manner. "SSA did not pay approximately 176,000 beneficiaries $81 million on the date policy first allowed the increased payment" (Social Security Administration, Office of the Inspector General 2024). However, it should be noted that its overall accuracy rate on payments is 99.7 percent (Leibenluft, O'Connor, and Romig 2025).

The Clawback Controversy

Social Security Administration clawbacks are benefit reductions enforced by the Social Security Administration to recover benefit overpayments. The clawbacks have received negative feedback. The Social Security Administration tried to end what some have called the "clawback cruelty" with new approaches (Longo 2024). For example, as of February 2025, the Social Security Administration no longer fully withheld benefits when beneficiaries could not repay the overpayment after receiving an overpayment notice. However, the Social Security Administration reversed these policies in March 2025, with the return to a 100 percent reduction in Social Security benefits for overpayments occurring after March 27, 2025. Beneficiaries can appeal the reduction if it causes undue financial hardship (Social Security Administration, Press Office 2025b).

The US can learn from international examples. In Canada, workers can claim social security benefits as early as age sixty. Canada has eliminated earnings restrictions for participants in its two main social security plans, the Canada Pension Plan (CPP) and the Quebec Pension Plan (QPP) (Latulippe and Turner 2019). CPP beneficiaries between ages sixty and sixty-five who receive benefits while working are required to continue contributing to the CPP. Such contributions become optional after age sixty-five (Government of Canada 2024h). The contributions made while working, plus receiving benefits, will increase the benefits beneficiaries will receive when they are no longer working. These benefit increases are known as the CPP post-retirement benefits and the QPP retirement pension supplement (Government of Canada 2024h).

Canada's policy changes indicate an awareness that the absence of earnings-related restrictions on CPP/QPP benefits "would allow older workers to combine earnings and a pension in a way that would suit both their needs and the growing demand for labor by employers" (Latulippe and Turner 2019, p. 394). Similarly, in the United Kingdom, workers can continue to work while receiving the State Pension (social security), and their earnings will not reduce their benefits (Citizens Advice 2025).

We propose that Congress repeal the retirement earnings test. This policy change would increase payroll tax revenues, decrease administrative costs, and increase benefits for some workers. It would also improve equity. Workers with shorter lifespans than average, who are likely to have lower-than-average income, would not have their lifetime benefits reduced, and clawbacks of overpaid benefits would occur less often. This proposal was advocated earlier by Steuerle and Bakija (1994). More recently, Greszler (2025) and others have favored ending the earnings test.

Social Security Administration actuaries have estimated that repealing the retirement earnings test would improve Social Security's finances (GAO 2024a). Because some beneficiaries reduce their work hours or leave employment to be exempt from the earnings test, ending it would increase older workers' earnings, raising payroll tax revenues.

In addition, administering the earnings test is expensive. According to the Social Security Administration's Office of the Inspector General, "In FY 2021, SSA spent approximately $70 million in administrative costs to enforce the earnings test. This estimated cost is conservative because there were many actions associated with administering the earnings test neither we nor SSA could quantify" (Social Security Administration, Office of the Inspector General 2024).

Repealing the earnings test would slightly increase Social Security's solvency: "The SSA Office of the Chief Actuary estimated this reform would close approximately 1 percent of Social Security's long-range shortfall" (Bipartisan Policy Center 2023). Over the long term, repealing the earnings test could eliminate hundreds of millions of dollars in administrative expenses and save millions of beneficiaries the financial and emotional stress of clawbacks.

Phased Retirement

As discussed in the previous proposal, many workers misunderstand the retirement earnings test. They view it as a tax that discourages work for people who want to claim Social Security benefits. Allowing workers to choose to receive partial benefits while working would eliminate the need to report earnings to the Social Security Administration, which is a major drawback of the earnings test.

By comparison, Germany has a statutory claiming age for social security benefits of sixty-three. Workers can temporarily reduce their social security pensions by up to 90 percent and continue working (BaFin, 2023).

Instead of an earnings test, we propose that workers be allowed to continue working and have the option to claim 25, 50, or 75 percent of the Social Security benefits they would otherwise receive. Their future benefits would be increased to compensate for the benefits they temporarily give up.

With this proposal, overpayments and clawbacks would not occur. This proposal could help workers to transition gradually into full retirement. They could receive a portion of their benefits while gaining an increase in future benefits due to not claiming full benefits initially.

The Social Security Advisory Board (2023) found that over half the early baby boomer cohort followed a nontraditional retirement path involving either partial retirement or a return to work before permanently leaving the labor force. According to the 2024 State of Retirement Planning study by Fidelity Investments, 66 percent of

Generation Z and millennials would prefer a phased retirement, and 57 percent of all respondents plan to work part-time in retirement (McKenna 2024). Thus, it appears that this proposal could help many workers who could use it to finance phased retirement.

An issue related to this proposal is how it would affect the benefits of spouses and survivors. For spousal benefits, we propose that they be tied to the worker's actual benefits received. However, for survivors' benefits, they would be tied to 100 percent of the worker's benefits rather than the temporarily reduced benefits.

With no earnings test, this arrangement would be easier for the Social Security Administration to manage. It would reduce administrative expenses by avoiding the need to track workers' earnings while they are receiving benefits. This proposal would also provide workers with more options for when to receive benefits without affecting the expected lifetime value of their benefits.

Our proposal could be adapted to the age range for receipt of partial Social Security benefits. Partial benefits could be an option up to the full retirement age of sixty-seven or the maximum benefit age of seventy.

We also propose to limit clawbacks of previous overpayments to 50 percent of monthly Social Security benefits. This limit would be a more compassionate and realistic approach, given the limited finances of many beneficiaries. In 2025, the Social Security Administration, reacting to public opposition to 100 percent clawbacks, reduced the maximum clawback to 50 percent of the person's benefit (Picchi 2025). We argue that the maximum should be set in law to prohibit the Social Security Administration from setting it at 100 percent.

These proposals could be fine-tuned by providing workers with more information about the earnings test. According to Slavov and Viard (2021b), "Until Congress eliminates the earnings test, we should take every possible step to increase public understanding of its true impact on lifetime benefits."

Benefit Clawbacks After Death

Only 0.3 percent of Social Security Administration benefit payments are overpayments (Romig 2025). However, when they occur, they can be a serious problem for the beneficiaries.

Social Security Administration regulations prohibit benefit payments for the month of a beneficiary's death, even though the beneficiary lived for part or nearly all the month (USA.gov 2023). A beneficiary must be alive for an entire month to be eligible for that month's benefits. According to AARP (2022), "Social Security benefits are paid a month behind. April's benefits are paid in May, and May's in June, and so on."

Surviving spouses or other family members are instructed to promptly notify the Social Security Administration about the death of a beneficiary. They also must notify the receiving financial institution if the Social Security Administration has made benefit payments via direct deposit. Benefit payments received after the beneficiary's death must be returned to the Social Security Administration since they are overpayments under current rules (Social Security Administration 2024gg).

In some rare cases, the Social Security Administration wrongly requests the return of appropriate benefit payments. According to one financial advice columnist, "In some circumstances . . .

Social Security 'claws back' money which rightfully belongs to the deceased" (Staff Reports 2024). The fact that a payment received in one month represents the previous month's benefit is likely to contribute to the confusion about whether a benefit payment needs to be sent back to the Social Security Administration.

We propose that a beneficiary who lives for one or more days of a given month be entitled to receive that month's benefit payment during the following month. The benefits would be paid to the deceased's survivor or estate. This change would reduce the prevalence of benefit clawbacks relating to a beneficiary's death.

The excess payment for days of the month when the beneficiary died could be viewed as a supplement to the Lump Sum Death Payment, which is $255, an amount that has not changed since 1954 (Benefits.gov 2024). Our proposal would offset the decline in the real value of the Lump Sum Death Payment (Social Security Administration 2024gg). The Office of the Chief Actuary (2024) estimated that in 2022, 43 percent of those eligible for death benefits did not receive them, presumably because they failed to claim them. Thus, for many, this proposal would serve as a substitute for death benefits.

Provide Better Information for Social Security Participants

The Social Security Administration needs to improve its communication with Americans, mainly to reduce confusion and enable families to make better financial and retirement decisions. For example, each year, the Social Security Administration mails to beneficiaries a Notice of Cost-of-Living Adjustment. The notice mailed at the end of 2024 provided the percentage increase in each beneficiary's benefit for 2025, the gross new benefit before deductions, the amount of any deductions, and the new net benefit. It did not provide the old benefit amount. If the program administrators had provided the old benefit amount, the beneficiary could have easily verified that the new amount was correct by comparing the two amounts.

Another example pertains to communication about deductions from gross monthly benefits. The Social Security Administration allows participants to set up a convenient online account, which they can use to obtain information about their Social Security benefits (Social Security Administration 2025b). For current beneficiaries, it provides a statement of the most recent monthly benefit, including the gross monthly benefit, deductions, and net monthly benefit. However, the online account does not provide an itemized listing of what the deductions are. The online account could provide more information about the deductions and the reasons for them.

Yet another example of lackluster communication relates to the communication dates. Social Security Administration offices are closed on Saturdays, Sundays, and national holidays. Nonetheless, some offices mail notices to participants stamped with dates when offices are closed. As a result, participants may question the validity of correspondence, particularly given the widespread problem of fraudulent (spam) notices.

We propose several ways to improve communication between the Social Security Administration and citizens. First, we propose that when the Social Security Administration provides a written notice of a new benefit amount, either by mail or online, it should also include the current benefit amount to make it easier to compare the current and new amounts. This simple change would make it easier for beneficiaries to verify that the new amount is correct and see how much their benefits will increase.

Second, we propose that the Social Security Administration provide, on the beneficiary's online account, an itemized listing of the deductions from gross monthly benefits. Given the large number of potential deductions, it is important for the Social Security Administration to provide that information so that beneficiaries can check the validity of the deductions and know the amounts for individual items.

Third, we propose that the Social Security Administration only use postmarks that correspond to dates when the administration's offices are open. This will reduce suspicion of scams or fraud in the minds of participants.

Fourth, we propose that when sending written communications to participants, the Social Security Administration should provide its mailing addresses, phone numbers, and hours of operation so that participants can more easily know how to resolve problems, learn more, and ask other questions.

Provide Free Financial Assistance

The National Commission on Fiscal Responsibility and Reform (2010, p. 52) proposed the following: "Direct the Social Security Administration to improve information on retirement choices, better inform future beneficiaries on the financial implications of early retirement, and promote greater retirement savings."

SOCIAL SECURITY FOR FUTURE GENERATIONS

Deciding when to claim Social Security benefits is challenging for many participants; however, the available online tools for retirement planning—including those that focus on when to claim Social Security benefits—may not fully meet the needs of some participants. The Social Security Administration's benefit calculators are useful, but additional resources are in demand (Social Security Administration 2025a).

Many participants would value the opportunity to receive more personalized guidance than online benefit calculators can provide, and they would generally prefer to receive it from the Social Security Administration. Martin and Kintzel (2016) compared free online tools for people deciding when to claim their Social Security benefits. They found that, "Although SSA remains neutral regarding the claiming decision, many individuals would prefer advice on the best age to claim." Social Security is complicated. If you speak with two different people on the Social Security Administration helpline, you may receive two different answers (Andrews 2022).

Since 1988, the Social Security Administration has provided a toll-free telephone number (800-772-1213) that people can call to obtain help with their benefits. The number is accessible Monday through Friday and receives twenty-eight million calls a year. Near the end of 2024, the average wait time was thirteen minutes (Social Security Administration 2025l). However, in 2025, wait times were substantially longer.

Private financial advisors tend to be expensive. Many people cannot afford their services. Furthermore, financial advisors may not act in their clients' best interests when providing advice about when to claim Social Security benefits (Blanchett and Fichtner 2023). It might be advantageous for the client to delay Social Security benefits (to receive the higher monthly amount); however, this decision would reduce the advisor's compensation if the client withdraws personal financial assets while postponing benefits. As a result, some financial advisors can be biased toward steering the client toward claiming Social Security benefits early so as to keep more money in the investment portfolio. Thus, "financial advisor compensation can have a direct impact on the quality of services provided" (Blanchett and Fichtner 2023, p. 55).

The US Bureau of Labor Statistics (2025) has noted that financial advisors have been facing job competition from robo advisors, indicating the success of these tools in providing financial advice.

We propose that the Social Security Administration should provide a free robo advisor that is designed for Social Security questions. That program would answer questions about when participants could claim their Social Security benefits, how different claiming options affect benefits, and other questions. The program could provide general information in simple language. The information provided by the robo advisor would be limited to official Social Security data. Our proposed program could be updated as needed to provide accurate information.

Raise the Full Retirement Age

In 1983, when the last major Social Security reform occurred, the full retirement age was gradually raised from sixty-five to sixty-seven. This policy change created some lasting confusion. The 1983 law created confusion about the age at which beneficiaries could receive *maximum* benefits. The law did not change that age, which is still seventy. The 1983 law had little to do with workers' retirement ages; they can still retire at age sixty-two or the age at which they can receive maximum benefits, which remains at seventy.

However, by raising the full retirement age, the government in 1983 found a nontransparent way of cutting Social Security benefits. That lack of transparency may be why the idea of raising it again today is a popular policy with some politicians, given the difficulty in enacting reforms. The Congressional Budget Office (2024) noted that all people affected by an increase in the full retirement age would receive a smaller amount of Social Security benefits over their lifetimes.

However, despite the lack of transparency in the past, the idea of raising the full retirement age now has merits—if life expectancy for *all* major demographic and economic groups increases. If people typically live longer than in the past, then it might make sense to delay retirement. Doing so could alleviate the financial costs of sustaining Social Security. However, it may be difficult for some older workers who want to postpone retirement to do so, due to ageism on the part of some employers.

Between 2016 and 2060, the Census Bureau projected life expectancy to increase by 6.1 years (Medina, Sabo, and Vespa 2020), which would be 1.4 years over a ten-year period. If that outlook occurs, and if today's full retirement age is left as is, then the length of time that people receive benefits will also increase. Table 6-1 shows the historical increase in life expectancy at age sixty-five. The increase in life expectancy raises Social Security's costs by raising the number of years that beneficiaries receive benefits.

Between 1940 and 2019, the life expectancy at age sixty-five for men rose by 6.2 years; for women, it rose by 7.3 years. Over a shorter period—comparing life expectancy in 2000 versus 2019—it rose by 2.2 years for men and 1.7 years for women. Thus, the table shows that if the full retirement age were increased by one year on average, then both men and women at age sixty-five would receive benefits for more years than if they had been sixty-five in 2000. If they delayed retirement one year to age sixty-six, they would still have a longer expected retirement period with no change in annual benefits.

Year	Men	Women
1940	11.9	13.4
2000	15.9	19.0
2019	18.1	20.7

Table 6-1: Life expectancy starting at age sixty-five. Source: American Academy of Actuaries (2022a)

In 2025, the Republican Study Committee in the House of Representatives proposed raising the full retirement age from sixty-seven to sixty-nine. This change would occur over eight years, raising the full retirement age by three months per year. It could start for those turning sixty-two in 2027 (Heilman 2025).

We propose raising the full retirement age from sixty-seven to sixty-eight at the rate of one month per year, with a delay of ten years. If life expectancy *has not increased for all major demographic and economic groups* by at least one year compared to 2020, then the start of this proposed change would be postponed. This approach would give fair deference to population groups with lower life expectancies, at least to some extent. Our proposal would not affect the date of Social Security's trust fund depletion, but it would improve its long-term financing.

Our proposal could be modified in various ways. One would be to increase the full retirement age to sixty-nine (the 2025 Republican idea). Congress could also set a lower or higher life expectancy; that is, the baseline for deciding whether to raise the full retirement age. Congress could also change the delay period before the new policy takes effect, or beneficiaries with low benefits could be exempted from this change. Another option, proposed by Biggs and Shoven (2025), is to raise the full retirement age and at the same time adjust the benefit formula so that there is no net effect on lower-income beneficiaries. This option would also have a larger negative effect for high-income beneficiaries than middle income beneficiaries.

Gradually Increase the Standard Early Retirement Age

In addition to longer lifespans, another factor today affects people's choices about when to retire. The average number of hours people work each week has not changed much in recent decades. The average workweek has been thirty-eight to thirty-nine hours since 2003 (GAO 2024b). The "standard" full-time workweek, such as in the federal government, remains at forty hours.

At the same time, average family wealth has increased considerably since Social Security started paying benefits in 1940. With greater wealth, people want more leisure. Because the average hours of work each week have not declined, people are choosing to retire earlier. Therefore, the increase in leisure time has occurred primarily during retirement. Arguably, the increased demand for lifetime leisure is the reason why the earliest retirement age was reduced to age sixty-two in 1956 for women and in 1961 for men, and why subsequent proposals to raise that age have been unpopular.

Again, it is helpful to consider what other countries are doing. Between 1983 and 2013, nine out of twelve OECD countries lowered the generosity of their social security benefits. These countries were Belgium, Canada, France, Germany, Italy, Japan, the Netherlands, Spain, and the United Kingdom (Borsch-Supan and Coile 2020). As stated earlier, the United States cut benefits by raising the full retirement age, so that study that did not include the US in its list of countries that cut benefits. This reflects the US policy's lack of transparency.

Some countries have raised the *early* retirement age. In a study of twelve OECD countries, ten of them raised the early retirement age for social security between 1996 and 2019. Those countries were Belgium, Denmark, France, Germany, Italy, Japan, the Netherlands, Spain, Sweden, and the United Kingdom (Borsch-Supan and Coile 2020).

We propose a new concept: the *standard early retirement age.* This new policy, which would be phased in, would set age sixty-three as the standard early retirement age. Implementation would only occur if life expectancy for all major demographic and economic groups has risen by at least one year. Our proposal would retain age sixty-two as the early retirement age. As is the case today, those who claim benefits at age sixty-two would receive reduced benefits that year and all subsequent years. This proposal is a more transparent alternative to the previous proposal, and it does not rely on the confusing concept of the full retirement age.

If we assume that life expectancy in 2035 has risen by at least one year for all major demographic and economic groups, starting in 2035, benefits at every age would gradually be moved back so that, eventually, the benefits people currently receive at age sixty-two would be provided at the standard early retirement age of sixty-three. Similarly, benefits at every higher age would be reduced by the same percentage. Starting in 2035, the standard early retirement age would be raised by a month every year until 2044, which is when the standard early retirement age would reach sixty-three. People would still be able to collect benefits at age sixty-two, but at a reduced level. People could offset this cut in annual benefits by postponing retirement by one year.

In 2022, 27 percent of retirees claimed Social Security benefits at age sixty-two (Royal 2024). Under the new plan, participants would still be able to claim retirement benefits at age sixty-two, but the language of standard early retirement age could encourage participants to retire at age sixty-three or later.

In alignment with Social Security actuaries, this proposal assumes that over the next thirty years, further improvements in life expectancy will occur. As shown in table 6-2, Social Security's actuaries predict that between 2023 and 2055 life expectancy at age sixty-five will increase by more than two years for both men and women. Thus, someone claiming benefits at age sixty-three in 2055 will have more than one year longer of expected retirement than a similar person claiming benefits at age sixty-two in 2023. For a person claiming benefits at age sixty-three, when this proposal is fully phased in, her or his monthly benefit would be 6.7 percent less than it otherwise would be for claiming at that age. The effect of this reduction on lifetime benefits would be mostly offset by their longer life expectancy.

Year	Men	Women
2023	17.9	20.5
2055	20.3	22.7

Table 6-2: Life expectancy at age sixty-five under the intermediate assumptions of Social Security's actuaries. Source: 2024 OASDI Trustees Report

This proposal will not affect the Social Security trust fund depletion date. It will, however, improve its long-term financing.

CHAPTER 7

Simplifying Social Security

This chapter presents proposals that would make Social Security less confusing. In the past, there was less concern about the difficulty many people had in making financial decisions, which has been highlighted more recently by research on financial literacy. Biggs (2013), in his critique of Social Security, wrote, "The program is simply very hard to understand." The World Bank (2025) agreed, telling its US employees that, "The US tax and Social Security systems are complex." The proposals in this chapter address that critique.

Eliminate Confusing Terminology

There are two common misconceptions about the full retirement age. First, many people think that maximum benefits are received at full retirement age (FRA). They understandably think that the word *full* refers to maximum benefits. When benefits are claimed at the full retirement age, the beneficiary receives 100 percent of a quantity known as the primary insurance amount (PIA). However, by postponing benefits beyond the FRA, people are eligible to receive more than 100 percent of the PIA. Thus, the word *full* is potentially misleading.

Even financial journalists may fail to distinguish between full and maximum benefits. For example, Konish (2023a) wrote, "Social Security's full retirement age—when beneficiaries may receive 100 percent of the benefits they have earned—is currently sixty-seven for people born in 1960 or later." Readers of that statement are likely to assume that 100 percent is the highest possible percentage, even though they can receive higher benefits by claiming later, up to age seventy.

Vernon (2024), writing for *Forbes* magazine, explained that the terms used by the Social Security Administration to describe the benefit-claiming ages can be misleading. The full retirement age is not the age at which maximum benefits are received, since the benefit amount can be increased after full retirement age through delayed retirement credits. Furthermore, the normal retirement age (NRA), another term for the FRA, is neither the average age nor the most common age at which people claim benefits.

Romig (2023a), writing for the Center on Budget and Policy Priorities, offered a more detailed explanation.

> The full retirement age is the age at which full Social Security benefits are paid. Workers can file sooner and collect permanently reduced monthly benefits, or later and get larger monthly benefits. These reductions and credits are designed to be roughly 'actuarially neutral,' meaning that a person with average life expectancy will get around the same lifetime benefits—either a smaller monthly benefit for a longer time, or a bigger monthly benefit for a shorter time. Under current law, retirees get 70 percent of their full benefit if they claim at sixty-two, 100 percent if they claim at sixty-seven, and 124 percent if they claim at seventy (with a sliding scale for every month

between those ages).

Because the word *maximum* can be understood as a synonym for *full*, the concept of full retirement age can be misleading.

The second common misconception is that raising the full retirement age is not a benefit cut when in fact it is. In 2024, House Republicans proposed Social Security reforms that included increasing the FRA in response to increasing life expectancies (Konish 2024). As stated earlier, raising the FRA is a nontransparent way of cutting Social Security benefits. Policymakers may think it is politically easier to raise that age than to state outright that they are cutting benefits. That approach may reflect the political reality of how difficult it is to reform Social Security.

Another common argument is that the FRA should be raised due to increasing life expectancy gains. This idea becomes questionable considering the data on the effect of income inequality on lifespans. Vernon (2024) noted that "recent gains in longevity have only benefited about half of the workforce, mostly leaving out lower-income workers and workers of color."

The concept of the full retirement age appears to be unimportant to most workers. A 2023 survey by the Nationwide Retirement Institute asked respondents whether they knew the age at which they would be eligible for full Social Security benefits. The results indicated that only "13 percent of adults correctly guess[ed] their FRA based on their year of birth. Fifty percent incorrectly stated a lower age and 4 percent incorrectly stated a higher age. Thirty-three percent said they did not know" (Nationwide Retirement Institute 2023, p. 14).

Changing terminology to improve the clarity of

communications would help participants, but simplifying the system by removing unhelpful and outdated concepts would be better. In 2018, Nationwide's annual survey revealed that many people have critical gaps in their knowledge of Social Security. For example, 88 percent of older adults did not know "what factors determine the maximum Social Security benefit an individual can receive" (Godbout 2018).

Tina Ambrozy, who was the president of sales and distribution at Nationwide in 2018, stated that, "Social Security is undoubtedly one of the most complex retirement topics facing American workers, and most are likely unable to grasp the thousands of rules that apply to Social Security" (Godbout 2018). American workers do not need to understand Social Security's thousands of rules. That is a problem for people who write books about Social Security. However, many American workers do not understand the substantially smaller set of rules that apply to their situations.

The language used by other countries is often better. The Government of Canada (2025b) wrote, "The standard age to start the (social security) pension is sixty-five. However, you can start receiving it as early as age sixty or as late as age seventy." The term *standard age* does not have the potentially misleading implication about benefit levels that the term *full retirement age* has.

Senator Bill Cassidy (2025), a Republican, and others introduced legislation to change the Social Security Administration's terminology from *early eligibility age, full retirement age,* and *delayed retirement credits* to *minimum monthly benefit age, standard monthly benefit age,* and *maximum monthly benefit age* to better reflect how the program works.

We propose two changes. First, we propose that the Social

Security Administration drop the concept of the full retirement age when communicating with participants. Instead of making the full retirement age the central focus, the Social Security Administration could use a single system of benefit adjustments from age sixty-two (the minimum benefit age) to age seventy (the maximum benefit age). This new system would be simpler than the current system, which is complicated by different frameworks for calculating benefits claimed at ages below and above full retirement age.

Second, we propose dropping the primary insurance amount (PIA) concept, which refers to benefits received at full retirement age. Participants would be more likely to understand the system if they only needed to know about the minimum and maximum benefit. The Social Security Administration could make these changes in its public communications while internally retaining the concepts of the FRA and PIA, if that terminology makes it easier for Social Security actuaries to calculate benefit amounts. Such technical details need not be referenced in Social Security communications to the public. Most people probably do not understand the primary insurance amount (PIA) concept, given that the full retirement age (FRA) concept is confusing.

Munnell (2022) wrote about the confusion related to the Social Security Administration's emphasis on the FRA, which she argued is no longer worth focusing on.

> So, if age seventy is the age at which Social Security pays the highest benefits, what is all this talk about the 'full retirement age?' Before the delayed retirement credit became actuarially fair, the full retirement age was a meaningful concept. It was the age at which lifetime benefits were the highest. Once the delayed retirement

credit became actuarially fair, the full retirement age became largely meaningless. It does not describe the age when benefits are first available. That is age sixty-two. It does not describe the age when monthly benefits are at their maximum. That is age seventy.

If the concept of the full retirement age were abandoned, policymakers could not use raising the full retirement age as a nontransparent way to cut benefits. Aaron (2010) has critiqued this "argument for cutting benefits across the board—misleadingly called 'raising the retirement age'" because it may have little impact on when people claim benefits.

One option would be to provide better education about these terms. However, the concepts—not just the terms—are problematic. The FRA is just one point on a line of increasing benefits in relation to age. The more serious problem, however, occurs when lawmakers use the term to hide benefit cuts.

Count All Covered Earnings

Social Security benefits are calculated based on the thirty-five years of the worker's highest covered earnings. The Social Security Administration estimates that for workers born between 1950 and 1959 and surviving to age sixty-seven, 62 percent had thirty-five or more years of covered earnings between ages twenty-two and sixty-seven (Congressional Research Service 2022a). Those workers pay Social Security payroll taxes on earnings during all those years. However, they will only receive an increase in benefits for the thirty-five years of highest earnings. This policy is particularly unfair to long-career, low-wage workers.

Similarly to Steuerle and Bakija (1994), we propose that the Social Security Administration should count all covered earnings when calculating benefits. However, we would apply this rule only to workers with more than forty years of covered earnings, and we would subtract the lowest five years.

We propose that all earnings be counted when calculating Social Security benefits for people with more than forty years of earnings. The lowest five years would be subtracted, and the remainder of indexed earnings summed and divided by thirty-five. Thus, if a person had forty-five years of covered earnings, the lowest five years would be dropped. The remaining forty years would be summed and then divided by thirty-five. This way, long-career, low-wage workers could raise their Social Security benefits by continuing to work. However, to limit the benefits of long-career high-earners, the current maximum average wages would be used.

A proposal by the Progressive Policy Institute (Ritz and Morris 2025) would also count all years of covered earnings, but that proposal would only base benefits on years rather than on earnings.

Though some older workers may still encounter age discrimination, this proposal could encourage greater labor force participation at older ages. Under current policy, older workers who have already worked forty years cannot increase future Social Security benefits by working an additional year, if their earnings in that year were lower than in prior years. In that case, the payroll tax would not be offset by an increase in future benefits and thus would operate as a tax on earnings, discouraging work at older ages.

Our proposal would also reduce the current redistribution from workers with long careers to workers with shorter careers by reducing the penalty on long careers. The effect of this option on high earners would be limited by the maximum allowable benefit.

Our proposal could be adjusted to focus on low-wage earners with long careers. We prefer this proposal more than others that increase the number of years counted in the benefit calculation. That type of proposal would bring more years of zero or low earnings into the benefit calculation, particularly for women, thereby reducing benefits.

Simplify the Presentation of the Benefit Formula

Workers' monthly Social Security benefits are calculated by using their primary insurance amount (PIA). The first step in that calculation is to divide the worker's average indexed monthly earnings (AIME) into segments. Average indexed monthly earnings are indexed for changes in wage levels rather than changes in price levels. Higher earners have their earnings divided into three segments, middle earners have their earnings divided into two segments, and lower earners have all their earnings in one segment. Then each segment is multiplied by a different percentage, with higher earnings segments multiplied by lower percentage factors. (The three percentage factors, going from low to high earnings, are 90 percent, 32 percent, and 15 percent.) Then the calculations for each worker's earnings segments are summed. Thus, the calculation includes several separate calculations. This approach is complex and nontransparent as to what percentage of earnings the worker will receive as benefits. That requires an additional calculation.

We propose to simplify the benefit calculation so that a single number would be multiplied by the person's average indexed earnings. The worker would be able to readily see what her earnings replacement rate and benefit would be. The simple calculation would multiply the worker's average indexed monthly earnings by the corresponding replacement rate for the benefit claiming age she had selected. The Social Security Administration's Office of the Chief Actuary could create a table showing the replacement rate at different levels of average indexed monthly earnings. It could also provide an online calculator that would indicate the replacement rate and benefit for each level of average indexed monthly earnings.

The workers' primary insurance amount is their monthly benefit at full retirement age (age sixty-seven for workers born in 1960 or later). This amount would be determined by multiplying the average indexed monthly earnings by the relevant replacement rate percentage factor. The average indexed monthly earnings would be provided online at the workers' individual Social Security accounts. With that information, they could determine their replacement rate relative to their Social Security covered earnings and how that rate would change with increases or decreases in their average indexed monthly earnings. With this proposal, the benefit amounts for each person would remain the same as the current benefit amount, with no effect on Social Security solvency.

Table 7-1 provides an example of how this proposal could work. People who know their AIME could use the replacement rates from that table to estimate what their PIA would be. That could be obtained by a single calculation of multiplying their AIME by a replacement rate from the table.

Average Indexed Monthly Earnings (AIME)	Primary Insurance Amount (PIA)	Replacement rate for AIME (PIA/AIME)
$1,000	$900	90%
$3,000	$1,671	56%
$4,000	$1,991	50%
$5,000	$2,311	46%
$6,000	$2,631	44%
$7,000	$2,951	42%
$8,000	$3,168	40%
$9,000	$3,318	37%
$10,000	$3,468	35%
$11,000	$3,618	33%
$12,000	$3,768	32%
$13,000	$3,918	30%

Table 7-1: Replacement rate and primary insurance amount (PIA) for different average indexed monthly earnings (AIMEs) for 2025. Source: Authors' calculations

Reduce Spousal Benefits in Higher-Income Families

The structure of Social Security benefits today is the result of compromises between individual equity and social adequacy. Benefits for spouses and survivors are received without any reduction in other spouse's benefits. By contrast, in workplace pensions, the option of survivors' benefits always comes with a reduction in the spousal benefits so that the total benefits package is roughly equal in value, whether or not a survivor's option is chosen.

Social Security's spousal benefits are based on need: Two people need higher benefits than one person. However, marriage rates have declined and divorce rates have increased. In addition, more women are qualifying for Social Security benefits based on their own earnings record. For these reasons, a smaller percentage of the population today receives spousal benefits compared to the past. If we compare single people and married couples with two earners who have similar earnings, these benefits are unfair to single people. A family with the same level of earnings will receive larger benefits if they qualify for spousal benefits than a single person.

However, the Pew Research Center (Cohn, Livingston, and Wang 2014) found that, despite a common perception that nonworking wives are married to high-income husbands, relatively few stay-at-home mothers are in highly educated, high-income families. It is more common that they are in families with relatively low wages and stay at home because they cannot afford childcare.

Thompson and Carasso (2002, p. 137) noted that Social Security spousal and survivors' benefits tend to be higher in the

United States than in other developed countries. However, benefits for single people tend to be lower. Among the sixteen developed countries they examined, they found that "for one-earner couples at the average earnings level, the spouse's supplement is higher in the United States than anywhere else. . . . The supplement amounts to 20 percent of the average wage in the United States, but it averages only 13 percent of the average wage in the other countries with such a supplement."

For example, the United Kingdom provides substantially lower benefits for spouses than the United States. The US and Belgium provide spousal benefits that are scaled to the earnings level of the working spouses, a feature not found in any of the other fourteen countries. Favreault, Sammartino, and Steuerle (2002b, p. 177) said, "A system designed to meet the needs of the US population in 1940 may not meet the needs of US families in 2040."

Currently, spousal benefits in the US are 32.5 percent of a worker's primary insurance amount (the benefit at the full retirement age) if the spouse claims those benefits at age sixty-two. This amount increases to 50 percent if the spouse claims benefits at full retirement age.

We propose reducing spousal benefit percentages to 25 percent and 40 percent for workers with earnings above the second bend point in the Social Security benefit formula. This would partially address the inequity faced by single workers (DePaulo 2017) and two-earner families with similar earnings. Because the reduction is only for a spouse's benefit, this would result in a reduction in family benefits of 7 percent if no offsetting changes are made by the spouse.

With this change, some spouses may offset the reduction by delaying claiming spousal benefits. Also, some spouses may offset the reduction by claiming benefits on their earnings record when that results in higher benefits.

A possible variation of this proposal is to apply a different criterion, depending on the person. For example, it could only affect people with more than a minimum amount of Social Security benefits, those having AIMEs above the first bend point in the PIA formula.

Raise the Eligibility Age for Survivors' Benefits

In 1980, 23.2 million people received OASI benefits. By 2023, that number had risen to 52.7 million people, an increase of 127 percent. By comparison, in 1980, 7.6 million people received OASI *survivors'* benefits, but by 2023 that number had fallen to 5.8 million, a decrease of 30 percent. Over those years, the percentage of survivors who claimed benefits fell from 21.4 percent of OASI beneficiaries to 8.7 percent (Social Security Administration 2025e). This decrease is partly due to an increase in female labor force participation and wages, but it is also due to a decrease in marriage rates.

The female labor force participation rate has increased over time, but in 2021 the labor force participation rate for women age forty-five to fifty-four was 72 percent, compared to 83 percent for men (US Bureau of Labor Statistics 2023d). Between 1960 to 2022, the percentage of women who were married fell from 65 percent to 46 percent (Loo 2024). Another study found that between 1995 and 2018, the percentage of adults age eighteen and older who were married declined from 58 percent to 53 percent while the percentage who were cohabiting rose from 3 percent to 7 percent (Horowitz, Graf, and Livingston 2019).

Tamborini and Whitman (2007) compared data for 2001 with data for 1985. They found an increase in the percentage of women who were never married or who were married for less than ten years, which is the number of years required to be eligible for Social Security survivors' benefits. The Social Security Administration (2013b) reported that a significantly larger proportion of women were ineligible for spousal and survivors' benefits in 2009 than in 1990 due to changes in marital trends. The percentage of women age sixty-five and older who had never married rose from 5.5 percent in 1990 to 6.4 percent in 2022 (Loo and Brown 2024). The number of widowed mothers and fathers receiving survivors' benefits declined from 154,000 in 2012 to 114,000 in 2021 (Urban and Collins 2023).

With that general background in mind, we can also look at other factors that influence our proposals, presented later in this section. First, we should consider the eligibility age for survivors' benefits. A person can claim survivors' benefits at age sixty, but she or he cannot claim spousal benefits until age sixty-two. To simplify Social Security's rules, we propose increasing the eligibility age for survivors' benefits to sixty-two.

Second, it is important to understand the rules pertaining to survivors' benefits after remarriage. Rosanes (2024) summarizes the legislative changes that have occurred over time.

> Originally, widows and widowers lost their eligibility for survivor benefits if they remarried, regardless of their age. This changed in July 1965 when a law was passed allowing widows to remarry after

turning sixty. This initial rule change, however, only permitted remarried widows and widowers to claim an amount equal to half of their deceased spouse's full retirement benefits. A bigger change in December 1977 allowed surviving spouses to remarry after age sixty and still collect the full survivor benefits. The amount is equivalent to 100 percent of their deceased spouse's full retirement benefit, which is also referred to as the primary insurance amount (PIA). This rule change did not apply to surviving divorced spouses. The final rule change was passed in January 1984. This allowed remarried surviving divorced spouses to claim the full survivor benefits as long as they were married for at least ten years before divorcing, and they waited until age sixty or later to remarry. Remarriage, however, nullifies a divorced spouse's right to claim spousal benefits on a living ex-spouse. This [is the] rule unless the later marriage ends in death, annulment, or divorce.

Third, many people's Social Security benefits are affected by what happens after remarriage following a divorce. Older people lose spousal or survivors' benefits if they remarry before age sixty following a divorce (Social Security Administration 2025r). This loss can force people to choose between remarriage and their Social Security benefits. If they remarry at ages sixty or sixty-one, they can receive survivors' benefits from their former marriage. If they remarry at age sixty-two or older, they can receive survivors' benefits from their former marriage or benefits based on their current marriage.

We propose changes to each of the three issues described above. First, regarding the eligibility age for survivors' benefits, we propose raising that age from sixty to sixty-two so that it is consistent with the eligibility ages for worker and spousal benefits. Warshawsky (2021) has also recommended this change. Having a different age is an unnecessary complication. With more women in the labor force, the wage gap between men and women is falling, and the general increase in life expectancy over many years reduces the need for such an early eligibility age. This change would have no effect on the eligibility age for survivors with disabilities, or survivors taking care of children under age eighteen, or for those taking care of children with disabilities under age nineteen.

Second, we propose raising the eligibility age for survivors' benefits after remarriage to age sixty-two. Thus, persons remarrying at sixty-two and older could choose between the survivors' benefits they would receive from their former spouse's earnings record, or from benefits based on their own earnings record, or from the benefits of the new spouse.

Third, we propose changing the rules pertaining to the eligibility age for benefits after a remarriage following divorce. People sixty-two and older who remarry after a divorce could continue receiving the Social Security benefits they currently receive, or they could receive their new spouse's benefits if those benefits are higher. This change would end the difference between remarrying following the death of a spouse and remarrying following divorce. It would permit older persons to remarry without having to consider that decision's effect on Social Security benefits. This change would primarily affect women because they are more likely to receive spousal benefits than men.

Establish Consistent Requirements for Spousal and Survivors' Benefits

Under the current system, the Social Security claiming options are complicated, so much so that financial advice columnists often recommend that people consult a financial advisor—which most people cannot afford—before making a decision. Andrews (2022), writing for AARP, stated, "Deciding when and how to file for retirement benefits is often tricky, especially if you have a spouse. Not thinking through the details can cost you thousands of dollars in lost benefits."

As with worker and spousal benefits, survivors' benefits are reduced when claimed at the earliest age. However, dually entitled survivors can claim survivors' benefits at an early age. When they reach the full retirement age, which is age sixty-seven for people born in 1960 or later, or if they postpone benefits to age seventy, they can claim benefits based on their earnings with no reduction for having taken the survivors' benefits earlier. According to the Social Security Administration (2025c), "If you're eligible for survivor and another benefit, you'll choose the payment that's best for you. The payments won't be added together. You can also switch benefits later. For example, you could start with survivor benefits and then change to retirement at age seventy when that payment is highest."

It used to be possible to use this strategy for spousal benefits. People could claim those benefits first and then switch to their own benefits. This strategy allowed them to take advantage of delaying their own benefits. A law passed in 2015, which fully took effect in 2024, outlawed that option (Markowitz 2018). We argue that such a strategy should no longer be available to people receiving survivors' benefits.

Nationwide Retirement Institute (2021), in an article explaining Social Security survivors' benefits, wrote, "There are several layers of complexity to the widow(er) benefit that make it difficult to determine whether to claim benefits early, when to wait and when to switch to the survivor's own benefit." One of those layers relates to workers who died before age sixty-two (Davies and Li 2022). Our proposal deals with the situation for workers who die at sixty-two years or older.

A second layer of complication pertains to the base for calculating spousal and survivors' benefits. Although Social Security benefits for spouses and survivors are based on the earnings record of each person's partner, spousal benefits are based on the partner's primary insurance amount (Social Security Administration 2013a). By contrast, survivors' benefits are based on the partner's actual benefits (Social Security Administration 2024cc). This difference often results in a smaller percentage of increase in survivors' benefits compared to spousal benefits.

It is complicated to use the primary insurance amount as the base for calculating spousal benefits while using the actual benefit as the base for calculating the survivors' benefits. This approach makes it difficult for participants to determine their benefit amounts. Most participants and their spouses presumably do not know what the primary insurance amount is, and they may not be sure what the term even means.

In response to these complications, we propose two solutions. First, we propose basing the benefit amount for *both* spousal and survivors' benefits on the age at which a person first makes any type of Social Security benefits claim. Thus, if recipients of survivors' benefits later claim benefits based on their own earnings, those benefits would be based on the first age at which they received any type of Social Security OASI benefits. This system would be simpler and more equitable relative to the treatment of people who only receive worker benefits.

Second, we propose using the same basis to determine both spousal and survivors' benefits. This would improve simplicity and transparency. Specifically, we propose that both types of benefits be based on the partner's actual benefit amount, which is simpler and more transparent for participants than basing both on the partner's primary insurance amount. Ideally, this would be done so that participants can easily figure out their benefit levels. This proposal would improve consistency in the policies for different benefit types and thereby make Social Security simpler to understand.

Simplify the Eligibility Requirement for Survivors' Benefits

To be eligible to receive survivors' benefits, a person must have been married for at least nine months at the time of the spouse's death (Jarrett 2025). As discussed earlier, the person also must be at least age sixty. An exception to the rule is when a person dies in the line of duty as an active military service member.

The nine-month rule for survivors' benefits is unusual within the Social Security regulatory framework. It is less than the requirement for receiving spousal benefits and the requirement for receiving Medicare benefits as a surviving spouse. The length-of-marriage requirement to receive spousal benefits is one year. The length-of-marriage requirement to be eligible for Medicare coverage based on a deceased spouse's earnings record is also one year (UnitedHealthcare 2025).

Because it is not general practice for the Social Security Administration to have partial-year requirements, the requirement is not intuitive. It would be easier for participants to understand if the rule was one year. Among other wealthy countries like the United States, we are unaware of any example of a partial-year requirement other than when a policy change is being phased in.

We propose raising the minimum length of marriage required for receiving Social Security survivors' benefits from nine months to one year. The current exceptions would continue to apply. This change would make the requirement consistent with the requirement for eligibility for Medicare benefits as a surviving spouse.

Survivors' Benefits for Unmarried Couples

Views about marriage have changed, and the number of unmarried couples has doubled between 1990 and 2024 (Hahn 2024). A survey of 906 Gen Z and millennial respondents, conducted by the Thriving Center of Psychology, found that roughly 40 percent believe marriage is an outdated tradition. Even though 83 percent said they would like to get married at some point, 85 percent also reported that they did not feel marriage is needed to "have a fulfilling and committed relationship" (Nazarro 2023).

This change in the prevalence of couples getting married will continue to affect people's eligibility for Social Security benefits. As stated by the Social Security Administration (2022c), "Marital status is important in determining entitlement to retirement, survivors, Medicare, and disability benefits."

Couples, including same-sex couples, can qualify for Social Security benefits through marriage or common-law marriage. A common-law marriage is considered valid under some state laws even when there is no formal ceremony or marriage license. The Social Security Administration also recognizes some nonmarital legal relationships, such as some civil unions (also called civil partnerships) and domestic partnerships. Common-law marriages and civil partnerships are recognized in some states after a couple has lived together for seven years and presents themselves as married, but many states do not recognize those relationships. Same-sex partners in some states are eligible for spousal and survivors' benefits from Social Security, even though they were not married or in a common-law marriage because state laws prevented them from getting married.

We propose that unmarried couples (including same-sex couples) who meet specific requirements be eligible for spousal and survivors' benefits. This proposal could be adjusted. For example, the Social Security Administration could require that couples cohabitate for at least seven years (perhaps less). They would not need to present themselves as being married, but they would have to show they had a stable, long-term cohabiting and financially interconnected relationship.

CHAPTER 8

Improving Information and Assistance

The proposals in this chapter would improve the administrative functioning of the Social Security Administration, facilitating its interactions with participants. Although administrative issues do not have the same priority as issues of equity and social justice, they are nonetheless important for people who interact with Social Security.

Mandate Staff Hiring When Customer Service Falters

For many years, participants have faced long wait times when they call the Social Security Administration's national 800 helpline. In December 2023, Lightman (2023) wrote, "Trying to get through to Social Security on its 800 number? Be very, very patient. Wait times have been averaging roughly thirty-five minutes."

More recently, the situation appears to be growing worse. As of early 2025, the staffing at the Social Security Administration was the lowest since 1972. The small pool of workers must provide service to a record number of participants. Despite this situation, the House of Representatives in late 2024 rejected funding for additional staffing (Jay and Wile 2024). Earlier that year, the House of Representatives refused a request from the Social Security Administration for more money to hire additional staff, which forced it to implement a hiring freeze. As a result of the understaffing, a call in late 2024 by one of the authors to the Social Security Administration's assistance line had a wait time of more than ninety minutes.

In February 2025, the Trump Administration announced that it was closing forty-seven Social Security Administration field offices (Levalley 2025). Field offices are the key sources of assistance where people go for interviews when they are filing applications. That same month, the Social Security Administration stated that it would lay off about seven thousand staff members in response to President Trump's executive order to reduce the federal workforce, which it did (Social Security Administration, Press Office 2025a). This staffing cut was the largest in Social Security's history, a 13 percent cut. The last time the Social Security Administration had such low staffing was in 1967 when it had 480 beneficiaries for every employee. In 2025, after the staffing cut, there were 1,480 beneficiaries for every staff person. Nearly half of the senior executives resigned, leading to a massive brain drain in the agency (Romig and O'Connor 2025). In early March 2025, on a call to the helpline by one of this book's authors, a recorded message stated that the estimated wait time would exceed two hours.

We propose requiring the Social Security Administration to increase helpline staffing by 5 percent if, over the previous three months, the average wait time on the customer service helpline is more than an hour. An alternative to this proposal would be to select a less lengthy wait time.

We also propose that the Social Security Administration study the possibility of increasing the hours of operation for its national helpline. The current hours are 8 am to 7 pm local time Monday through Friday. By extending the hours, the Social Security Administration could potentially reduce the average wait times. Doing so would require funding for additional staff.

Beyond facing long wait times on the helpline, participants also must be patient to receive a determination about their benefits. Therefore, our proposal would legally require the Social Security Administration to increase benefits-determination staff by 5 percent if during the previous three months the average wait time for staff to resolve a benefits claim is more than two months.

Our proposal could be adjusted by setting shorter wait times to determine the hiring requirement. Instead of basing the hiring decision on an average time metric, the requirement could be based on the percentage of people whose benefit claims are handled within a set number of weeks. In that case, the number of weeks and the percentage would be policy variables.

Mobile Service Units

For some people and some services, it is easiest, and in some cases required, for participants to resolve problems by meeting in person with a Social Security Administration help desk employee. For many people living in rural areas, going to a Social Security Administration office requires driving an hour or longer. The Social Security Administration offers Video Service Delivery Centers (VSDCs) to make its services more accessible in some rural areas and Native American reservation communities (Social Security Administration 2023a).

We propose that the Social Security Administration provide mobile service units for rural and other underserved areas. Many beneficiaries, particularly older adults and individuals with disabilities, may struggle with online systems or face transportation barriers that make in-person office visits difficult. The Social Security Administration's mobile service units, like mobile health care units, would help with applications, appeals, and general inquiries. Mobile units could partner with local organizations, such as libraries and senior centers, to set up temporary service points.

Social Security Applications at Birth

A decades-old rule has allowed parents to apply for Social Security numbers at hospitals shortly after the birth of a child. According to Bystry (2021), writing for the Social Security Administration, "We've made it easy. If your child is born in a hospital, the most convenient way to apply for a Social Security number is at that hospital before you leave." This rule is called the Enumeration at Birth program (Social Security Administration 2022d). New parents at a hospital or birthing center, or those using a licensed midwife, can request a Social Security number during the birth registration process.

In 2025, the Social Security Administration ended that policy in Maine, forcing parents to take their newborn children to a field office to register them for a Social Security number. As of early 2025, Maine only had eight Social Security Administration field offices (Eckstein 2025). The Social Security Administration reversed that policy a few days later due to objections (Zehra 2025).

We propose legislation that ensures that parents can apply for Social Security numbers for their children in hospitals, birthing centers, or with registered midwives. This legislation would ensure that the Enumeration at Birth program cannot be changed at the option of the Social Security Administration.

Improve Information Technology

Much of the Social Security Administration's information technology (IT) infrastructure is decades old. Social Security's core programming language, known as COBOL (Common Business Oriented Language), is extremely outdated (Luhby 2025). The first version of COBOL was released in 1960 (China and Goodwin 2025). Maintaining these systems is costly and complex, requiring specialized knowledge that is increasingly rare.

The Social Security Administration manages highly sensitive personal and financial data, making it a prime target for cyberattacks. Weaknesses in identity verification systems create risks of identity theft and fraudulent benefit claims. The Social Security Administration has expanded its digital services, but its online platforms sometimes suffer from usability problems, outages, and slow processing times.

The Social Security Administration's IT problems could undermine future reforms. Slow adoption of new systems may stall reforms that rely on automated calculations or benefit adjustments. Addressing these IT challenges will likely require significant investment in modernization, cybersecurity upgrades, and workforce development to support Social Security reform efforts.

The Social Security Administration Office of the Inspector General (2024, p. 179) has analyzed the IT needs of the Social Security Administration. It summarized its report as follows: "[The] SSA continues relying on outdated applications and technologies to process its core workloads (for example, retirement and disability claims) and knowledge of its dated applications and legacy infrastructure will diminish as developers retire. Without complete and timely modernization of its legacy systems, SSA runs the risk of increased maintenance costs and decreased capacity to support business and processing needs."

Recent technology modernization at the Social Security Administration, financed by the Technology Modernization Fund, has focused on digitizing forms. The goal is to make them easier to access and to streamline beneficiary communications (US General Services Administration 2024). According to Clare Martorana, federal chief information officer and technology modernization fund board chair, the "SSA has been burdened by paper processes for too long, impacting their ability to upload documents, adjudicate claims online, and communicate digitally with their customers" (US General Services Administration 2024).

In 2024, the Social Security Administration Office of the Inspector General (2024, p. 173) reported that "our contract auditor assessed SSA's Information Security program as 'not effective.' The contractor identified deficiencies that could limit SSA's ability to protect its information systems and data. . . . The contract auditor recommended SSA continue refining its enterprise architecture system inventory, software, and hardware asset inventories; implementing its cyber-security risk management strategy; and improving its process for integrating and formalizing risk-based decisions into cyber-security program monitoring activities."

In addition to these information technology problems, the Social Security Administration cut its technology personnel team roughly in half in 2025 (Luhby 2025). These cuts were much greater than the overall cuts of 13 percent, which were generally considered to be severe (Romig and O'Connor 2025).

We propose that the Social Security Administration update its information technology. In addition, we propose that legislation would require the Social Security Administration to maintain adequate information technology staff.

Identity Theft

Identity fraud cost an estimated $47 billion in 2024, with roughly 18.2 million victims. Social Security numbers are a primary target of criminals hoping to perpetrate identity fraud. Long wait times at the Social Security Administration make trying to resolve problems caused by these crimes even more difficult.

Senators Chuck Grassley, a Republican, and Maggie Hassan, a Democrat, have sponsored legislation that, if passed, will require the Social Security Administration to improve the assistance it provides victims after their Social Security numbers are stolen and used for fraud. The Improving Social Security's Service to Victims of Identity Theft Act would compel the Social Security Administration to provide a single point of contact to assist victims, track the individual's case to completion, and "coordinate with other specialized units to resolve case issues as quickly as possible" (Ianzito 2025).

We propose requiring the Social Security Administration to improve the assistance it provides to participants whose Social Security numbers have been stolen.

In the next chapter, we look at proposals for improving Social Security related to social justice.

CHAPTER 9

Social Justice and Equity Proposals

In this chapter, we present two proposals designed to resolve issues faced by people who have been convicted of crimes, including those who were wrongfully convicted, and their spouses. We also present proposals relating more generally to the equity of benefits received.

Wrongful Convictions

International Wrongful Conviction Day, celebrated on October 2, raises awareness of the causes of and remedies for wrongful conviction. It recognizes the tremendous personal, social, and emotional costs of wrongful conviction imposed on innocent people and their families. Wrongful Conviction Day began as a project of the Innocence Network, an affiliation of roughly seventy organizations dedicated to providing pro bono legal and investigative services to individuals seeking to prove their innocence when they have been convicted of crimes. These efforts hope to rectify the causes of wrongful convictions and to support the exonerated after they are freed (Wrongful Conviction Day 2024). Stevenson (2014) discussed many of these problems with the criminal justice system, but many persist more than a decade later.

SOCIAL SECURITY FOR FUTURE GENERATIONS

When a person receiving Social Security benefits is convicted of a crime and incarcerated for more than thirty days, that person's benefits are suspended. However, if the person has a spouse or child who receives benefits, those benefits continue (Social Security Administration 2023b).

When a person is convicted of a crime and the conviction is subsequently overturned, the person is exonerated and the crime is removed from the legal record. However, if the person was receiving Social Security benefits before the conviction is overturned, that person would not receive those lost benefits for the period of incarceration. The person also would not receive any Social Security work credits during the time of incarceration, reducing his or her future benefits.

In 2023, US courts granted 153 exonerations. Of these, eight were group exonerations that involved 471 people. Thus, the courts exonerated more than six hundred people of crimes they did not commit (The National Registry of Exonerations 2024). In 85 percent of those exonerations in 2023, the conviction was marred by official misconduct. For example, official misconduct was tied to the actions of Chicago Police Department officers who planted drugs or weapons on people after they refused to pay bribes. Perjury or false accusations were the second leading cause of wrongful conviction. Other factors were mistaken witness identification, false confessions, false or misleading forensic evidence, and ineffective assistance of counsel (The National Registry of Exonerations 2024). False confessions are sometimes given by people younger than age eighteen who have been intimidated into confessing to get a lighter sentence, even though they did not commit a crime. In 22 percent of false confessions, exculpatory DNA evidence was ignored (Moskovska 2024).

Racism is a major factor in wrongful convictions. In nearly 84 percent of exoneration cases, the wrongfully convicted individual was a person of color. Although 13 percent of the prison population is Black and 13.7 percent of the total population is Black, roughly 50 percent of wrongfully convicted and exonerated persons are Black. Moreover, 15 percent of murders by Blacks involved a White person, but 31 percent of Black people exonerated of a murder conviction had been wrongfully convicted of murdering a White person. It takes three years longer on average for a Black man to be exonerated than it takes for a White man to be exonerated (Moskovska 2024).

In some wrongful conviction cases, the individual had been sentenced to death or life without parole. On average, the wrongfully incarcerated individuals lost 14.6 years of freedom. Some cases involved incarceration of more than twenty years. One case in 2023 involved incarceration of more than forty-eight years (The National Registry of Exonerations 2024).

We propose legislation that would require the Social Security Administration to credit earnings for the time a person is wrongfully incarcerated. This would help restore the lives of exonerated individuals. We do not make a specific proposal for the amount of credit, but one option would be to credit them for two thousand hours of work per year at the federal minimum wage. Another option would be to credit them with earnings at an amount that would have lifted them out of poverty. Also, if they are sixty-two or older, they could receive payment for the Social Security benefits they would have received starting at age sixty-two. If they had previously claimed Social Security retirement benefits, they would be credited for the payments they had missed.

Compensation for false incarceration, if ever obtained, often occurs years after exoneration (The National Registry of Exonerations 2024). We argue that this proposal is a small remedy for a major social injustice. Without this remedy, exonerated people risk suffering financially in their future years for a crime they never committed.

An alternative to this proposal would be to fund compensatory benefits through a general revenue transfer to the Social Security Administration instead of being funded by the OASI Trust Fund.

Spouses of Incarcerated Persons

In a publication titled "What Prisoners Need to Know," the Social Security Administration (2023c, p. 2) stated, "If you receive Social Security, we'll suspend your benefits if you're convicted of a criminal offense and sentenced to jail or prison for more than thirty continuous days. We can reinstate your benefits starting with the month following the month of your release. Although you can't receive monthly Social Security benefits while you're incarcerated, benefits to your spouse or children will continue as long as they remain eligible."

Hansen (2022), writing for the Prison Journalism Project, described how, after he was convicted of a felony and incarcerated, his wife was evicted from her apartment due to being unable to pay rent. He argued that the current policies are unjust and harmful because the family members of an incarcerated worker should not be punished for a crime that they did not commit. "It is important to point out that citizens who go to prison for a felony are not victims," he wrote. "But this law has turned our loved ones into victims. It rips needed funds away from them. . . . If I'm released after my minimum sentence of fifteen years, I will have lost $180,000, some of which are my own earnings, stored by the government for my retirement. I may be a felon, but this extra punishment is above and beyond reason. If the government wants to take our earned money, then at least give it to our families who need it."

We propose that the spouse of an incarcerated beneficiary receive *survivors'* benefits, not spousal benefits, during the period of incarceration. This would promote fairness for family members. We argue that the financial impact of incarceration on family members is like the financial effect of a worker-beneficiary's death. Spousal benefits do not exceed one-half of the worker's primary insurance amount (PIA). They are reduced if the spousal beneficiary has claimed benefits before reaching full retirement age (Social Security Administration 2013a). By contrast, a surviving spouse generally receives 100 percent of the deceased worker's benefits provided that the spouse has reached full retirement age (Social Security Administration 2024cc). Thus, the survivor's benefit amounts are more likely to provide adequate income to the spouses of incarcerated beneficiaries. After the end of the incarceration, the spouse would be switched back to receiving spousal benefits.

Our proposal could be adjusted in a relatively simply way. The extra benefits could be funded by a transfer of general government revenue to the OASI Trust Fund or by an income transfer from the federal government directly to the spouse.

Spouses with High Government Pensions

The Social Security Fairness Act was signed into law in early 2025. It provides, among other changes, spousal benefits to people who have relatively high pensions from government jobs not covered by Social Security when the spouse is receiving Social Security benefits. For example, consider a spouse with a federal government pension of more than $100,000 a year who is married to a worker-beneficiary spouse with a Social Security benefit of $36,000 a year at full retirement age. The spouse with the federal government pension can qualify for a spouse's benefit from Social Security of $18,000 a year if the spouse claims it at full retirement age.

This option is available even though that person has paid little or no Social Security taxes and has had a long career earning a relatively high salary while working in a government job not covered by Social Security. That person is provided a generous spousal Social Security benefit, despite having a large government pension. By comparison, it would not be possible for a person with a generous *private sector* pension of over $100,000 a year to qualify for Social Security spousal benefits.

Before the passage of the Social Security Fairness Act, under the Government Pension Offset law, the hypothetical spouse described above, who worked in a government job, would not have been eligible to receive a full spousal benefit from Social Security. That benefit would have been reduced by two-thirds compared to the person's government pension. In this example, the spouse's Social Security benefit would be reduced to zero. When the Government Pension Offset law was passed in 1977, the offset was 100 percent, but it was reduced to two-thirds in 1983 (Social Security Administration, Research, Statistics, & Policy Analysis 2024).

We propose reducing Social Security spousal benefits by one-third of the government pension amount for those receiving government pensions who were not covered by Social Security. This would be a middle-of-the-road approach, with spousal benefits being lower than what is allowed by the Social Security Fairness Act (which is 100 percent) but higher than the amount allowed by the Government Pension Offset law (zero). This proposal would provide Social Security spousal benefits to people with low government pensions; however, it would eliminate the situation in which a person with a large government pension could also receive a relatively large Social Security spousal benefit.

Protecting the Accuracy of Participants' Social Security Records

In early 2025, the Social Security Administration knowingly falsified the Social Security records of approximately six thousand immigrants who were legally living in the United States to indicate that they had died. The SSA did this to cancel their Social Security numbers, which had been lawfully obtained, in order to prevent the numbers' owners from working in the formal labor force (Gibson, C. 2025).

We propose that Congress pass legislation prohibiting the Social Security Administration from knowingly falsifying participants' records. If participants are suspected of having committed crimes, those issues should be addressed directly through standard procedures in the legal system.

Protect the Privacy of Participants

The Privacy Act (5 U.S.C. §552a), also known as the Privacy Act of 1974, states that the Social Security Administration is legally responsible for safeguarding the information in its administrative files against violation of individual privacy. Other legal protections are provided by other laws: the Social Security Act; the Confidential Information Protection and Statistical Efficiency Act; Title 13 of the United States Code governing the Census Bureau; and the Internal Revenue Code covering earnings data considered to be tax return information (McNabb, Timmins, Song, and Puckett 2009).

The Social Security Administration has two strategies for producing public-use data files. One involves working with other federal agencies to develop synthetic files, which have the statistical properties of the original dataset but are artificially generated so as not to breach the confidentiality of individuals' information. It has used a different methodology to produce three traditional public-use microdata files based on its administrative data. The agency makes several changes in the data for developing the public-use files to ensure that individuals cannot be identified. Those changes include removing information such as the Social Security number, name, address, bank account information, and date of birth; top coding (removing extremely high values and substituting a ceiling value); and rounding benefit and earnings amounts. The files are reviewed by a Disclosure Review Board, using a detailed checklist on disclosure potential, looking specifically for unique records and overlap with other publicly available data (McNabb, Timmins, Song, and Puckett 2009).

In February 2025, the Department of Government Efficiency (DOGE), which President Trump had created a few weeks earlier through an executive order, requested access to Social Security Administration data on individuals. The reasons for the request and why it was granted were not made publicly available. Social Security's Acting Commissioner Lee Dudek granted DOGE read-only access to the private Social Security Administration data of individuals (Dudek 2025). Social Security's previous acting commissioner had resigned several days earlier because she refused to comply with DOGE's request to provide access to information about individuals (Hussein 2025).

Nancy Altman, president of Social Security Works, an advocacy group for the preservation and expansion of Social Security benefits, wrote:

> There is no way to overstate how serious a breach this is. The information collected and securely held by the Social Security Administration is highly sensitive. SSA has data on everyone who has a Social Security number, which is virtually all Americans, everyone who has Medicare, and every low-income American who has applied for Social Security's means-tested companion program, Supplemental Security Income. If there is an evil intent to punish perceived enemies, someone could erase your earnings record, making it impossible to collect the Social Security and Medicare benefits you have earned (Hussein 2025).

Subsequently, in June 2025, the Supreme Court, in a split decision, ruled that DOGE could temporarily access Social Security confidential data on individuals while a lower court was considering whether such access was legal (Totenberg and Ononye 2025).

Also in June 2025, ten Congressional Democrats, including Senator Ron Wyden, sent a letter to the tech company Palantir raising concerns that this private company was building a mega-database that would include personal income tax records and Social Security records combined for individuals (Bracken 2025).

We propose an amendment to the Social Security Act that would strictly limit access to Social Security Administration data on individuals. Access would be granted only to employees of the Social Security Administration who need the information to assist a participant, or for other administrative purposes related to processing Social Security benefits. Our proposal would not limit access to the data for research purposes when all personal identifying information has been deleted to prepare public-use files.

We also propose legislation that would prohibit the combination of Social Security records on individuals with other government databases containing personal information, such as personal income tax records except when all personal identifying information has been removed and the data is to be used for research purposes.

Deemed Wages for Volunteer Emergency Responders

The Social Security Caregiver Credit Act of 2023 amended the Social Security Act "to credit individuals serving as caregivers of dependent relatives with deemed wages for up to five years of such service" (Congress.gov 2023b). The bill specifies that deemed wages are capped at half the national average annual earnings. Caregivers must provide at least eighty hours per month of care to be eligible. The deemed wages recognize the value of unpaid work by caregivers. This concept extends the concept of spousal benefits, where spouses can receive Social Security benefits in recognition of the unpaid work they do for their families.

Another group that provides valuable, unpaid work is volunteer emergency responders, including firefighters, police officers, search and rescue teams, and disaster relief workers. Governments enjoy reduced costs, thanks to the valuable work of volunteer emergency service providers. Some volunteer firefighters receive pensions based on their volunteer work (Turner and Wood 2023).

Of the approximately 676,900 volunteer first responders, about 65 percent are firefighters. The time donated by volunteer firefighters saves localities an estimated $46.9 billion per year. Most fire departments (64 percent) operate with only volunteer firefighters (National Volunteer Fire Council 2025). Volunteers in fire departments work as firefighters, emergency medical technicians (EMTs), rescue squad members, and fire police who control traffic at emergency scenes.

We propose providing deemed earnings credits to volunteer emergency responders who meet minimum requirements for annual hours of work and minimum years of work for up to five years of service. A Social Security tax could be levied on government agencies that benefit from these volunteers. The proposal would serve as recognition for valuable unpaid service, and it would provide an incentive to help offset the decline in the number of volunteer firefighters.

The minimum annual hours requirement, and possibly other

requirements, would be policy choice options. For example, formal certification could be a requirement.

Survivors' Benefits for Military, Police, and Firefighters

If a member of the military dies in combat, or if a police officer or firefighter dies in the line of duty, the Social Security survivors' benefits for that person's spouse will be based on a shortened earnings history. The Social Security Administration already makes one distinction for military deaths during active duty. Generally, a person must have been married at least nine months before the spouse's death to qualify for survivors' benefits. In recognition of the deceased person's sacrifice, that nine-month rule does not apply if the death occurred in the line of duty (Social Security Administration 2025h).

We propose establishing minimum Social Security survivors' benefits for the surviving spouses of military members who die in combat, from combat-caused injuries, while on active duty, or from mental trauma resulting from combat. We also propose establishing the same minimum survivors' benefits for the surviving spouses of police and firefighters. In addition, we recommend extending the exclusion to the nine-month rule for marriage for eligibility for survivors' benefits to police and firefighters. Eligibility for this benefit would not be affected by remarriage.

The minimum benefits level could be adjusted, depending on policy preferences. One option would be to allow the survivor to receive full survivors' benefits at age sixty-two rather than having to wait to age sixty-seven (the full retirement age for those born after 1962). Another option would be to credit the deceased people with wages for years when the national average annual wage exceeded their own wages.

In the next chapter, we address the needs of low-wage earners.

CHAPTER 10

Supporting Low-Wage Workers

Some workers with very low annual wage earnings must pay the Social Security payroll tax even though they receive no credit toward future benefits. In 2025, annual cash wages of less than $150 paid to seasonal farm workers were not subject to the Social Security OASI payroll tax (IRS 2025b). Self-employed workers and most other workers had to pay the Social Security payroll tax if their annual earnings were $400 or more. Church employees had to pay the Social Security payroll tax if their annual earnings in 2025 were $108.28 or more (IRS 2025b). Farm workers' wages were covered if their employers paid them more than $150 a year or if the total wages paid by the employer to all workers was more than $2,500 a year, even if an individual's wages were less than $150 a year (Social Security Administration 2022b). By comparison, for household employees, the minimum earnings subject to Social Security payroll taxation in 2025 was $2,800 a year (IRS 2025e).

In 2025, a worker needed at least $1,810 in covered annual earnings to earn one work credit toward eligibility for Social Security benefits (Social Security Administration 2025k). Thus, with the current requirements, it is possible for low-earning workers to be required to pay Social Security OASI taxes on their low earnings but receive no credit toward eligibility for future benefits.

We propose raising the minimum level of annual earnings that is taxable by the Social Security payroll tax so that it matches the level required to earn one credit toward future Social Security benefits. Thus, for 2025, that minimum would be $1,810 a year. People who earn less than the minimum would not pay Social Security taxes. Higher minimums for certain groups, such as household workers, could be maintained.

Support Low-Earning Self-Employed Workers

The Qualified Small Business Tax Credit for Increasing Research Activities provides small businesses with a tax credit against the employer's share of the Social Security OASI payroll tax. For taxable years beginning after December 31, 2015, and before January 1, 2023, the maximum research credit that a small business could elect in a tax year to be applied toward payroll taxes was $250,000. The maximum amount of payroll tax research credit that a qualified small business can apply against payroll tax liability increased from $250,000 to $500,000 for tax years beginning after December 31, 2022 (IRS 2025c). This tax credit reduces the payroll tax payments made by qualifying small businesses. However, the reduction in payroll tax payments is made up to the Social Security OASI Trust Fund through general revenue payments from the Treasury Department.

We propose a Social Security payroll tax credit for low-wage, self-employed workers. Our proposal is similar to the Small Business Tax Credit. Employed workers only pay the worker's half of the Social Security payroll tax, but self-employed workers must pay both portions. They can deduct the employer's share of the payroll tax that they pay when calculating their Adjusted Gross Income for federal income tax returns; however, this deduction is of no benefit to low-wage, self-employed workers who do not have a federal income tax liability. For this reason, we propose a credit for the employer's share of the payroll tax for low-wage self-employed workers. This credit would be paid out of general revenue funds by the Treasury Department to the OASI Trust Fund.

Survivors' Benefits for Lower-Income Beneficiaries

Under current policy, if a person's spouse dies and that person is eligible to receive survivors' benefits when they reach age sixty, the surviving spouse would lose that eligibility if they remarry before age sixty.

We propose legislation that would allow lower-income beneficiaries to remarry at any age and claim survivors benefits at age sixty-two based on the earnings of the deceased spouse. This requirement would most affect low-income women. Surviving spouses could also choose to claim benefits based on their own earnings record or on the earnings record of a new spouse. Age limits could be placed on this proposal, such as for remarriage before age thirty. Policymakers could also adjust the income levels that allow or disallow beneficiaries' eligibility for this proposal.

The Special Minimum Benefit

The special minimum benefit was enacted in 1972 to provide adequate retirement benefits to low earners. When it was enacted, the special minimum benefit for workers with thirty years of coverage was equal to 96 percent of the poverty threshold. A study at the turn of the twenty-first century found that since 1990, three-quarters of the recipients were women (Olsen and Hoffmeyer 2001/2002).

To be eligible for a special minimum benefit, a person must have at least eleven years of covered earnings, with the benefit increasing with more years of covered earnings, up to thirty years. Beginning in 1979, the value of the minimum benefit increased with price growth to $886 per month in 2020 for a worker with thirty years of covered earnings. The number of beneficiaries receiving the special minimum benefit has declined from about two hundred thousand in the early 1990s to about 32,100 in 2019. Fewer new beneficiaries are receiving the price-indexed special minimum benefit because wage growth typically exceeds price growth. Thus, wage-indexed regular benefits are usually higher (Social Security Administration 2021b).

All new special minimum beneficiaries since 1998 qualified because they were subject to the Windfall Elimination Provision. That provision reduced Social Security benefits for individuals receiving a pension based on employment not covered by Social Security (Springstead, Whitman, and Shoffner 2014). Because the Windfall Elimination Provision ended in 2025 with the passage of the Social Security Fairness Act, the special minimum benefit provision no longer has any effect, with no one benefiting from it.

The University of Maryland's Program for Public Consultation (2024) found that 71 percent of voters in six swing states favored raising the minimum monthly benefit from $1,066 to $1,570 (as an initial value) for those who have worked thirty or more years. "The minimum benefit would rise with inflation and always be set at 125 percent of the federal poverty line" (Program for Public Consultation 2024). This change, which would *increase* the funding shortfall by 7 percent, was supported by most high earners and low earners. Those with household incomes under $50,000, the people who could benefit from this proposal, were somewhat more likely to support it (77 percent) than those with household incomes over $150,000 (69 percent).

We propose that the special minimum benefit be increased for workers with thirty or more years of covered earnings and subsequently be wage-indexed so that it keeps up with regular Social Security benefits. The National Commission on Fiscal Responsibility and Reform (2010), known as the Simpson-Bowles Commission, made a proposal similar to ours.

This proposal could be altered by lowering the required number of years of covered earnings, or by prorating the minimum benefit for fewer years or more years—for example between eleven and forty years.

The next chapter focuses on ways to improve Social Security by adjusting actuarial factors.

CHAPTER 11

Proposals Relating to Changes in Actuarial Factors

Social Security benefits are calculated by using various actuarial factors. Although they may seem like obscure technical issues, they can have important implications for beneficiaries. This chapter focuses on ways to reform Social Security by adjusting the actuarial factors.

Delayed Retirement Credit

Many people mistakenly believe that the delayed retirement credit (i.e., claiming benefits beyond full retirement age) is an 8 percent annual increase. For example, people might think that if they delay benefits from age sixty-nine to seventy, then they will receive 8 percent more at age seventy.

That is not true. The total increase in age-seventy benefits for people who have a full retirement age of sixty-six is 32 percent *of age sixty-six benefits*. In other words, the person does not add 8 percent to the previous year's benefits; rather, the person receives 8 percent more than the age sixty-six amount.

This calculation, if done by a bank, would likely be illegal. Perhaps for that reason, this misconception is so widespread—even among Social Security experts. For example, writing for *Kiplinger Personal Finance*, Lakeford and Levalley (2025) wrote, "For every year you delay taking your Social Security benefits past full retirement age, you get a bump of 8 percent in your benefit until age seventy." To be clear, that statement is wrong.

Table 11-1 shows the actual percentage increases by age. If a person's primary insurance amount is $1,000, they would receive an $80 per month increase in benefits for each year of postponed benefits up to age seventy. That $80 per month increase is an 8 percent increase in the first year of delay, but the second year of delay is an $80 increase on a monthly benefit of $1080, assuming the person stopped working so that the PIA was the same. That results in a 7.4 percent increase.

Age	Commonly misperceived rate (%)	Actual rate (%)	Actuarially fair rate (%)			
			3% real		1% real	
			M	F	M	F
66 to 67	8.00	8.00	6.78	6.29	5.38	4.91
67 to 68	8.00	7.41	7.00	6.49	5.59	5.10
68 to 69	8.00	6.90	7.19	6.70	5.81	5.31
69 to 70	8.00	6.45	7.47	6.92	6.05	5.52

Table 11-1: Crediting rates for various delayed retirement credit approaches, 2021. Source: Andrews and others (2024)

As the table above shows, for each year that people delay benefits beyond the full retirement age of sixty-six, they will receive a *lower percentage* increase compared to the previous year. Thus, the common misperception results in a substantial overstatement of the value of each one-year delay. The last columns of the table show that an actuarially fair increase would be for each age. It would *increase with age* because there are fewer years during which people who delay benefits can receive an increase in benefits.

People who consider delaying benefits from age sixty-nine to seventy will presumably want to know how much their benefits will increase. The calculation would involve a comparison of the loss of one year of benefits versus the percentage increase in annual benefits. The Social Security Administration (2023b), in its publication "Retirement Benefits," states, "We'll add 8 percent to your benefit for each full year you delay receiving Social Security benefits beyond full retirement age." As table 11-1 shows, that statement *is not true.* If you delay benefits from age sixty-nine to seventy, your benefit will increase by 6.45 percent. A correct statement of the current arrangement would be as follows: "If you wait until age sixty-nine to start benefits. you will get 116 percent of your PIA. If you wait until age seventy, you will get 124 percent of your PIA."

We propose that the delayed retirement credit be changed so that beneficiaries would receive an 8 percent increase per year compared to *the previous year's benefit amount.* For a person who delays benefits to age seventy, this would result in a 36 percent increase compared to the age sixty-six retirement age. By comparison, the current rule's outcome would be a 32 percent increase. Thus, our proposal would allow a person receiving $2,000 a month at age sixty-six to receive $80 more per month than what she or he would receive under current policy. That difference could easily amount to $20,000 more during the person's remaining lifetime.

Our proposal could be adapted. Instead of 8 percent, the adjustment factor could be reduced to 7 percent. This reduction makes sense because interest rates have declined generally. Also, life expectancy has increased for the upper-income workers who are most likely to postpone retirement to older ages. Dushi, Frieberg, and Webb (2021), while considering that workers who delay benefits typically have higher incomes, found that the current adjustment factors are too high for workers who have higher life expectancies.

Another option would be to keep the same adjustment factors but drop the misleading claim that people will receive an 8 percent increase per year. The Social Security Administration should publish the actual increase in benefits for a one-year delay.

Early Retirement Actuarial Factors

To explain the actuarial adjustment factors for early retirement, the Social Security Administration (2025c) writes out a complicated and confusing formula. To avoid burdening our readers with the description, we will only present the main two sentences: "In the case of *early retirement*, a benefit is reduced [by five-ninths] of one percent for each month before normal retirement age, up to thirty-six months. If the number of months exceeds thirty-six, then the benefit is further reduced [by five-twelfths] of one percent per month."

The main thing to notice is that the Social Security Administration explains the adjustment for early retirement backward from the way most people presumably think about it. People generally consider whether they should continue working past age sixty-two and how much they would gain by delaying benefits. By contrast, the Social Security Administration communicates about the question in terms of how much earlier than age sixty-seven (the full retirement age) people might wish to retire.

The presumed goal of the actuarial adjustment factors is to ensure that a person with average life expectancy will receive the same lifetime expected value of benefits no matter when that person retires. In that situation, the actuarial adjustment factors do not influence the person's decision as to when to retire and collect benefits. For each year a person delays benefits, she reduces the future time during which she will receive higher benefits because of the delay. For that reason, the actuarial adjustment factors need to *increase for higher ages* because of the shorter period for which they are in effect.

In table 11-2, we calculate the current actuarial factors for delayed retirement past age sixty-two up to the full retirement age of sixty-seven. The actuarial factor for delaying benefits from age sixty-two to sixty-three is 7.1 percent. However, the factor for delaying benefits from age sixty-three to sixty-four falls to 6.7 percent. It then goes up to 8.4 percent for people who delay benefits from age sixty-four to sixty-five because the person is within three years of the full retirement age of sixty-seven. The pattern does not follow the pattern of actuarially fair adjustment factors increasing for each year of delayed benefits.

1	2	3	4	5	6	7
Benefit Claiming Age	Social Security Administration primary insurance amount actuarial adjustment factors	Percent of PIA	Current Actuarial Factors for Delayed Retirement (annual increase)	Proposed Reform of Actuarial Factors for Delayed Retirement	Percent of Age 62 Benefit with Proposed Reform	Percent of Age 62 Benefit Currently
62	-5.0%	70.0%	--	--	100.0	100.0
63	-5.0%	75.0%	7.1%	6.7%	106.7	107.1
64	-6.7%	80.0%	6.7%	7.1%	114.3	114.3
65	-6.7%	86.7%	8.4%	7.2%	122.5	123.9
66	-6.7%	93.3%	7.6%	7.6%	131.8	133.3
67	--	100.0%	7.2%	8.4%	142.9	142.9

Table 11-2: Actuarial adjustment factors for delayed Social Security benefit claiming. Source: Author's calculations using Social Security Administration primary insurance amount actuarial adjustment factors (column 2)

We propose that the Social Security Administration explain the early retirement decision in terms of working past age sixty-two rather than in terms of retiring earlier than age sixty-seven. In other words, the Social Security Administration should explain the options in terms of how benefits will increase when people delay retirement past age sixty-two. We also propose that the adjustment factors for delayed retirement should increase each year after age sixty-two, as is required to maintain actuarial neutrality. This way, the factors would not influence retirement age choices for people with average life expectancies.

In column 5 of table 11-2, we show our proposed adjustment factors. They rise with each year of delayed retirement past age sixty-two. This is an example of what the pattern should look like. Columns 6 and 7 in table 11-2 compare side-by-side the results of our adjustment factors with the results of current adjustment factors for delayed retirement. The results are essentially identical.

Simplify the Actuarial Adjustments for Different Benefits

The different types of Social Security benefits (retired worker, spouse, survivor) have diverse sets of actuarial adjustments for those who claim benefits early or delay their claims. This is an overly complex system. Regardless of when people choose to claim benefits, the expected value of lifetime benefits should stay the same.

In relation to benefits for retired workers, the Social Security Administration Office of the Chief Actuary (2025c) explained that those who claim retirement benefits before the full retirement age may receive as little as 70 percent of their primary insurance amount due to the monthly benefit reduction for early claiming. "A worker can choose to retire as early as age sixty-two, but doing so may result in a reduction of as much as 30 percent." If a person who turns sixty-two in 2025 claims early benefits that year, five years before the normal retirement age, then the Social Security Administration would reduce that person's benefits by 30 percent.

In relation to calculating spousal benefits, the adjustment process to account for early benefits is different. "A spouse can choose to retire as early as age sixty-two, but doing so may result in a benefit as little as 32.5 percent of the worker's primary insurance amount. . . . For a spouse who is not entitled to benefits on his or her own earnings record, this reduction factor is applied to the base spousal benefit, which is 50 percent of the worker's primary insurance amount" (Social Security Administration, Office of the Chief Actuary 2025a).

If a worker and spouse were both born in 1960 or later and thus have a full retirement age of sixty-seven, and if they claim their retirement benefits at age sixty-two, the worker's benefits will be reduced by 30 percent and the spouse's benefits will be reduced by 35 percent (Social Security Administration, Office of the Chief Actuary 2025b).

The current rules for claiming spousal benefits early is unfair to low-income women who have lower life expectancies; the benefit reduction at age sixty-two is arguably too large. The current adjustment, however, is *favorable* to high-income women, who have longer life expectancies, because the adjustment for delayed benefits is overly generous, particularly for those women.

In relation to calculating survivors' benefits, the Social Security

Administration (2025q) uses yet another set of actuarial adjustments. "Payments start at 71.5 percent of your spouse's benefit and increase the longer you wait to apply. For example, you could get over 75 percent at age sixty-one, over 80 percent at age sixty-three, and over 90 percent at age sixty-five. You can get up to 100 percent when you reach your full retirement age for survivor benefits (between ages sixty-six and sixty-seven)."

If we compare all three categories described above, we see that retired workers who delay benefits past full retirement age up to age seventy will accumulate delayed retirement credits that increase the monthly benefit amounts. By contrast, a spouse who delays spousal benefits past full retirement age will not see an increased monthly benefit amount. Royal (2025) explained that "if you wait until after your full retirement age [to claim spousal benefits], the benefits will not increase. The wage earner may benefit from delaying benefits until age seventy, but the spouse applying for benefits will not." Markowitz (2024b) noted, "The most your spouse can receive on your work record is 50 percent of your primary insurance amount."

If the retired worker postpones retirement benefits, the surviving spouse's benefits will increase by the worker's delayed retirement credits. "[The] delayed retirement credits you've accumulated do affect what your surviving spouse—or even your surviving divorced spouse—will receive when you pass on. The SSA computes [the survivor's] benefit based on your primary insured amount plus any delayed retirement credits you've obtained up to the month of your death" (Western & Southern Financial Group 2024). Thus, the spousal benefits cannot be increased if a spouse delays the claim, but survivors' benefits can be increased if the worker-beneficiary delays benefits.

We propose using a single set of actuarial adjustments for different types of Social Security OASI benefits. Our proposal promotes simplification and equity because the penalty for claiming benefits early and the credit for delaying retirement would be the same for survivors, spouses, and retired workers. This change would end the less favorable treatment of spouses who receive no increase in benefits for delaying benefits past full retirement age.

The next chapter presents Social Security reform proposals inspired by aspects of the US private pension system.

CHAPTER 12

Proposals Inspired by the US Pension System

Inadequate retirement savings continue to be a problem for many Americans. An AARP survey indicated that one in five Americans who are at least age fifty have no retirement savings other than Social Security (AARP 2024). Another survey asked retirees to describe what financial advice they would give their younger selves. According to the survey, "The majority (70 percent) would advise changing savings habits by saving or investing more or earlier" (Bearden 2022).

A related issue is whether American retirees are adequately covered by annuities. Many proposals have been advanced to encourage annuitization by workers with 401(k) plans (e.g., Iwry and Turner 2009), but relatively few people annuitize even part of those plans. Catch-up contributions to Social Security would increase beneficiary annuitization in retirement.

Low-income workers are less likely than high-income workers to have access to an employer-sponsored retirement savings plan (GAO 2023a). Given the inadequacy of retirement savings for many workers, additional measures, ideally at the federal level, are needed to promote financial security in retirement. This is especially true because many people must retire earlier than planned due to health issues or other unforeseen circumstances. In 2024, 58 percent of retirees reported having retired earlier than expected (Collinson and

Cho 2024). As we have described, those who claim Social Security benefits early receive permanently reduced benefits.

Catch-up contributions to Social Security could be an approach for some people to increase their retirement savings. This idea is inspired by pension law: Retirement savings plans, such as 401(k)s, allow annual catch-up contributions for those who are age fifty and older (IRS 2024f). According to the IRS (2024f), "Plan participants must make catch-up contributions to a retirement plan via elective deferrals." The IRS (2024h) added that, "Elective deferrals by a participant in excess of limits imposed under the plan document or by statute are allowed . . . These contributions, commonly referred to as 'catch-up' contributions, include elective deferrals to a 401(k) plan, 403(b) plan, governmental 457(b) plan, SARSEP, SIMPLE-401(k), and SIMPLE-IRA."

Catch-up contributions are recognized as a way of helping people who have not saved enough for retirement. According to Roberts (2024), "Catch-up contributions are crucial if you are just starting to prepare for retirement in your fifties or if you need to rebuild your retirement savings for any reason." Unlike retirement savings plans, Social Security lacks this option.

Social Security catch-up contributions are not a new idea (Ghilarducci, Webb, and Papadopoulos 2018; Sun and others 2019; Turner 2019). The extent to which Social Security's replacement rate is less for high earners may make them want to opt out of catch-up contributions. Alternatively, low earners who need additional income to meet their immediate expenses could find it financially difficult to participate, even if it would be best for their futures.

From an international perspective, the United Kingdom allows voluntary contributions to its National Insurance (social security)

Proposals Inspired by the US Pension System

program only by those who need to fill in gaps in their record to have enough qualifying years to receive the UK State Pension, and to qualify for certain benefits. Gaps in National Insurance records may occur due to living or working outside the UK, unemployment, low-paying employment, or self-employment with earnings so low that no contributions were made (GOV.UK 2025).

We propose allowing workers who are at least age fifty with annual earnings below the Social Security taxable maximum earnings to voluntarily purchase Social Security earnings credits. These voluntary contributions would increase individuals' credited earnings for purposes of calculating their future Social Security benefits. The amount contributed by an individual could vary from one year to another according to each person's preferences and needs. Voluntary contributions could be made when a person files an annual federal income tax return.

Catch-up contributions in pensions primarily benefit high-income workers because those people usually contribute the maximum amount allowed annually. By contrast, catch-up contributions for Social Security would not benefit workers earning above the taxable maximum and thus already making the maximum allowable contributions.

Our proposal would give workers the option to purchase earnings credits annually when they file federal income taxes. Workers would purchase these credits at a rate based on the payroll taxes they would pay if they had received actual earnings as a self-employed worker. The purchased credits would be included in the Social Security benefit calculation just like credits from actual earnings. The purchasing limit would be the Social Security maximum taxable earnings. In other words, the combination of a worker's actual and credited earnings could not exceed this threshold. In 2025, maximum taxable annual earnings were $176,100 (Social Security Administration 2024c).

Compared to purchasing an annuity, which often involves a one-time payment of a relatively large sum, our proposed catch-up contributions would involve one or more smaller payments. Because these contributions could be made incrementally over many years, people could change their minds if they no longer wished to contribute. This system could appeal to those who are reluctant to purchase an annuity because of the size of the commitment.

Most workers who are at least age fifty would have the option of making catch-up contributions during any given year because their earnings are below the taxable maximum. "Every year, roughly 6 percent of covered workers have earnings above the taxable maximum" (Social Security Administration 2024dd). However, the percentage would be higher for older workers. It is important to add that approximately 80 percent of covered workers will never earn more than the taxable maximum. "Almost 20 percent of current and future covered workers are projected to have earnings above the taxable maximum in at least one year" (Social Security Administration 2024dd).

To implement this proposal, it would be necessary to change IRS Form 1040 to allow people with earnings below the Social Security taxable maximum to purchase additional earnings credits (Turner 2019). The OASDI payroll tax rate for self-employed workers was 12.4 percent in 2025 (Social Security Administration 2024k). Since 12.4 percent of $1,000 equals $124, it is logical to allow people to purchase earnings credits in $1,000 increments at $124 per credit. The Social Security Administration would adjust the price of earnings credits in response to changes in the payroll tax rate. For calculating federal income tax payments, half of the voluntary catch-up contributions would be tax-deductible. This approach would mirror the calculations applicable to the earnings of self-employed workers (Turner 2019).

Voluntary contributions are preferable because forced contributions could financially hurt some workers. Voluntary annual contributions based on the purchase of earnings credits would give covered workers who are at least age fifty the freedom to decide how much to contribute if their annual earnings are below the taxable maximum.

This approach makes sense considering the potential for unforeseen economic setbacks, such as health issues, caregiving responsibilities, natural disasters, and pandemics. The Covid-19 pandemic was associated with many job losses and an economic recession (Center on Budget and Policy Priorities 2024a). Under this proposal, those who earned less than they usually do for one or more years during a pandemic would have the opportunity to make catch-up contributions to Social Security by making voluntary contributions, if they were able to do so.

Voluntary Employer Super Contributions

In March 2023, 73 percent of civilian workers had access to retirement benefits from their employers, with 56 percent participating in these plans (US Bureau of Labor Statistics 2023a).

A survey by ShareBuilder 401(k) found that only a small percentage of small businesses offered 401(k) plans (Umpierrez

2024). Some employers with few employees may not want to take on the complexity and cost of sponsoring a retirement savings plan. This survey of five hundred small business owners at companies with up to fifty employees found that only 24 percent provided 401(k) plans for their employees. When asked why they had not done so, 55 percent responded that their businesses were too small to access a plan, and 28 percent said they could not afford to provide a company matching contribution. Another 22 percent said that providing a 401(k) plan would be too expensive.

The 2023 Small Business Retirement Survey of more than seven hundred small companies found that over half believed the annual cost of offering a retirement savings plan exceeded $10,000, and only 7 percent thought the cost was under $5,000 (Sprick 2024a). Some states have provided automatic IRA plans, but these plans do not permit employer contributions, and the employee opt-out rate has been high (Sprick 2024a).

We propose allowing employers to make voluntary Social Security *super contributions* for their employees who are at least age fifty. Super contributions would be above what employers would normally make based solely on the employees' earnings. If they made these contributions, they would be required to make them for all employees who are at least age fifty and who earn less than the Social Security taxable maximum earnings. These contributions could be determined as a percentage of the employees' earnings, as a percentage of the employer's contributions for the employees, or as a flat contribution for each employee. The super contributions would increase the credited earnings the employees had with Social Security, raising their future retirement benefits. Small employers often have uncertain or variable revenue, so this proposal would make it easy to adapt their financial commitment to changes in company revenue.

The OASDI payroll tax rate in 2025 was 6.2 percent for employers and the same for employees. That 6.2 percent was divided so that 5.3 percent went to the OASI Trust Fund and 0.9 percent went to the Disability Insurance Trust Fund. For example, if an employer contributed an extra 5 percent of employees' earnings, that would increase the total employer's and employees' Social Security OASDI contributions by 40.3 percent (=5/12.4) and therefore increase the employees' credited earnings for the year by the same percentage. The maximum annual salary taxable by Social Security in 2025 was $176,100. Thus, workers earning $125,516 would be credited with the maximum taxable earnings of $176,100. Workers earning $125,516 or less would receive the full 5 percent credit, and workers earning above that amount would receive less than 5 percent. Workers earning at least the maximum taxable earnings would receive no super contribution.

This proposal for increasing future Social Security retirement benefits would be simpler for many small employers than offering a retirement savings plan. Because business owners could set their contributions and easily adjust them, our recommendation could make it less expensive and more flexible than the current system. It would provide employers and employees with an alternative to state-facilitated auto-IRAs.

Maximum Age for Delayed Retirement Credits

Workers who postpone Social Security benefits after reaching full retirement age receive a delayed retirement credit up to age seventy. The Social Security Amendments of 1972 provided a delayed retirement credit up to age seventy-two. Then, in 1983, Congress lowered the age to seventy (Congressional Research Service 2022b). At that time, few people claimed Social Security benefits past age seventy. The Bipartisan Policy Center (2016) recommended gradually raising the maximum benefit age to seventy-two, by one month every two years.

Today's workers can postpone withdrawals from retirement savings accounts. As a result, their accounts can grow due to investment returns until age seventy-three. At that age, they are usually required to start taking required minimum distributions (RMDs). In 2032, the age at which required minimum distributions must begin will change to seventy-five (Internal Revenue Service 2025e).

By comparison, in the United Kingdom people can defer social security pension benefits as long as they wish, with no maximum age. They continue receiving credits for higher benefits when they eventually claim benefits (UK Government 2025a). In 2020, Japan passed legislation to raise the maximum age for deferral of benefits with a benefit increase from age seventy to seventy-five (Social Security Administration 2020).

We propose raising the age at which beneficiaries can receive maximum Social Security benefits from seventy to seventy-two. Some of the reforms we have proposed in this book involve targeted cutbacks, but this recommendation would allow some people to offset those cutbacks by further postponing benefits. It would also provide an incentive for some people to continue working for more years.

Many countries have found innovative ways to reform their social security programs. That is the focus of our next chapter.

CHAPTER 13

Lessons from Other Countries

Social security policies in countries that are comparable to the United States can serve as models for our Social Security reforms. This chapter presents some of those ideas.

Update the Program Name

The Social Security Act was signed in 1935, ninety years ago as of 2025. When President Franklin Roosevelt successfully ran for his last term in 1944, his opponents attacked him for being too old. He was sixty-two (Goodwin 1995). We now have had two presidents, Biden and Trump, who were elected in their late seventies. People's views as to when old age begins have changed.

People can now claim benefits at age sixty-two, compared to age sixty-five in the original Social Security Act. People on average live much longer now, and most participants do not consider themselves old when they claim benefits. We argue that it is time to update the name of the Old-Age and Survivors Insurance (OASI) program.

Life expectancy has improved considerably since 1940, when Social Security first started paying benefits. Life expectancy at age sixty-five can be measured in two ways. The first, which is the traditional method, is to use *period life tables*. Those tables are based on the mortality rates at different ages for a particular year. This common approach is relatively simple to calculate, but it assumes that there will be no future improvements in life expectancy due to reductions in mortality rates. As a result, it generally understates life expectancy. The second way to measure life expectancy is called *cohort life expectancy*. It is more difficult to calculate because it requires predicting or projecting future mortality rates. However, it is a superior measure because it recognizes that life expectancy is expected to improve over time due to future declines in mortality rates.

We use the cohort life expectancy measure to compare the life expectancies at age sixty-five in 1940 and 2024. In 1940, cohort life expectancy at age sixty-five was 12.7 years for men and 14.7 years for women. In 2024, it was 19.2 years for men and 21.8 years for women (OASDI Trustees 2024). Thus, between 1940 and 2024, life expectancy at age sixty-five increased by 51.2 percent for men and 48.3 percent for women. These are large increases.

As a result of these improvements, people who retire at age sixty-two or even in their mid-to-late sixties rarely consider themselves to be old. Many people in their early to mid-seventies do not consider themselves to be old. A Pew Research Center (2009) survey found that people's perceptions of the onset of old age varied widely. Respondents under age thirty believed, on average, that old age begins before sixty. Middle-age respondents believed that old age begins at seventy. Adults who are sixty-five or older believed, on average, that old age begins at seventy-four.

Many countries (e.g., Australia, France, Germany, Ireland, Japan, Spain, and the United Kingdom) do not use the words *old age* in the names of their social security programs. They tend to use the words *pension, retirement, social insurance,* or *national insurance* instead.

We propose updating the name of the OASI to the Retirement and Survivors Insurance program (RSI). This would reflect the major improvements in US life expectancy since 1940. Our proposal would retain "Social Security" as the popular name for the program. The Social Security Administration appears to recognize implicitly the desirability of such a change. When it mails a Notice of Award to new OASI beneficiaries, the heading on the letter is "Retirement, Survivors and Disability Insurance." The letter does not refer to old-age benefits. The booklet sent with the letter is titled "What You Need to Know When You Get Retirement or Survivors Benefits." A paper by Alleva (2017) published online for the Social Security Administration's Office of Retirement and Disability Policy is titled "Social Security Retirement Benefit Claiming-Age Combinations Available to Married Couples." The Social Security Administration, in its statistics, refers to retirement benefits rather than old-age benefits. Thus, it seems the Social Security Administration has already unofficially adopted the concept of our proposal.

Likewise, the AARP avoids using "old-age benefits" in an article titled "The Basics of Social Security Retirement Benefits" (Dono 2025). Similarly, the Center for Retirement Research at Boston College refers to "retired-worker benefits" (Chen, Munnell, and Gok 2025).

Reduce Maximum Benefits for Individuals and Families

Over the years, policymakers and others have proposed various changes to the formula for calculating individual benefits. The goal is to increase Social Security's solvency while promoting equity across income groups. One example is a proposal to decrease benefits for high earners (American Academy of Actuaries 2022b). Pethokoukus (2025) of the American Enterprise Institute argued, "With rising wealth, Social Security should focus on the poor rather than sending large checks to high-income retirees." According to the investment bank UBS, in 2024, there were one thousand new millionaires each day (Cerullo 2025).

Some people have also raised concerns about Social Security benefits for high-earning families. A high-earning worker may have a high-earning spouse, in which case both receive Social Security benefits based on their own earnings history. In the past, it was more common for a high-earning worker to have a spouse who did little or no work outside the home or who worked in a relatively low-paying job. In that case, the spouse would receive relatively generous Social Security spousal benefits based on the earnings of the high-earning spouse. This feature is sometimes criticized as being unfair to single people. It is particularly disadvantageous to low-earning couples because usually both spouses are working and do not receive the subsidy for a nonworking spouse (Warshawsky 2016). However, Social Security has always provided benefits to some vulnerable groups (e.g., spouses with limited work experience, survivors, and children) who have not paid for those benefits.

According to the Social Security Administration (2021a), "A wife with no work record or low benefit entitlement on her own work record is eligible for between one-third and one-half of her spouse's Social Security benefit." Spousal benefits may be up to 50 percent of the worker-beneficiary's primary insurance amount (PIA) if the spouse delays benefits until the full retirement age. Workers who receive delayed retirement credits for benefit-claiming delays past the full retirement age (between sixty-six and sixty-seven, depending on the person's birth year) receive an increase in benefits but do not increase the spouse's benefits.

Steuerle (2015) argued that Social Security spousal benefits are unfair not only to single people, but also to two-worker couples. "A one-worker couple earning $80,000 annually gets tens of thousands of dollars more in expected benefits than a two-worker couple with each spouse earning $40,000, even though the two-worker couple pays the same amount of taxes and typically has higher work expenses."

These spousal benefits may be regarded as increasingly obsolete historical artifacts that should be updated. A Congressional Research Service report further explained the issue.

> Social Security benefits are designed in a way that can result in inequities between households with similar earning profiles. Spouse's and survivor's benefits were added to the Social Security system in 1939. At that time, the majority of households consisted of a single earner—generally the husband—and a wife who was not in the paid workforce but instead stayed home to care for children. However, in recent decades, women have increasingly assumed roles

as wage earners or as heads of families (Isaacs 2017).

The Social Security Administration (2024s) examined the projected effects of a proposal to reduce the maximum spousal benefit from one-half to one-third of the worker-beneficiary's primary insurance amount (PIA), decreasing replacement rates. The American Academy of Actuaries (2010) explained how this proposed reform would reduce Social Security's long-range funding shortfall while promoting "greater parity between single-earner and two-earner families."

Looking internationally, the US provides higher Social Security benefits to high earners than other countries. For example, the social security benefits of high earners are considerably lower in Canada than in the United States. In 2024, Canadians who began receiving their Canada Pension Plan benefits at age sixty-five could receive a maximum annual benefit of C$16,375 (US$12,118) (Government of Canada 2024). At age sixty-five, Canadians can also receive benefits from the Old Age Security (OAS) program, where the maximum annual benefits are C$8,620 (US$6,379) (Government of Canada 2024). Thus, the annual maximum for these two programs combined was $18,497. However, Canada reduced OAS benefits for high earners, with the reduction going down to zero for the highest earners. The most that those people can receive is $12,118 a year.

Writing about spousal benefits, Steuerle (2015) said, "In many European countries that created benefit systems around the same stereotypical stay-at-home woman, the spouse's benefits are more equal among classes. In the United States, spouses who marry the richest workers get the most." Canada does not have a direct equivalent to the US spousal benefits in Social Security (Social

Security Administration 2019).

Our proposal has three elements. First, regarding individual benefits, we propose changing the individual benefit formula to create an additional bend point. This change would reduce the benefits of people with a career of high earnings who claim benefits in the future. This proposal could be phased in with a five-year delay. The primary insurance amount (PIA) factor associated with average indexed monthly earnings (AIME) above this new bend point could be 10 percent (reduced from 15 percent).

It is difficult to determine the percentage of beneficiaries this proposal would affect; however, an earlier proposal estimated that about 25 percent of beneficiaries would be affected (Debt Reduction Task Force 2010). Waldron (2012) found that in 2007, 28.7 percent of OASI beneficiaries had earnings above the second bend point. When split by gender, the figure was 46.1 percent of men compared to 10.4 percent of women. Adding a third bend point would change the benefit formula for individuals so that it would be consistent with the formula for Social Security family benefits, which already has three bend points (Social Security Administration 2024h).

The second element of our proposal pertains to family benefits. We propose limiting the combined retired-worker and spousal benefits of high-earning workers. Our proposed maximum would apply only to couples with a worker-beneficiary and a spouse who qualifies for spousal benefits. Social Security provides spousal benefits for people in traditional marriages, same-sex marriages, and some other marital arrangements, such as civil unions and domestic partnerships (Bystry 2021). The maximum we propose would not apply to couples when both individuals claim retirement benefits based on their own earnings records.

In 2024, the maximum benefit of a high-earning worker claimed at full retirement age (between ages sixty-six and sixty-seven, depending on the person's birth year) was $45,864 annually, and the maximum combined benefit at that age, including spouse's benefit, was $68,796 (Social Security Administration 2024). We propose setting a lower limit for the maximum combined benefit, including the spousal benefit. The maximum spousal benefit would be determined by a percentage reduction of the maximum benefit the couple could receive if they both claimed benefits at their full retirement age. The proposal would set an upper limit on primary insurance amounts used to determine a worker's and spouse's benefits. If that limit were reduced by 10 percent, the maximum based on 2024 benefits for the couple would be $61,916 annually, and if it were reduced by 15 percent, it would be $58,477. These amounts are still substantial benefits for high-earning families. As for all our proposals, this change would not affect current beneficiaries.

The limit we propose has multiple advantages. It addresses equity concerns regarding single-earner, high-income couples receiving overly high benefits. The proposed limit is aligned with Social Security's goal of redistribution through a progressive benefit formula that replaces a higher percentage of earnings for low-income workers than high-income workers.

The third aspect of our proposal pertains to price-indexed maximum benefits. With current policy, the earnings used to calculate Social Security benefits are wage indexed rather than price indexed. As Biggs (2025) pointed out, this results in an increase over time in replacement rates for a given level of real (price-indexed) wages. The taxable maximum earnings ceiling for Social Security is also wage-indexed, causing it to rise in real value over time. For example, between

2015 and 2025, the real value of the Social Security taxable maximum earnings rose by roughly $21,000 measured in 2025 dollars.

Many people may find the maximum annual Social Security benefit to be surprisingly high, given the perception that the program is designed primarily to help provide lower- and middle-income Americans with an adequate retirement income. In 2025, the maximum annual Social Security benefit obtainable for someone retiring at age seventy was $61,206 (Social Security Administration 2024ff). By comparison, in 2023, the median income of persons age sixty-five and older was $54,710 (US Census Bureau 2024).

Regarding the maximum level of individual and family Social Security benefits, we propose price-indexing rather than wage-indexing. With this change, the real value of maximum benefits (corrected for inflation) would remain constant over time. Because wages generally rise faster than prices, this change would reduce the replacement rate for the top Social Security beneficiaries. This alternative is not a benefit cut relative to current benefit levels, but it is a benefit cut relative to what the maximum wage-indexed benefits would have been in the future.

We also propose raising the tax rate on Social Security benefits to 50 percent for households with taxable annual income of $1 million or more.

Longevity Insurance Benefits

In the US, 4 percent of the population is age eighty or older (Caplan and Rabe 2023). The National Commission on Fiscal Responsibility and Reform (2010) and Turner (2013), among others, have proposed a non-targeted benefit increase for retirees who are at least age eighty-two.

Among those who are at least age sixty-five, poverty rates increase with increasing age. According to Ochieng and others (2024), the official poverty rate and the Supplemental Poverty Measure showed that poverty is higher among people ages eighty and older than people age sixty-five to age seventy-nine. The Supplemental Poverty Measure (SPM) was developed by the Census Bureau to provide a more comprehensive understanding of poverty in the United States. Unlike the official measure, which relies solely on cash income, the SPM considers various factors, including noncash benefits, necessary expenses, and geographic differences in the cost of living.

Muller and Turner (2022) showed that the higher mortality rates of people in poverty cause the official measure to understate the risk of falling into poverty at older ages. Selective survival bias thus influences the estimates of elder poverty. Observed rates of poverty at older ages are reduced because those who have lived in poverty have disproportionately high mortality rates. The risk of falling into poverty at older ages is obscured by cross-sectional data that fail to provide a complete picture. Those who previously lived in poverty may have died, while those currently not in poverty may fall into poverty at older ages.

Social Security began with a benefit eligibility age that was higher than it is now, even though life expectancy was much shorter when the program began. Consequently, like President Franklin Roosevelt, who died at age sixty-three, many workers did not live long enough to be eligible to receive retirement benefits.

Social Security benefit payments began in 1940 with an

eligibility age (earliest claiming age) of sixty-five. Men who were twenty years old in 1900, and thus sixty years old in 1940, had a life expectancy of only sixty-two years (Turner 2016b). Such a high eligibility age relative to the life expectancy is a characteristic of a longevity insurance program. According to Chen and Turner (2015), social security programs that began as longevity insurance have evolved into programs that provide broad-based social insurance or income replacement in retirement as life expectancies have increased. Table 13-1 provides historical data relating to the change in life expectancy over time in the US.

Year Cohort Turned 65	Percentage of Population Surviving from Age 21 to Age 65		Average Remaining Life Expectancy for Those Surviving to Age 65	
	M	F	M	F
1940	53.9	60.6	12.7	14.7
1950	56.2	65.5	13.1	16.2
1960	60.1	71.3	13.2	17.4
1970	63.7	76.9	13.8	18.6
1980	67.8	80.9	14.6	19.1
1990	72.3	83.6	15.3	19.6

Table 13-1: Social Security Administration data on life expectancy.
Source: Social Security Administration (2024m)

Some life insurance companies provide longevity insurance annuities in the United States, the United Kingdom, and other countries (Blake and Turner 2014; Chen, Hughes, and Turner 2016; Kintzel and Turner 2020). A financial instrument called a *tontine* can also be used to provide longevity insurance benefits (Turner, Fullmer, and Forman 2021). A tontine involves a group of individuals who pool money to invest in a fund, often to receive annuity-like payments. As members of the tontine die, their share of the investment is not inherited but redistributed to the remaining living participants, increasing their individual payouts.

Relative to the private sector, the federal government has important advantages in providing longevity insurance annuities because it can create programs that avoid *adverse selection* issues (Turner and others 2017). Adverse selection occurs when people who expect to have a long life are more likely than other people to purchase annuities.

Recipients of social security benefits in Ireland who are at least age eighty receive an Age 80 Allowance (Irish Government 2024; Turner and others 2016). The United Kingdom provides the Over 80 pension, a separate, means-tested pension for people over age eighty (UK Government 2024a). Germany uses Riester pensions, which are voluntary defined contribution plans that can be used as a longevity insurance annuity with payments that begin at age eighty-five (payments can begin earlier) (BaFin 2023).

Other similar ideas have been proposed in the US. In 2010, the National Commission on Fiscal Responsibility and Reform (2010) proposed a version of longevity insurance benefits. In 2016, Representative Reid Ribble, a Republican, introduced H.R. 5747, known as the Save Our Social Security Act or "S.O.S. Act of 2016" (Social Security Administration 2024t). The proposed legislation, not enacted into law, involved increased Social Security benefits that would be phased in from age eighty-two to age eighty-six.

We propose that the Social Security Administration provide longevity insurance benefits to low-benefit OASI beneficiaries who are at least age eighty-two. This proposal would apply to people in the bottom half of beneficiaries by benefit level. The benefits would be capped so as not to exceed monthly benefits above the bottom half. Starting at age eighty-two, people who receive low benefits would receive an additional $50 per month, increasing to $100 per month at age eighty-seven and $150 per month at age ninety-two.

In line with this proposal, we propose that the Social Security Administration could change the name of the program from Old-Age and Survivors Insurance (OASI) to Retirement, Survivors and Longevity Insurance (RSLI) (Turner 2016b). This adjustment would help promote public awareness of the longevity insurance benefit.

The US Social Security program functions within a broader economic context. In the next chapter, we focus on ways to reform other government programs that affect Social Security.

CHAPTER 14

Reforming Government Programs That Affect Social Security

In this chapter, we consider proposals to reform other government programs that either adversely affect Social Security or could more positively affect Social Security.

Prohibit Automatic Enrollment in Medicare

Under the Social Security Act, a private Medicare Advantage insurance company can automatically enroll people who had previously been enrolled in either a commercial insurance plan or Medicaid before they turned sixty-five. The enrollment can be automatic unless people opt out. As stated by Moeller (2016), "The Centers for Medicare & Medicaid Services (CMS) should change this and, at a minimum, provide opt-in protection to beneficiaries. If not, the real-world effect of this rule is that not reading every piece of your mail—even mail you are not expecting and did not ask to be sent to you—can cost you enormous amounts of money and even your financial solvency."

In late 2024 and early 2025, UnitedHealthcare, the largest

health insurer in the United States and owner of Government Employees Health Association (GEHA), attempted to enroll its age-sixty-five and older clients in Medicare (GEHA 2024). It automatically enrolled them in a Medicare Part D (prescription drug) plan, unless they opted out. Medicare Part D plans are only offered by private health insurance companies (UnitedHealthcare 2025).

That was just the beginning of the problems. For many older clients who opted out, because of a "computer glitch," UnitedHealthcare reenrolled those people. As a result, in early 2025, the Social Security Administration sent them notices about their premiums for Medicare Part B (medical insurance). For clients in their seventies with higher incomes, the cost of being enrolled in Part B, even though they were already enrolled in health insurance from UnitedHealthcare, exceeded $600 a month. This amount would be subtracted from monthly Social Security benefits, substantially reducing those benefits. This action was taken even though the client had not contacted the Social Security Administration to request this change, and had, in fact, requested that the insurance company not make this change.

This created problems both for the Social Security Administration, which had extra work dealing with the situation, and for the older people involved, who needed to spend time and emotional energy fixing the problem caused by their health insurance company.

We propose banning health insurance companies from automatically enrolling their clients in Medicare. Enrollment in Medicare should occur only when the person makes a direct request to Medicare to do so.

Increase Supplemental Security Income Benefits

Supplemental Security Income (SSI) is a program run by the Social Security Administration that provides means-tested benefits to low-income people who are at least age sixty-five, and to low-income adults of any age with disabilities or who are blind. In 2025, it provided benefits to 1.6 million people age sixty-five and older (Portalatin-Perez 2025). The program is funded by general government revenue. If this program were more generous and available at age sixty-two, it would reduce the need for the Social Security OASI program to address issues related to low-income people who qualify for Social Security benefits.

The maximum monthly benefit for SSI in 2025 was $967 for individuals and $1,450 for couples. The annual amounts are thus $11,604 for individuals and $17,400 for couples. Some states supplement these benefit amounts. SSI also has a financial assets limit (excluding a home) of $2,000 for individuals and $3,000 for couples (Social Security Administration 2025o). Because the benefit levels are so low, this program places pressure on Social Security OASI to provide more generous benefits for its low-income beneficiaries.

For every two dollars earned from work, SSI benefits are reduced by about one dollar. Above a low-income level, SSI benefits are reduced dollar-for-dollar by Social Security benefits. The first $20 per month of Social Security benefits and other unearned income is exempt (Social Security Administration 2024ee). SSI's Social Security rules reduce or eliminate the positive effect of Social Security benefits on the income of some low-income SSI recipients.

We propose four changes to SSI. First, Congress should reform the SSI program so that it provides more generous benefits, reducing the need for Social Security OASI to provide increased benefits for low-income retirees. Second, policymakers should reduce the Supplemental Security Income offset to one dollar for every two dollars of Social Security benefits. This would make it the same offset as for workers' earnings. Third, we propose raising the exempt amount to $800 a month. This would reduce the need for some of the reforms we have proposed, such as raising the minimum benefit for workers with twenty years or more of covered earnings. Finally, we propose lowering the eligibility age for SSI benefits to age sixty-two because low-income people tend to have shorter life expectancies and retire at younger ages. Our proposal could be adjusted by increasing or lowering the SSI benefit amount.

The Disability Insurance and Health Insurance Trust Funds

Part of the revenue from the federal income taxation of Social Security OASI benefits is transferred to the Disability Insurance (DI) and Health Insurance (HI) Trust Funds. In 1993, Congress enacted legislation that increased the limit of benefits "subject to taxation from 50 percent to 85 percent for single taxpayers with incomes over $34,000 and for taxpayers filing jointly with incomes over $44,000." Any additional tax revenue is deposited in Medicare's Hospital Insurance Trust Fund (Social Security Administration 2025p).

We propose transferring 100 percent of the revenue from the

federal income taxation of Social Security OASI benefits to the OASI Trust Fund.

Taxation of Unemployment Insurance Benefits

Unemployment insurance benefits are taxable under the federal income tax and some state income taxes. However, people who receive unemployment insurance benefits are not required to pay the Social Security payroll tax on those earnings, even though those benefits are related to work (Social Security Administration 2022e). By comparison, the government does impose taxes on other work-related earnings, even when a person is not working. For example, people must pay Social Security taxes on earnings from sick leave, annual leave, and administrative leave.

We propose that people who have annual incomes above a certain threshold should be required to pay Social Security taxes on unemployment insurance benefits, as part of the Social Security self-employment tax. Our proposal could be adjusted by raising or lowering the income threshold, such as $60,000 a year for a single taxpayer and $80,000 for a person filing a joint tax return. The thresholds should be price-indexed for future years.

In addition to long-term solvency questions, Social Security faces an urgent need for new revenue. There are ways to provide the revenue. That is the topic of our next chapter.

CHAPTER 15

New Revenue Sources for the Short-Run Shortfall

Many of the proposals presented so far have limited effects in the short run. Starting with this chapter, we focus on proposals that could have a more immediate effect on increasing revenue for Social Security. Providing new revenue sources now to deal with the Social Security financing problem could prevent the need for drastic measures. As Walker (2025) writes, "It appears increasingly likely that the timing of program changes may effectively require at least a temporary general revenue infusion to avoid sudden across-the-board benefit reductions at trust fund depletion. Especially if lawmakers wait until the last minute to act, it may be impossible to phase in revenue increases or benefit cuts fast enough."

Tap Unclaimed Retirement Savings Accounts

When workers change jobs, they often lose track of their pension accounts with former employers. The former employers also lose track of the workers. As a result, a high proportion of lost retirement savings accounts likely will never be matched with their owners or their owners' beneficiaries. These funds have received preferential tax treatment, and they have been earmarked for use in the retirement income system. When people do not claim their funds, the funds fail to serve the retirement income system.

Many workers change jobs frequently, especially when they are young, which can cause them to lose track of their retirement savings accounts from previous jobs. In January 2024, the median number of years that wage and salary workers remained with their employers was 3.9 years, the shortest duration since January 2002 (US Bureau of Labor Statistics 2024a).

Many retirement account owners have 401(k) accounts that they were never aware of (because they were automatically enrolled in an account) or forgot about. According to the Charles Schwab Corporation (2023), "If left unattended for too long, old [401(k)] accounts can be converted to cash—and even transferred to the state as unclaimed property—forgoing their future growth potential."

Unclaimed individual retirement accounts (IRAs) are also a major issue. Due to variations in state dormancy and escheatment laws, many people are unclear about what happens to unclaimed IRAs. The period over which an IRA must have been unattended before it is considered dormant and thus eligible for escheatment varies by state (Boyte-White 2023). To define when an IRA is dormant, many states use the required minimum distribution beginning date, which is age seventy-three in 2025 (D'Amato 2023).

It is problematic that "most states do not automatically notify account owners about dormant accounts" (Hallez 2021). Forced transfers of inactive 401(k)s to IRAs—a conversion of one type of retirement account to another without the account owner's consent—have sparked criticism by the Government Accountability Office (GAO). This process, though questionable, is legally permitted. "Federal statute permits plans to rollover accounts of more than $1,000 but not over $5,000 to an IRA on behalf of participants who have not instructed, for example, to have them rolled over to a new employer's plan or a preexisting IRA, or sent directly to them" (GAO 2014a, p. 2).

Statistics on unclaimed retirement savings plans are astonishing. The financial technology company Capitalize (2023) provided the following estimates related to unclaimed 401(k)s.

> As of May 2023, we estimate that there are 29.2 million left-behind or forgotten 401(k) accounts holding approximately $1.65 trillion in assets, up from 24.3 million and $1.35 trillion in May 2021. This represents 25 percent of all 401(k) plan assets, up from 20 percent in May 2021. The number of forgotten 401(k)s increased by over 20 percent since May 2021 driven by a period of heightened job switching (e.g., 'The Great Resignation') with 3.8 million and 4.4 million accounts left behind in 2021 and 2022 respectively.

That remarkable amount exceeds the large size of US credit card debt (Turner 2024). In mid-2024, Americans' credit card debt reached $1.182 trillion (Schulz 2025). Yet the credit-card debt crisis generally receives more media attention than the larger amount in unclaimed 401(k)s.

The current solutions to this problem are unsatisfactory. According to Hallez (2021), "Few [U.S. states] automatically match unclaimed retirement accounts with their owners. In most cases, only about 3 percent of accounts are claimed within two years of being turned over to the state." It is possible that account owners do not know when their unclaimed retirement accounts have been converted to IRAs or transferred to the state, or they do not understand how to claim the funds after this has happened.

The SECURE 2.0 Act, passed in 2022, required the Department of Labor to create an online Retirement Savings Lost and Found Database. The department's Employee Benefits Security Administration (EBSA) requested that plan administrators voluntarily provide the information to assist with developing the online search tool (EBSA 2024b). However, because sharing plan information is voluntary, employer participation has been low, perhaps because of concerns about cybersecurity or the legal risks related to security and privacy laws (Turner 2024).

People can sometimes find unclaimed IRAs and 401(k)s through the National Association of Unclaimed Property Administrators (Farmer 2021). The unclaimed property website for a specific state can be found through the NAUPA website (Amend 2023). The Government Accountability Office reported that survey data provided by seventeen states showed that, in 2016, 84 percent of the retirement accounts transferred to these states were assets and uncashed checks from employer-based defined contribution plans, and 16 percent were transfers from IRAs (GAO 2019b, p. 12).

We propose that unclaimed 401(k) accounts and other unclaimed pension accounts be transferred to the Social Security Administration to fund OASI benefits. This change could also raise public awareness about the problem of unclaimed retirement accounts and hopefully help people reconnect with their funds before the transfer. Knowing that all lost pension funds could be found in one place would help account owners find them. And our proposal would allow account owners or their beneficiaries to claim the funds even after they have been transferred to the OASI. Either way, unclaimed funds would be used for their original purpose of providing retirement income.

To facilitate this proposal, a nationwide standard definition for establishing the dormancy of retirement accounts would need to be established. This definition is necessary to avoid confusion related to variations in state-specific laws. It may be possible to enact a new federal law that would use a combination of the participant's current age and the number of years for which the account has been inactive to determine whether the account is dormant. One example of a dormant account could be an eighty-year-old participant whose account has been abandoned for ten years or any account that has been abandoned for twenty years.

Those funds could be taxed as benefit payments or distributions before being transferred to the Social Security Administration, but we propose to transfer them untaxed to better reduce the OASI funding shortfall.

Financial Market Investments

The Social Security OASI Trust Fund is invested exclusively in US government bonds. Weaver (2001) argued that collective investment of Social Security funds in the stock market would have three advantages compared to a system of mandatory individual retirement accounts. First, the financial costs of managing the system would be considerably lower than the greater cost of managing millions of individual accounts with different investment mixes. Second, the cost of providing information to participants would be considerably lower because investment decisions would be centralized. Third, the defined benefit approach of Social Security would be preserved, which has lower risks for participants than the financial market risks for individual accounts.

Part of the Canada Pension Plan Trust Fund is invested in the stock market. The Canada Pension Plan is Canada's main social security plan for all parts of Canada except Quebec Province, which has a separate social security plan. The Canada Pension Plan Investment Board is an investment management organization that has managed Canada Pension Plan investments since 1999. Its ten-year average rate of return as of 2024 was 9.2 percent. By comparison, Social Security's effective interest rate earned in 2023 on the government bonds it held was 2.3 percent (Social Security Administration 2025d). The Canada Pension Plan invests globally in stocks, bonds, and infrastructure. In part due to the success of its investments, the Canada Pension Plan is projected to be financially sustainable for at least the next seventy-five years (Canada Pension Plan Investments 2024). Munnell (2024a), however, stated that the fund would have done better over the long run if, instead of active management, it had used passive management by investing in index funds, which have lower management costs.

Munnell (2023b), among others, has proposed investing part of the Social Security Trust Funds in the stock market. Republican Senator Bill Cassidy made such a proposal (Konish 2023b). He and Democratic Senator Tim Kaine, in 2025, also proposed investing $1.5 trillion over the next five years into an investment fund that would then be given seventy years to grow (Folley and Fields 2025).

We propose that the part of the OASI Trust Fund deriving from the transfer of lost pension accounts (our previous proposal) be invested in stock and bond markets. Instead of using payroll tax revenue to create the fund proposed by Cassidy and Kaine, it could be created by using assets from lost pension fund accounts. We do not believe that payroll tax revenue or revenue from the personal income taxation of Social Security benefits should be invested in the stock market. Those two types of revenue should be invested exclusively in government bonds.

Because the Social Security Administration does not have the personnel required to manage those investments, the Thrift Savings Plan would take over that role. It would use the same model it uses for managing the investments of federal government workers, members of the military, and members of Congress. The Thrift Savings Plan has low fees on its investment options of less than five basis points (Thrift Savings Plan 2024a). (A basis point is 0.01 percent.) The money transferred to Social Security from lost pension funds could be entirely invested in the Thrift Savings Plan's longest target date fund. As of 2025, that is the 2070 target date fund, which has a net expense ratio of less than five basis points. This arrangement would presumably be simple for the Thrift Savings Plan to manage. It would ensure the funds were passively managed, without political interference and at low cost. This approach could lower the already low fees of the Thrift Savings Plan due to economies of scale.

Contrary to some lawmakers' proposals, we do not recommend instituting mandatory individual retirement accounts as part of Social Security (e.g., Warshawsky 2022).

Cap Retirement Savings Accounts

Some wealthy Americans know how to use tax-advantaged retirement savings accounts to amass huge fortunes. Policymakers have become aware of IRAs and 401(k)s with extremely large account balances. "In recent decades, with the advent of the Roth IRA and relaxed restrictions on IRA rollovers, ultrawealthy Americans have reportedly built tax-sheltered accounts worth many millions—or even billions—of dollars" (Daugherty 2024).

Steuerle (2025) argued for considering pension reform at the same time as Social Security reform to have a broader perspective on policy for retirement income. Roth IRAs were created to help the middle class save more for retirement. Their exploitation by the wealthiest Americans to "sidestep the tax system" is not aligned with their intended usage (Elliott, Callahan, and Bandler 2021a). Some affluent entrepreneurs have used Roth IRAs to greatly increase their wealth. For example, PayPal founder Peter Thiel's Roth IRA, reportedly worth $5 billion at the end of 2019, has been described as a "$5 billion tax-free piggy bank" (Elliott, Callahan, and Bandler 2021a). Thiel may still own a self-directed Roth IRA (IRA Financial Group 2023). Some investors who own Roth IRAs may invest the annual contributions in purchasing a huge number of extremely low-cost shares of a start-up company (Elliott, Callahan, and Bandler 2021a). If the company's stock price skyrockets, colossal financial gains will occur in the Roth IRA. These gains remain tax free if the account owner does not withdraw them before age fifty-nine and a half.

The IRA of Republican Senator Mitt Romney is estimated to

hold between $25 million and $125 million (IRA Financial Group 2023). Romney's wealth grew from special types of investments that he could access as the cofounder of the private equity investment firm Bain Capital (IRA Financial Group 2023). Most investors lack such investment opportunities.

"While benefits obtainable from a defined contribution plan or IRA are not limited, the intended outcome of these contribution limits is to indirectly limit individual account balances" (Turner 2024). Yet current policies, which limit annual contributions but do not directly limit individual account balances, have not succeeded in preventing the accumulation of enormous account balances. Evidence indicates that "there is no effective cap on the amount that can be received from a defined contribution plan or IRA in the United States, particularly for wealthy people who have access to non-publicly available investments" (Turner 2024). To effectively address this problem, direct limits on account balances will be necessary.

To prevent the federal government from losing too much tax revenue, it has long been a principle in pension policy and tax law to limit the amount of tax preference an individual can receive. Many believe it is unjust that "the government spends a large amount of money subsidizing a whole range of retirement plans whose benefits flow overwhelmingly to America's most affluent" (Mechanic 2021). The owners of retirement savings accounts with the largest account balances have had disproportionately large tax subsidies estimated to have exceeded $100 million for some owners over the period they are anticipated to have held the accounts (Turner, McCarthy, and Stein 2016). These tax subsidies are so large due to the unusually high rate of return on the investments of the funds in the accounts

(Turner, McCarthy, and Stein 2016). Regulations should be adjusted to reflect the principle of limiting the amount of tax preference an individual can receive for the sake of the government's finances and in the pursuit of equity in a nation with sizable and growing wealth inequalities.

Most Americans have much smaller retirement savings than what the wealthiest account owners hold in their IRAs and 401(k)s. The Federal Reserve's 2022 Survey of Consumer Finances (SCF) found that the "median retirement savings for Americans in 2022 was $86,900" (Parker 2024b). In 2007, the median retirement account balance of high-income households was equal to four times that of middle-income households (GAO 2023a). In 2019, the median retirement account balance of high-income households had grown so that it was equal to nine times that of middle-income households (GAO 2023a).

Turner, McCarthy, and Stein (2014) examined data on households with 401(k) accounts and IRAs and estimated that, in 2010, approximately 176,000 households had combined retirement savings of over $3 million per household. Thus, taken as a whole, these tax-advantaged retirement savings accounts likely held over $500 billion (Turner, McCarthy, and Stein 2014). Estimates based on more recent data would be higher. By comparison, consider an extreme example of what it would take to achieve a relatively large retirement savings account. If a person contributed $50,000 a year for thirty years and earned 10 percent every year, at the end of thirty years, that investor would have accumulated $8,224,701.

Ireland has a limit on account balances, which is known as the Standard Fund Threshold (KPMG 2024). Since December 2005, the threshold has been "a lifetime limit on the total capital value of pension benefits that an individual could draw from tax-relieved pension products" (KPMG 2024). If this limit is exceeded, "the excess is subject to penal taxation at an effective income tax rate of up to 68.8 percent" (KPMG 2024). The Standard Fund Threshold in 2024 was €2 million ($2.6 million). That amount is set to rise to €2.8 million in 2029 (Mercer 2025).

Some US lawmakers, such as Democratic Senator Ron Wyden, the chair of the Senate Finance Committee, have tried to stop the use of Roth IRAs by wealthy people who seek to avoid taxation (Elliott, Callahan, and Bandler 2021c). In 2016, Wyden proposed the Retirement Improvements and Savings Enhancements Act, which did not pass. This bill "would have required owners of Roth accounts worth more than $5 million to take out money over time, capping the accounts' growth" (Elliott, Callahan, and Bandler 2021c).

We propose a $10 million ceiling on the total amount in an individual's IRA and employer-provided defined contribution accounts. If the total amount across all such accounts owned by the same individual exceeds $10 million, further contributions would not be permitted, and distributions from those accounts would be required. Account balances exceeding the $10 million maximum would be reduced to that maximum through mandatory withdrawals made over a period not to exceed ten years. Because these accounts have received income tax subsidies—to encourage the accumulation of assets to finance retirement—tax revenue from withdrawals made to reduce oversized account balances would be transferred from the IRS to the OASI Trust Fund. Not all such withdrawals would be taxable because the withdrawals from Roth IRAs and Roth 401(k)s are tax-free. Nevertheless, considerable revenue could be generated.

We have chosen ten years as the time limit for reducing oversized account balances so that, for example, a person who is age forty would need to reduce his balance to the maximum by age fifty. This period would spread the possible tax consequences over a decade. The required withdrawals would start at 10 percent of the amount that exceeds the cap on December 31 of the previous year. It would increase by 10 percent per year so that, by the end of the tenth year, 100 percent of the remaining excess would be withdrawn.

We propose $10 million as the initial value of the limit because that amount would not affect most investors. The Employee Benefit Research Institute's data, based on the Federal Reserve Board's Survey of Consumer Finances, indicated that in 2022, only 3.2 percent of retirees had over $1 million in their retirement accounts, while only 0.1 percent of retirees had over $5 million (Mancini 2024). The total number of individuals who own IRAs (either traditional IRAs or Roth IRAs) worth at least $5 million is estimated to be more than twenty-eight thousand (Elliott, Callahan, and Bandler 2021b). Thus, the proposed taxation would impact relatively few people while still generating considerable revenue.

Withdrawals from traditional IRAs are subject to income taxation. The tax varies, depending on the federal income tax brackets, the type of IRA, the account owner's age, and other factors (Epstein 2024). There are exceptions, but early withdrawals (before age fifty-nine and a half) from traditional IRAs generally result in a 10 percent penalty and the federal income tax (Epstein 2024). An early withdrawal penalty of 10 percent applies to traditional 401(k)s as well (Parker 2024a). However, this early withdrawal penalty would not apply to forced withdrawals under our proposal, though the federal income tax still would apply. Contributions to 401(k) plans are made with pre-tax dollars, so they are tax deferred. Thus, the federal income tax also applies to traditional (not Roth) 401(k) withdrawals (Parker 2024a).

Our proposal, which limits IRA and 401(k) account balances to $10 million in aggregate per person, would increase the solvency of the OASI Trust Fund. Our ceiling is a reasonable complement to the limits placed the annual contributions to such accounts. If tax revenues from the mandatory withdrawals are transferred to the OASI Trust Fund, taxes on retirement account balances that exceed the $10 million maximum will fund retirement benefits for participants of varying incomes.

A policymaking option could be to lower the ceiling to, for example, $5 million. That amount would still exclude most retirees from a higher tax burden.

Taxing High Earners

The United States has one of the most unequal income distributions in the developed world (DeSilver 2013). In the fourth quarter of 2023, "the top 10 percent of households by wealth" owned "66.9 percent of total household wealth while the bottom 50 percent of households owned only 2.5 percent of total household wealth" (Kent 2024). On average, for every $1 of wealth owned by White families, Black families owned 23 cents, and Hispanic families owned 19 cents (Kent 2024).

The 1983 Social Security reforms included setting the taxable maximum at a level that taxed 90 percent of all wage earnings. In 1982, 90 percent of all wage earnings were payroll taxed. By

2017, this proportion had fallen to 84 percent (Peter G. Peterson Foundation 2023b). In 2021, it had fallen to 81 percent, which indicates that "a record share of earnings was not subject to Social Security taxes" (Bivens and Gould 2023). Over the years, rising wage inequality has decreased the proportion of Social Security taxable earnings "as more earnings for higher-wage workers spilled over the cap" (Bivens and Gould 2023).

All wage earnings are subject to the Medicare tax. For Medicare Part A, the tax rate is 2.9 percent, with no tax ceiling on the wages and salaries. If annual wages exceed certain thresholds—$250,000 for married taxpayers who file joint returns and $200,000 for unmarried people—an additional 0.9 percent tax is levied on the amount above the threshold. The taxes are split equally between the employer and the employee (Congressional Budget Office 2018).

For an international comparison, consider that the United Kingdom provides a social security benefit based on contributions (Hobson, Kennedy, and Mackley 2022). Social security taxes are levied on all earnings above the taxable maximum at 2 percent a year, with no effect on future benefits. These taxes are paid entirely by the employee (UK Parliament 2024). In tax year 2023-2024, the United Kingdom taxed workers at a rate of 2 percent for all earnings above £50,270 a year ($67,362) for National Insurance Contributions (social security contributions) (UK Government 2024b).

We propose placing a Social Security tax of 0.5 percent per year, split between employers and employees, on earnings above the taxable maximum. Because the earnings of workers who make more than the taxable maximum tend to rise over their careers, this change would generally only apply later in life. Our proposal could be adjusted by raising the earnings level at which the tax took effect, which, for example, could be raised to $500,000 a year. In addition, policymakers could raise or lower the tax rate.

Funding Administrative Costs

Historically, Social Security has financed its administrative expenses from payroll tax payments and, more recently, from income tax payments on Social Security benefits. In 1957, Social Security (OASI) administrative expenses were 2.2 percent of total costs, but by 2018 and years since then, they had fallen to 0.4 percent, their level in 2023 (Social Security Administration 2025i).

Munnell (2023b) argued for partial use of general revenue to finance Social Security. According to the Committee for a Responsible Federal Budget (2014), "The general fund has occasionally reimbursed the Social Security Trust Funds in specific cases to compensate it for policy changes that would otherwise lower its balance."

In its survey of social security programs in the Americas, the Social Security Administration (2019) wrote, "Government contributions may be used in different ways to defray a portion of all expenditures (such as the cost of administration)." Denmark uses general revenue to finance social security benefits and administrative expenses (Bunn, Bray, and Haddinga 2023). In the United Kingdom, National Insurance contributions are made on a pay-as-you-go basis. When necessary, general revenues from the Treasury can be used to increase the balance of the National Insurance Fund (NIF): "To maintain the working balance of the fund, the Treasury can also 'top up' the NIF with a grant (known as a 'supplement') by a specific percentage of expected benefit expenditure" (Masala 2024, p. 6).

We propose that general revenue funding be allowed for Social Security, but exclusively for Social Security's administrative expenses. Because of the difficulty of dealing with the current financial shortfall, it may be helpful, if not necessary, to use some general revenue to finance Social Security. We propose doing so in a limited way. This proposal would preserve the tradition of no general revenue funding for Social Security benefits (other than income tax payments on Social Security benefits). As an example of this approach, the Thrift Savings Plan for federal government employees, members of Congress, and the military is partially subsidized by the federal government by providing administrative services by the government agencies employing the participants.

With this arrangement, if general tax revenues were used to fully cover administrative expenses, workers would know that all their payroll tax payments were going to provide benefits. General tax revenues could provide a more stable source of funding for administrative expenses, which could otherwise be constrained by trust fund balances, particularly in times of financial stress. A dedicated general tax allocation could make it easier to invest in administrative technology and infrastructure improvements without eroding the trust fund. However, this funding could be affected by political swings, so our proposal retains the use of the OASDI Trust Fund as an alternative source of funding for administrative expenses.

If lawmakers wanted to adjust our proposal, they could use federal revenue to cover some expense categories, such as property rental or ownership expenses. Another option could be to automatically trigger using federal revenue for administrative expenses if the projected date of trust fund depletion was within ten years.

EPILOGUE

Social Security for Future Generations

This book approaches Social Security reform from multiple perspectives. It discusses using lost pension money in unclaimed retirement savings accounts, such as 401(k) accounts, for helping to finance Social Security. This money has already been designated through tax preferences to support retirement income. The book proposes voluntary catch-up contributions up to the maximum contributions as determined by the maximum taxable earnings for Social Security contributions. These extra contributions for people who are at least age fifty would primarily benefit middle-class workers.

Our goals include reducing inequality in retirement savings and reducing poverty at older ages. Therefore, one of our proposals is designed to help low-income beneficiaries who are age eighty and older, who primarily are women. The US needs policies that provide more equitable treatment of two-earner versus one-earner high-income households. We reject the idea of a flat benefit program, with everyone receiving the same level of benefits, but we propose raising the lowest benefits and reducing the highest benefits. Lawmakers, we believe, can change the taxes and benefits for the highest-earning workers. Benefit cuts for those workers and levying a small tax on annual earnings above the taxable maximum would reduce the advantages of those workers.

Our proposals target changes that we argue are justified on grounds of equity. Low-income workers need higher benefits because high-income workers receive most of the tax subsidies in the private pension system. In other words, high-income workers receive a disproportionate share of the public subsidies in the retirement income system. These targeted changes, on net, would reduce the need for across-the-board payroll tax hikes and benefit cuts. We are advocating a diversified approach to reform, with proposals affecting different aspects of the Social Security OASI program and the Social Security Administration.

As we have shown in the book, there are numerous ways to simplify the way that Social Security communicates with workers and beneficiaries. The terms *normal retirement age* and *full retirement age* are confusing because nothing about them is normal or full. The term *primary insurance amount* may be useful for actuaries, but it is yet another technical term. Instead, Social Security communications with the public should focus on minimum benefits, receivable at age sixty-two, and maximum benefits, receivable at age seventy, with benefit levels determined by a replacement rate rather than by a calculation with multiple bend points.

Any successful reform must have elements that appeal to both political parties. For this reason, the book includes proposals traditionally favored by Republicans and proposals traditionally favored by Democrats. For example, the proposal to invest funds transferred from lost pensions in financial markets is in line with Republican proposals to invest part of the OASI Trust Fund in the stock market. The proposal to raise benefits for low- and middle-income beneficiaries in their eighties and older through longevity insurance benefits is in line with proposals favored by Democrats to provide better support for older widows.

We have not proposed some common ideas that have been analyzed by other writers. For example, it is often suggested that all new state and local government workers should be covered by Social Security (e.g., Peter G. Peterson Foundation 2022). This proposal would make Social Security a truly national program. It would resolve issues related to the equitable treatment of workers who qualify for state or local government pensions while working in jobs not covered by Social Security. We support that proposal. We also do not propose an increase in the payroll tax rate because we are not sure of what the increase would be, given our other proposals. However, we support a payroll tax rate increase as part of a diversified reform package.

Social Security has fully paid promised benefits for decades, providing needed retirement income for millions of American families. Yet, population aging, measured by the increase in the old-age dependency ratio, makes future reforms more difficult. Further delay also increases the difficulty of reforms.

One of our goals has been to provide ideas that might facilitate the reform process. For example, the traditional idea that a reform needs to resolve financing issues for the next seventy-five years is a higher, more difficult-to-achieve standard than used by many countries. Given the difficulty of legislating Social Security reform, we propose that the reform period be reduced to forty years, which is still a substantial period of time.

We hope that examining Social Security from different perspectives will facilitate reform by providing policymakers with more options. Reform is urgently needed. Procrastination raises the magnitude of the changes required. Social Security is a promise—

SOCIAL SECURITY FOR FUTURE GENERATIONS

but many Americans are worried that the promise will not be kept. It is time to get to work on keeping the promise for future generations.

APPENDIX 1

Summary of Proposals

Chapter 4 Proposals: Improving the Reform Process

Automatic Adjustments for Social Security. The automatic adjustment mechanism could involve a trigger, such as the projected date of trust fund depletion being less than or equal to ten years from the present. The resulting adjustment could be an increase in the payroll tax rate of 0.25 percent for both employers and employees. If the projected trust fund depletion date were less than five years away, the cost-of-living adjustment could be reduced, and the payroll tax rate could be increased.

Use a Forty-Year Period to Evaluate Solvency Proposals. Each proposal should require the trust fund to be financially stable or show signs of improvement in the fortieth year. The new policy goal would be to maintain solvency for more than forty years. This proposal is consistent with the practice in some other countries.

Reduce Required Senate Votes. To facilitate the passage of Social Security reforms, we propose that Congress should reduce the number of required Senate votes from sixty to fifty-seven. The existing sixty-vote requirement for *structural* changes to Social Security should be retained. This proposal would still encourage bipartisan participation in the reform process while making it easier to pass needed changes.

Require Congress to Appoint Bipartisan Reform Commission. A bipartisan commission would recommend reform options and propose legislation for Social Security if the projected trust fund depletion date is ten or fewer years away. The commission could be a technical commission composed of economists, actuaries, and other Social Security policy experts. A technical commission would provide political cover for politicians, who would not be responsible for generating policy recommendations. The commission would hold public hearings and produce a report in one year.

Amend the Congressional Budget Act. This law governs the enactment of Social Security amendments. Our proposal would require benefit increases to be matched by increases in revenue or cuts in other benefits. This would ensure that the overall package has a neutral or positive effect on Social Security solvency.

Chapter 5 Proposals: Social Security Contributions and the Tax Code

Allow Workers to Make Voluntary Social Security Contributions. We propose that Congress allow workers with at least nine years of covered earnings at age sixty or older to make voluntary Social Security contributions. This would allow them to "buy" additional years of covered earnings and therefore meet the requirement of ten years of covered earnings.

Increase the Minimum Number of Contribution Years. We propose that lawmakers should gradually raise the minimum number of contribution years for Social Security eligibility from ten to twelve years—for people who want to start receiving benefits between age sixty-two and sixty-four. The law could stipulate that this change would begin ten years after the law is passed. For people who prefer to receive benefits at age sixty-five or older, the law would not change; they would still be required to have ten years of covered work to be eligible for benefits.

Raise the Payroll Tax Ceiling. Following the National Commission on Fiscal Responsibility and Reform (2010), Munnell (2024c), and others, we propose raising the payroll tax ceiling to cover a higher percentage of wages. This change should occur gradually, during a transition period. We propose that at least 85 percent of wages be covered. This change would raise revenues and the future benefits of those affected.

Social Security Taxes for People Younger than Twenty-One. We propose that all workers under age twenty-one pay both income tax and Social Security tax, and apply that rule to all work arrangements.

End the Student Exemption. We propose that Congress treat the earnings of students and nonstudents of the same age consistently; specifically, we propose ending the student exemption from the Social Security payroll tax.

Increase Payroll Taxes on Fringe Benefits. We propose that Congress increase the percentage of fringe benefit compensation that is subject to Social Security payroll taxes. This proposal is in line with the current treatment of adoption costs and employee contributions to 401(k) plans. We also propose a gradual increase in the *types of fringe benefits* that are subject to the Social Security payroll tax. For example, lawmakers could first count the employer's cost of group-term life insurance as income subject to the Social

Security payroll tax. Later, employer-subsidized transportation to work could be included.

Apply Payroll Taxes to Cafeteria Plans. In alignment with ideas from the Peter G. Peterson Foundation (2022), we propose making contributions to cafeteria plans subject to the Social Security payroll tax, which would be consistent with the treatment of 401(k) contributions.

Apply Payroll Taxes to Employer Contributions to Retirement Savings. We propose that Congress subject employer contributions to 401(k) plans and similar retirement savings plans to the Social Security payroll tax paid by employers and employees—up to the payroll tax ceiling.

Require Some Employers to Pay Social Security Taxes for Contract Workers. In situations where a large employer has long-term relationships with many full-time independent contract workers, we propose that the employer be required to make equivalent payments of the employer share of the contract worker's Social Security taxes. Also, the employer must withhold the employee's share of Social Security tax payments from the employee's earnings and submit that money to the Internal Revenue Service. This rule could apply to employers with at least one hundred long-term independent contract workers.

Apply the SECA Tax to Pass-Through Business Earnings. We propose that the Social Security Self-Employment Contributions Act (SECA) payroll tax apply to all earnings and distributions to pass-through business owners up to the taxable maximum.

Summary of Proposals

Chapter 6: Ideas from Financial Literacy Research

Repeal the Retirement Earnings Test. This policy change would increase payroll tax revenues, decrease administrative costs, and increase benefits for some workers.

Abandon the Earnings Test. Instead of an earnings test, we propose that workers be allowed to continue working and have the option to claim 25, 50, or 75 percent of the Social Security benefits they would otherwise receive. Their future benefits would be increased to compensate for the benefits they temporarily give up.

Limit Clawbacks. We propose to limit clawbacks of previous overpayments to 50 percent of monthly Social Security benefits. This limit would be a more compassionate and realistic approach, given the finances of many beneficiaries. As a related matter, we propose that a beneficiary who lives for one or more days of a given month be entitled to receive that month's benefit payment during the following month. The benefits would be paid to the deceased's survivor or estate. This change would reduce the prevalence of benefit clawbacks relating to a beneficiary's death.

Help Beneficiaries Compare Existing and New Benefit Amounts. When the Social Security Administration provides a written notice of a new benefit amount, either by mail or online, it should also include the current benefit amount to make it easier to compare the current and new amounts. This simple change would make it easier for beneficiaries to verify that the new amount is correct and see how much their benefits will increase.

Itemize Deductions on Beneficiaries' Online Accounts. We propose that the Social Security Administration provide, on the beneficiary's online account, an itemized listing of the deductions from gross monthly benefits. Given the large number of potential deductions, it is important for the Social Security Administration to provide that information so that beneficiaries can check the validity of the deductions and know the amounts for individual items.

Improve Written Correspondence. We propose that the Social Security Administration only use postmarks that correspond to dates when the administration's offices are open. This will reduce suspicion of scams or fraud in the minds of participants. As a related matter, we propose that when sending written communications to participants, the Social Security Administration should provide its mailing addresses, phone numbers, and hours of operation so that participants can more easily know how to resolve problems, learn more, and ask other questions.

Provide a Free Robo Advisor. We propose that the Social Security Administration provide a free robo advisor designed to answer Social Security questions. That program would answer questions about when participants could claim their Social Security benefits, how different claiming options affect benefits, and other questions.

Raise the Full Retirement Age. With a delay of ten years, we propose raising the full retirement age from sixty-seven to sixty-eight at the rate of one month per year. If life expectancy *has not increased for all major demographic and economic groups* by at least one year compared to 2020, then the start of this proposed change would be postponed.

Establish a New "Standard Retirement Age." This new policy, which would be phased in, would set age sixty-three as the standard retirement age. Implementation would only occur if life expectancy for all major demographic and economic groups has risen by at least one year. Our proposal would retain age sixty-two as the *early* retirement age.

Chapter 7: Simplifying Social Security

Improve Communication about the Full Retirement Age. We propose that the Social Security Administration drop the concept of the full retirement age when communicating with participants. Instead of making the full retirement age the central focus, the Social Security Administration could use a single system of benefit adjustments from age sixty-two (the minimum benefit age) to age seventy (the maximum benefit age).

Abandon the Primary Insurance Amount (PIA). By dropping the primary insurance amount (PIA) concept, participants would be more likely to understand the system. They would only need to know about the minimum and maximum benefit ages. The Social Security Administration could make these changes in its public communications while internally retaining the concepts of the full retirement age and the primary insurance amount, if doing so makes it easier for Social Security actuaries to calculate benefit amounts.

Include All Earnings for People with More Than Forty Years of Earnings. We propose that all earnings be counted when calculating Social Security benefits for people with more than forty years of earnings. The lowest five years would be subtracted, and the remainder of indexed earnings summed and divided by thirty-five. Thus, if a person had forty-five years of covered earnings, the lowest five years would be dropped. The remaining forty years would be summed and then divided by thirty-five. This way, long-career, low-wage workers could raise their Social Security benefits by continuing to work. However, to limit the benefits of long-career high-earners, the current maximum average wages would be used.

Simplify the Benefit Calculation. Under our proposal, a single number would be multiplied by the person's average indexed earnings. The worker would be able to readily see what their earnings replacement rate and benefit would be. The simple calculation would multiply the worker's average indexed monthly earnings by the corresponding replacement rate for the benefit claiming age they had selected.

Reduce Spousal Benefit Percentages. To partially address the inequity faced by single workers and two-earner families with similar earnings, we propose reducing spousal benefit percentages to 25 percent and 40 percent for workers with earnings above the second bend point in the Social Security benefit formula.

Raise the Eligibility Age for Survivors' Benefits. We propose raising that age from sixty to sixty-two so that it is consistent with the eligibility ages for worker and spousal benefits. As a related matter, we propose raising the eligibility age for survivors' benefits after remarriage to age sixty-two. Thus, people who remarry at sixty-two and older could choose between the survivors' benefits they would receive from their former spouse's earnings record, or from benefits based on their own earnings record, or from the benefits of new spouse.

Change Eligibility Rules Pertaining to Remarriage and Divorce. Persons sixty-two and older who remarry after a divorce could continue receiving the Social Security benefits they currently receive, or they could receive their new spouse's benefits if those benefits are higher. This change would end the difference between remarrying following the death of a spouse and remarrying following divorce.

Change Some Rules Pertaining to Spousal and Survivors' Benefits. We propose basing the benefit amount for *both* spousal and survivors' benefits on the age at which a person first makes any type of Social Security benefits claim. Thus, if recipients of survivors' benefits later claim benefits based on their own earnings, those benefits would be based on the first age at which they received any type of Social Security OASI benefits. This system would be simpler and more equitable relative to the treatment of people who only receive worker benefits. In addition, we propose using the same basis to determine both spousal and survivors' benefits. Specifically, we propose that both types of benefits be based on the partner's actual benefit amount, which is simpler and more transparent for participants than basing both on the partner's primary insurance amount.

Raise the Minimum Length of Marriage for Survivors' Benefits. We propose raising the minimum length of marriage required for receiving Social Security survivors' benefits from nine months to one year. The current exceptions would continue to apply. This change would make the requirement consistent with the requirement for eligibility for Medicare benefits as a surviving spouse. As a related matter, we propose that unmarried couples (including same-sex couples) who meet specific requirements be eligible for spousal and survivors' benefits.

Chapter 8: Improving Information and Assistance

Increases to Helpline Staffing. We propose requiring the Social Security Administration to increase helpline staffing by 5 percent if, over the previous three months, the average wait time on the customer service helpline is more than an hour, or possibly less.

Provide Mobile Service Units. We propose that the Social Security Administration provide mobile service units for rural and other underserved areas.

Facilitate Social Security Registration for Newborn Children. We propose legislation that ensures that parents can apply for Social Security numbers in hospitals, birthing centers, or with registered midwives for their newborn children. This legislation would ensure that the Enumeration at Birth program cannot be changed at the option of the Social Security Administration.

Update Information Technology. We propose that the Social Security Administration update its information technology. In addition, we propose that legislation would require the Social Security Administration to maintain adequate information technology staff.

Provide Better Help for Victims of Identity Theft. We propose requiring the Social Security Administration to improve the assistance it provides to participants whose Social Security numbers have been stolen.

Summary of Proposals

Chapter 9: Social Justice and Equity Proposals

Help Wrongfully Incarcerated People. To help restore the lives of those exonerated of crimes they did not commit, we propose legislation that would require the Social Security Administration to credit earnings for the time a person is wrongfully incarcerated.

Provide Spousal Benefits to the Spouses of Incarcerated People. To promote fairness for family members, we propose that the spouse of an incarcerated beneficiary receive *survivors'* benefits, not spousal benefits, during the period of incarceration. We argue that the financial impact of incarceration on family members is like the financial effect of a worker-beneficiary's death.

Change Rules Pertaining to Recipients of Government Pensions. For those receiving government pensions who were not covered by Social Security, we propose reducing Social Security spousal benefits by one-third of the government pension amount.

Prohibit the Falsification of Participants' Records. We propose that Congress pass legislation prohibiting the Social Security Administration from knowingly falsifying participants' records.

Strictly Limit Access to Social Security Data. We propose an amendment to the Social Security Act that would strictly limit access to Social Security Administration data on individuals. Access would be granted only to employees of the Social Security Administration who need the information to assist a participant, or for other administrative purposes related to processing Social Security benefits.

Prohibit the Integration of Social Security Records with Other Government Databases. We propose legislation that would prohibit the combination of Social Security records on individuals with other government databases containing personal information, such as personal income tax records, except when all personal identifying information has been removed and the data is to be used for research purposes.

Establish Minimum Survivors' Benefits for Military Spouses. The spouses of military members who die in combat, from combat-caused injuries, while on active duty, or from mental trauma resulting from combat should be guaranteed a minimum spousal benefit. We also propose establishing the same minimum survivors' benefits for the surviving spouses of police and firefighters. In addition, we propose extending the exclusion to the nine-month rule for marriage for eligibility for survivors' benefits to police and firefighters.

Chapter 10: The Need to Support Low-Wage Workers

Raise the Minimum Taxable Earnings Level. We propose raising the minimum level of annual earnings that is taxable by the Social Security payroll tax so that it matches the level required to earn one credit toward future Social Security benefits. Thus, for 2025, that minimum would be $1,810 a year.

Provide a Payroll Tax Credit for Some Self-Employed Workers. Similarly to the Small Business Tax Credit, we propose a Social Security payroll tax credit for low-wage, self-employed workers.

Change Survivors' Benefits for Lower-Income Beneficiaries.

We propose legislation that would allow lower-income beneficiaries to remarry at any age and claim survivors benefits at age sixty-two based on the earnings of the deceased spouse.

Increase the Special Minimum Benefit for Some Workers. We propose that the special minimum benefit be increased for workers with thirty or more years of covered earnings and subsequently be wage-indexed so that it keeps up with regular Social Security benefits.

Chapter 11: Proposals Relating to Changes in Actuarial Factors

Change the Delayed Retirement Credit. We propose that the delayed retirement credit be changed so that beneficiaries receive an 8 percent increase per year compared to *the previous year's benefit amount.*

Improve Communication about Early Retirement Decisions. We propose that the Social Security Administration explain the early retirement decision in terms of working past age sixty-two rather than in terms of retiring earlier than age sixty-seven.

Use a Single Set of Actuarial Adjustments. We propose using a single set of actuarial adjustments for different types of Social Security OASI benefits. Our proposal promotes simplification and equity across different types of OASI benefits. The penalty for claiming benefits early and the credit for delaying retirement would be the same for survivors, spouses, and retired workers.

Chapter 12: Proposals Inspired by the US Pension System

Allow Some Workers Over Age Fifty to Purchase Earnings Credits. We propose allowing workers who are at least age fifty with annual earnings below the Social Security taxable maximum earnings to voluntarily purchase Social Security earnings credits.

Allow Employers to Make Super Contributions. We propose allowing employers to make voluntary Social Security super contributions for their employees who are age fifty and older. Super contributions would be above what they would make based solely on the employees' earnings. If they made these contributions, they would be required to make them for all employees who are at least age fifty and who earn less than the Social Security payroll taxable maximum earnings.

Raise the Age for Receiving Maximum Benefits. We propose raising the age at which beneficiaries can receive maximum Social Security benefits from seventy to seventy-two. Some of the reforms we have proposed in this book involve targeted cutbacks, but this recommendation would allow some people to offset those cutbacks by further postponing benefits.

Chapter 13: Lessons from Other Countries

Update the Name of the OASI. To reflect the major improvements in US life expectancy since 1940, we propose updating the name of the OASI to the Retirement and Survivors

Insurance program (RSI). Our proposal would retain "Social Security" as the popular name for the program.

Change the Individual Benefit Formula. We propose changing the individual benefit formula to create an additional bend point. This change would reduce the benefits of people with a career of high earnings who claim benefits in the future. This proposal could be phased in with a five-year delay.

Limit Benefits of Some High-Earning Workers. We propose limiting the combined retired-worker and spousal benefits of high-earning workers. Our proposed maximum would apply only to couples with a worker-beneficiary and a spouse who qualifies for spousal benefits.

Use Price-Indexing Rather than Wage-Indexing. We propose price-indexing rather than wage-indexing the maximum level of individual and family Social Security benefits. With this change, the real value of maximum benefits (corrected for inflation) would remain constant over time. Because wages generally rise faster than prices, this change would reduce the replacement rate for the top Social Security beneficiaries.

Raise the Benefits Tax Rate on Some People with High Incomes. We propose raising the tax rate on Social Security benefits to 50 percent for households with taxable annual income of $1 million or more.

Provide Longevity Insurance to Some Beneficiaries. We propose that the Social Security Administration provide longevity insurance benefits to low-benefit OASI beneficiaries who are at least age eighty-two. This proposal would apply to people in the bottom half of beneficiaries by benefit level. The benefits would be capped so as not to exceed monthly benefits above the bottom half.

Chapter 14: Reforming Government Programs That Affect Social Security

Ban Health Insurance Companies from Enrolling Clients in Medicare. We propose banning health insurance companies from automatically enrolling their clients in Medicare. Enrollment in Medicare should occur only when the person makes a direct request to Medicare to do so.

Four Changes to the SSI Program. First, Congress should reform the SSI program so that it provides more generous benefits, reducing the need for Social Security OASI to provide increased benefits for low-income retirees. Second, policymakers should reduce the Supplemental Security Income offset to one dollar for every two dollars of Social Security benefits. This would make it the same offset as for workers' earnings. Third, we recommend raising the exempt amount to $800 a month. This would reduce the need for some of the reforms we have proposed, such as raising the minimum benefit for workers with twenty years or more of covered earnings. Finally, we recommend lowering the eligibility age for SSI benefits to age sixty-two because low-income people tend to have shorter life expectancies and retire at younger ages.

Transfer Revenue to the OASI Trust Fund. We propose transferring 100 percent of the revenue from the federal income taxation of Social Security OASI benefits to the OASI Trust Fund.

Require Some Taxes on Unemployment Benefits. We propose that people who have annual incomes above a certain threshold should be required to pay Social Security taxes on unemployment insurance benefits, as part of the Social Security self-employment tax.

Summary of Proposals

Chapter 15: New Revenue Sources for the Short-Run Shortfall

Transfer Unclaimed 401(k) and Pension Accounts to Social Security. We propose that unclaimed 401(k) accounts and other unclaimed pension accounts be transferred to the Social Security Administration to fund OASI benefits.

We propose that the part of the OASI Trust Fund deriving from the transfer of lost pension accounts (previous proposal) be invested in stock and bond markets.

Place a Ceiling on IRA Amounts. We propose a $10 million ceiling on the total amount in an individual's IRA and employer-provided defined contribution accounts. If the total amount across all such accounts owned by the same individual exceeds $10 million, further contributions would not be permitted, and distributions from those accounts would be required. Account balances exceeding the $10 million maximum would be reduced to that maximum through mandatory withdrawals made over a period not to exceed ten years. Because these accounts have received income tax subsidies—to encourage the accumulation of assets to finance retirement—tax revenue from withdrawals made to reduce oversized account balances would be transferred from the IRS to the OASI Trust Fund.

Apply an Additional Social Security Tax on Some Earnings. We propose placing a Social Security tax of 0.5 percent per year, split between employers and employees, on earnings above the taxable maximum.

Use General Revenue Funding for Social Security

Administration. We propose that general revenue funding be allowed for Social Security, but exclusively for Social Security's administrative expenses.

APPENDIX 2

Why Population Aging Makes Social Security Reform More Difficult

Population aging makes Social Security reform more difficult to achieve. This appendix explains why, in economic terms. The explanation lies in the structure of the Social Security benefit formula in a system with pay-as-you-go financing.

Pay-As-You-Go Financing

Social Security is financed on a pay-as-you-go basis. The revenues roughly equal the program's outlays when the system is functioning properly. Thus, the system is unfunded; that is, it does not have a reserve fund that helps meet its future liabilities, as is required for private sector pension plans. When considering Social Security reform, it is helpful to understand why pay-as-you-go financing is acceptable for Social Security but is not acceptable for private sector pension plans, or for state and local government pension plans.

Social Security and private sector pension plans differ considerably. Unlike for the sponsors of private pension plans, the US federal government is not at risk of ceasing to exist, and it has taxing authority to collect needed revenues. Furthermore, compared to state and local government pension plans, where the sponsoring jurisdiction also has taxing authority but people can move to lower tax jurisdictions, the federal government can increase the Social Security payroll tax rate without the risk that taxpayers will leave.

The next section presents a simple model for analyzing these issues relating to population aging and Social Security financing. Some readers will not be familiar with these types of models. The main thing to know is that the Social Security benefit formula is structured to maintain a constant benefit replacement rate (the ratio of benefits to previous earnings). To accomplish this, the payroll tax rate must increase at the same percentage rate as the old-age dependency ratio (the ratio of beneficiaries to workers). Thus, the problem of trust fund depletion with population aging is inherent in the structure of the Social Security pay-as-you-go benefit formula.

The Social Security Benefit Formula

With pay-as-you-go financing, Social Security faces the budget constraint that the annual inflow of revenue must equal the outflow of benefits:

$$BN = twL \qquad (1)$$

where B is the average annual benefit, N is the number of Social Security beneficiaries, BN is the total annual benefit payments, t is the payroll tax rate, w is average annual wage income taxable by Social Security, L is the total number of Social Security-covered workers in the labor force, and twL is the total annual Social Security payroll tax contributions. This constraint is a hard or fixed constraint determined by the financing requirements of a pay-as-you-go system.

Equation (1) can be rewritten in terms of the average individual's tax payments tw:

$$tw = B\frac{N}{L} \qquad (2)$$

In this analysis, we use the concept of *shadow prices*, which refers to economic resources not ordinarily priced in the market. Shadow prices are measured in terms of the value of economic resources that must be given up to obtain a dollar's worth of the economic resource being priced. They are useful in analysis because they provide insights into the amount of the priced resource individuals desire.

The shadow price to the individual for a marginal increase in Social Security benefits is the marginal increase in the worker's tax payments tw with respect to a marginal increase in benefits B for current beneficiaries. Using that insight, Turner (1984) showed that the old-age dependency ratio N/L acts as a shadow price p for Social Security benefits B in the context of a pay-as-you-go system:

$$p = \frac{N}{L} \qquad (3)$$

To demonstrate the intuition of this concept, when the ratio of beneficiaries to workers is one to ten, it costs each worker on average $0.10 to raise the average benefit level by $1. By comparison, when the ratio is one to two, it costs each worker $0.50 to raise the average benefit level by $1. Thus, the cost (or price) to workers of providing benefits to retirees rises with the old-age dependency ratio.

The pay-as-you-go constraint in equation 1 can be written in percentage change terms using E to represent the derivative of the natural logarithm ($E = d(ln)$):

$$E(BN) = E(twL) \qquad (4)$$

Equation (4) is a dynamic budget constraint. It indicates that for Social Security to maintain financial balance over time, the growth rate in total real benefit payments must equal the growth rate in total real payroll tax payments.

Splitting the dynamic budget constraint into its components, equation 4 becomes

$$E(B) + E(N) = E(t) + E(w) + E(L) \qquad (5)$$

The growth rate in total Social Security contributions (the right-hand side of equation 5) equals the sum of the growth rates of the payroll tax rate, average real wages, and the number of Social Security-covered workers in the labor force. The growth rate in total benefits (the left-hand side of equation 5) equals the sum of the growth rate of benefits per beneficiary and the growth rate of the number of beneficiaries. Expressing the equation in terms of the percentage change in average benefits gives

$$E(B) = E(t) + E(w) + E(L) - E(N) \qquad (6)$$

Because the policy interest concerning benefit levels relates to the replacement rate which equals the ratio of benefits to wages, equation 6 can be rewritten as

$$E\left(\frac{B}{w}\right) = E(t) - E\left(\frac{N}{L}\right) \qquad (7)$$

This final equation shows that, to maintain a constant replacement rate (left-hand side), the payroll tax rate must increase at the same percentage rate as the old-age dependency ratio (right-hand side).

The Old-Age Dependency Ratio: Historical Data and Projections

The 2023 Social Security Trustees' Report (2023) provided historical data and projections of the old-age dependency ratio. In 1950, it was 0.138, rising to 0.210 in 2000, an increase of 52.2 percent over 50 years. In 2020, it was 0.291, an increase of 38.6 percent over 20 years. In 2050, under the intermediate projections, it is projected to be 0.384, an increase of 82.9 percent over the 50 years from 2000 and an increase of 32.0 percent over the 30 years from 2020. These projections provide an estimate of the percentage increase in the payroll tax rate that would be needed if that were the only change made to the Social Security program to maintain solvency.

Year	Old-Age Dependency Ratio
1950	0.138
2000	0.210
2020	0.291
2050	0.384

Table A-2: Old-age dependency ratio, 1950-2050. Data for 1950 to 2020 are historical data, while the datum for 2050 is based on the intermediate projection of the Social Security actuaries.

Politically, needed Social Security reforms are difficult to achieve. Some lawmakers, such as Senator Bernie Sanders (2024), have proposed changes that would increase Social Security benefits.

The analysis of this section shows why these proposals would be difficult to enact. The reason is the projected increases in the old-age dependency ratio. Those increases make it difficult to achieve solvency through Social Security reforms, specifically because of the increases in the payroll tax rate that would be required if the benefit replacement rate is to be maintained or increased.

This appendix thus highlights the importance of the old-age dependency ratio when considering Social Security reforms. It indicates that the Social Security benefit formula is structured so that it is not possible to maintain the system with a constant payroll tax rate and increasing replacement rates, which result from the wage indexing of initial benefits at retirement. Periodic reforms are thus required.

Acknowledgements

We are grateful to Glenn McMahan, our editor, and the rest of the staff at Upriver Press for providing valuable support and input throughout the production of this book. Richard Burkhauser provided valuable comments on an early draft of the entire manuscript, and Stephen Goss provided valuable comments on our proposals. Kevin Hartmann Cortés participated in writing the first section of the chapter on fairness. Barbara Smith provided very helpful input during the early stages of the book preparation.

We are indebted to the scholars who have preceded our work on this book. In particular, we want to thank those whom we cite and with whom we have previously coauthored research. They include Emily Andrews, Clive Bailey, Kamila Bielawska, David Blake, Ellen Bruce, Richard Burkhauser, Tianhong Chen, Yung-Ping Chen, Agnieszka Chłoń-Domińczak, Jonathan Forman, Richard Fullmer, Teresa Ghilarducci, Colin Gillion, Yael Hadass, Gerard Hughes, Mark Iwry, Dale Kintzel, Marion Labouré, Denis Latulippe, Dongsoo Lee, David McCarthy, Courtney Monk, Dana Muir, Leslie Muller, David Rajnes, Martin Rein, Robert Schmitt, Sally Shen, Norman Stein, Wei Sun, Marek Szczepański, Saisai Zhang, and Natalia Zhivan.

About the Authors

John A. Turner, director of the Pension Policy Center, began his research career at the Social Security Administration. He researched pensions at the Department of Labor, worked on numerous social security systems at the International Labour Organization (ILO) in Geneva, Switzerland, and researched Social Security at AARP. His ILO book *Social Security Pensions: Development and Reform* (2000, with colleagues) focuses on middle- and lower-income countries. It is one of the most cited books on social security reform published in the twenty-first century, with more than six hundred citations, including its Spanish, French, and Japanese editions. He has published fourteen books and more than two hundred articles on social security and pension policy. He has received several honors, including being a Fulbright Senior Scholar and a Netspar Fellow, and an award from the *Journal of Risk and Insurance* for best article of the year. He is the only two-time award winner of the American College of Employee Benefits Counsel prize for best proposal for simplifying employee benefits law. Volunteers for Economic Growth Alliance, an umbrella organization with more than one hundred thousand volunteers, selected him as Volunteer of the Year for training pension regulators in East Africa. He has a PhD in Economics from the University of Chicago.

Serena E. McCarthy is a senior research analyst with the Pension Policy Center. Previously, she was a STEM Outreach Coordinator and a graduate teaching assistant at American University, specializing in science writing consultation. She has experience with literature research on a variety of topics. She graduated Phi Beta Kappa from Vassar College with a BA in psychology, with general honors and departmental honors. She has an MA in biology and an MS in biotechnology management, both from American University. She is the daughter of David D. McCarthy, who was a senior research analyst with the Pension Policy Center.

Works Cited

Aaron, Henry J. 2010. "Social Security: A Consensus Based on Confusion—Part I." Brookings Institution. https://www.brookings.edu/articles/social-security-a-consensus-based-on-confusion-part-i/.

Aaron, Henry J., and Robert D. Reischauer. 2001. *Countdown to Reform: The Social Security Debate.* The Century Foundation Press.

AARP. 2012. "The Future of Social Security: 12 Proposals on the Table in Washington." https://goyff.az.gov/sites/default/files/meeting-documents/materials/social_security_options.pdf.

AARP. 2022. "My Spouse Died Last Month. Do I Have to Return the Social Security Payment Deposited into Our Bank Account This Month?" https://www.aarp.org/retirement/social-security/questions-answers/returning-social-security-payment.html.

AARP. 2023. "AARP Social Security Solvency and Adequacy Principles." In Chapter 4: Savings and Retirement Security. *AARP Policy Book 2023-2024.* https://policybook.aarp.org/policy-book/savings-and-retirement-security/aarp-social-security-solvency-and-adequacy-principles.

AARP. 2024. "New AARP Survey: 1 in 5 Americans Ages 50+ Have No Retirement Savings and Over Half Worry They Will Not Have Enough to Last in Retirement." AARP Press Room. https://press.aarp.org/2024-4-24-New-AARP-Survey-1-in-5-Americans-Ages-50-Have-No-Retirement-Savings.

AARP. 2025. "Social Security Opinions and Attitudes on Its 90th Anniversary." https://www.aarp.org/content/dam/aarp/research/topics/work-finances-retirement/social-security/social-security-90th-anniversary-survey.doi.10.26419-2fres.00976.001.pdf.

Age UK. 2024a. "Changes to State Pension Age." https://www.ageuk.org.uk/information-advice/money-legal/pensions/state-pension/changes-to-state-pension-age/.

Age UK. 2024b. "Factsheet 19: State Pension." https://www.ageuk.org.uk/globalassets/age-uk/documents/factsheets/fs19_state_pension_fcs.pdf.

Age UK. 2024c. "State Pension: How and When Can You Pay." https://www.ageuk.org.uk/globalassets/age-uk/documents/information-guides/ageukig53_state_pension_inf.pdf.

Alleva, Brian J. 2017. "Social Security Retirement Benefit Claiming-Age Combinations Available to Married Couples." Research & Statistics Note No. 2017-01. Social Security Administration, Office of Research, Evaluation, and Statistics. https://www.ssa.gov/policy/docs/rsnotes/rsn2017-01.html.

Amend, Patricia. 2023. "5 Steps for Tracking Down Old 401(k)s and Other Lost Money." AARP. https://www.aarp.org/retirement/planning-for-retirement/info-2022/find-forgotten-401k-and-other-money.html.

American Academy of Actuaries. 2010. "Social Security Reform: Possible Changes in the Benefit Formulas and Taxation." Issue Brief. https://www.actuary.org/sites/default/files/files/Social_Security_Reform_Issue_Brief_6-15-10.4.pdf/Social_Security_Reform_Issue_Brief_6-15-10.4_0.pdf.

American Academy of Actuaries. 2012. "A Guide to Analyzing Social Security Reform." Issue Guide. https://www.actuary.org/sites/default/files/files/Issue_Guide_SocialSecurity_Reform.pdf.

American Academy of Actuaries. 2017. "Women and Social Security." Issue Brief. https://www.actuary.org/sites/default/files/files/publications/Women_and_Social_Security_051217.pdf.

American Academy of Actuaries. 2018. "Social Security–Automatic Adjustments." Issue Brief. https://www.actuary.org/sites/default/files/files/publications/SS_Automat_Adj_IB_05042018.pdf.

American Academy of Actuaries. 2020. "Assumptions Used to Evaluate Social Security's Financial Condition." Issue Brief. https://www.actuary.org/sites/default/files/2020-11/Assumptions_Evaluation_of_Soc_Sec.pdf.

American Academy of Actuaries. 2022a. "Raising the Social Security Retirement Age." https://www.actuary.org/wp-content/uploads/2011/09/SocialSecurityRetirementAge.pdf.

American Academy of Actuaries. 2022b. "Social Security Reform: Benefit Formula Options." https://www.actuary.org/sites/default/files/2022-08/SocSecReformBenefits0822.pdf.

American Academy of Actuaries. 2023. "Reforming Social Security Sooner Rather Than Later." Issue Brief. https://www.actuary.org/sites/default/files/20ameamer23-11/pension-brief-social-security-reform-sooner.pdf.

Anderson, Brian. 2024. "2 Ways a Harris Presidency Could Impact Social Security." *401k Specialist*. https://401kspecialistmag.com/2-ways-a-harris-presidency-could-impact-social-security/.

Andrews, Emily S., John A. Turner, Robert Schmitt, and Wei Sun. 2024. "Delayed Social Security Claiming: Why Do So Few Participants Delay Claiming Past Age 65?" *Journal of Retirement*, Summer 2024, 12(1): 7-21. https://www.pm-research.com/content/iijretire/12/1/.

Andrews, Michelle. 2022. "5 Ways to Beat the Social Security Bureaucracy." AARP. https://www.aarp.org/retirement/social-security/info-2022/customer-service-complaints-and-improvements.html.

Antonelli, Angela M. 2018. "The Aging of America: A Changing Picture of Work and Retirement." Georgetown University Center for Retirement Initiatives. https://cri.georgetown.edu/the-aging-of-america-a-changing-picture-of-work-and-retirement/.

AP-NORC Center for Public Affairs Research. 2023. "Younger Generations Are Not Confident That Social Security or Medicare Will Be There for Them." https://apnorc.org/projects/ayounger-generations-are-not-confident-that-social-security-or-medicare-will-be-there-for-them-a/.

Arnold, R. Douglas. 1998. "The Political Feasibility of Social Security Reform." In Arnold, R. Douglas, Michael J. Graetz, and Alicia H. Munnell (eds.). *Framing the Social Security Debate.* Washington, DC; National Academy of Social Insurance.

BaFin (Germany's Federal Financial Supervisory Authority). 2023. "Riester Pensions." https://www.bafin.de/EN/Verbraucher/Altersvorsorge/Riester/riester_node_en.html.

Baker, McKenzie. 2024. "China: China Extends Statutory Retirement Age – What Does This Mean for Employers?" https://insightplus.bakermckenzie.com/bm/pensions_10/china-china-extends-statutory-retirement-age-what-does-this-mean-for-employers.

Bauer, Elizabeth. 2021. "Do We Need to Fix Americans' Social Security Knowledge? Placing a Survey into Context." *Forbes.* https://www.forbes.com/sites/ebauer/2021/04/20/do-we-need-to-remedy-americans-social-security-knowledge-placing-a-survey-into-context/.

Bearden, Bridget. 2022. "Retiree Reflections." Employee Benefit Research Institute (EBRI). https://www.ebri.org/content/retiree-reflections.

Bellon, Tina. 2022. "Uber, Canadian Union Reach Deal to Support Gig Worker Benefits, Flexibility." Reuters. https://www.reuters.com/business/autos-transportation/uber-canadian-union-reach-deal-support-gig-worker-benefits-flexibility-2022-01-27/.

Benefits.gov. 2024. "Social Security Lump Sum Death Payment." https://www.benefits.gov/benefit/4392#.

Beshears, John, James J. Choi, David Laibson, and Brigitte C. Madrian. 2024. "Influencing Retirement Savings Decisions with Automatic Enrollment and Related Tools." The Reporter. NBER. https://www.nber.org/reporter/2024number3/influencing-retirement-savings-decisions-automatic-enrollment-and-related-tools.

Bielawska, Kamila. 2021. Monitorowanie i ocena systemów ubezpieczeń społecznych – przegląd kryteriów proponowanych przez Komisję Europejską i Bank Światowy oraz propozycje ich rozszerzenia w kontekście starzenia się populacji [Monitoring and assessment of social security systems – review of the criteria proposed by the European Commission and the World Bank and proposals for their extension in the context of an aging population], *Ubezpieczenia w Rolnictwie. Materiały i Studia*, Article 1 75. https://doi.org/10.48058/urms/75.2021.6.

Bielawska, Kamila, Sally Shen, and John A. Turner. 2022. "Issues of Trust: Pension Plans, Participants and Service Providers Over the Past 25 Years." *The Evolution of Supplementary Pensions: 25 Years of Pension Reform*, edited by James Kolaczkowski, Michelle Maher, Yves Stevens, and Jacob Werbrouck. Edward Elgar; Cheltenham, England.

Biggs, Andrew G. 2008. "The Social Security Earnings Test: The Tax That Wasn't." American Enterprise Institute for Public Policy Research. *Tax Policy Outlook* No. 3. https://www.aei.org/wp-content/uploads/2011/10/20080717_No-323312TPOJulyg.pdf.

Biggs, Andrew G. 2013. "A New Vision for Social Security." *National Affairs*, Summer. https://www.aei.org/wp-content/uploads/2013/06/-a-new-vision-for-social-security_142215308127.pdf.

Biggs, Andrew G. 2025. *The Real Retirement Crisis: Why (Almost) Everything You Know About the US Retirement System is Wrong*. AEI Press, Washington, D.C.

Biggs, Andrew G. and John Shoven. 2025. "How to Raise the Social Security Retirement Age While Protecting the Poor."

Stanford Institute for Economic Policy Research. https://siepr.stanford.edu/publications/policy-brief/how-raise-social-security-retirement-age-while-protecting-poor.

Bipartisan Policy Center. 2016. "Securing our Financial Future: Report of the Commission on Retirement Security and Personal Savings." http://bipartisanpolicy.org/library/retirement-security/.

Bipartisan Policy Center. 2023. "The Retirement Earnings Test." https://bipartisanpolicy.org/explainer/retirement-earnings-test/.

Bivens, Josh, and Ellen Gould. 2023. "A Record Share of Earnings Was Not Subject to Social Security Taxes in 2021. Inequality's Undermining of Social Security Has Accelerated." Economic Policy Institute. https://www.epi.org/blog/a-record-share-of-earnings-was-not-subject-to-social-security-taxes-in-2021-inequalitys-undermining-of-social-security-has-accelerated/.

Blake, David, and John A. Turner. 2014. "Longevity Insurance Annuities: Lessons from the United Kingdom." *Benefits Quarterly* 30(1): 39-47. https://openaccess.city.ac.uk/id/eprint/17148/8/.

Blanchett, David, and Fichtner, Jason J. 2023. "Biased Advice? The Relationship Between Financial Professionals' Compensation and Social Security Retirement Benefit Claiming Decisions." *Retirement Management Journal* 12(1): 54-64. https://download.ssrn.com/24/03/05/ssrn_id4749066_code510892.pdf.

Board of Governors of the Federal Reserve System. 2022. "Federal Reserve System Budgets." https://www.federalreserve.gov/publications/2022-ar-federal-reserve-system-budgets.htm.

Borsch-Supan, Alex H., and Courtney Coile. 2020. "Social Security Programs and Retirement Around the World: Reforms and Retirement Incentives – Introduction and Summary." NBER Working Paper 25280. https://www.nber.org/system/files/working_papers/w25280/w25280.pdf.

Bosworth, Barry, and R. Kent Weaver. 2011. "Social Security on Auto-Pilot: International Experience with Automatic Stabilizer Mechanisms." Center for Retirement Research at Boston College Working Paper 2011-18. https://crr.bc.edu/wp-content/uploads/2011/11/wp_2011-18-508.pdf.

Boyte-White, Claire. 2023. "What Are the Dormancy and Escheatment Rules for IRAs?" Retirement Planning > IRAs. Investopedia. https://www.investopedia.com/ask/answers/110415/what-are-dormancy-and-escheatment-rules-iras.asp.

Bracken, Matt. 2024. "Data Tracking, AI, and Modernization: How SSA Has Ditched Its Paper-Based Past." Fedscoop. https://fedscoop.com/social-security-administration-securitystat-ai-modernization/.

Bracken, Matt. 2025. "Democrats Push Palantir for Answers on Reports of IRS 'Mega-Database.'"

British Broadcasting Corporation (BBC). 2024. "How Much Is the State Pension Going UP and What Is the Triple Lock?" https://www.bbc.com/news/business-53082530.

Brown, Courtenay. 2024. "French Government Collapses as Political Chaos Reaches Boiling Point." MSN. https://www.msn.com/en-us/news/news/content/ar-AA1vheO4?ocid=sapphireappshare.

Brown, Jeffrey. 2014. "The Social Security Earnings Test Is Not a Tax." *Forbes*. https://www.forbes.com/sites/jeffreybrown/2014/08/08/the-social-security-earnings-test-is-not-a-tax/.

Brown, S. Kathi. 2012. "The Impact of Claiming Age on Monthly Social Security Retirement Benefits: How Knowledgeable Are Future Beneficiaries?" AARP Research. https://www.aarp.org/research/topics/economics/info-2014/social-security-claiming-age-retirement-benefits.html.

Bruce, Donald, and Xiaowen Liu. 2014. "Tax Evasion and Self-Employment in the US: A Look at the Alternative Minimum Tax."

Internal Revenue Service, Statistics of Income Division Publication. https://www.irs.gov/pub/irs-soi/14rescontaxevasion.pdf.

Bruce, Ellen A., and John Turner. 2004. "Lost Pension Money: Who is Responsible? Who Benefits?" *UIC Law Review* 37(3): 695-725. https://repository.law.uic.edu/cgi/viewcontent.cgi?article=1394&context=lawreview.

Bruce, Ellen A., John A. Turner, and Dongsoo Lee. 2005. "Lost Pensions: An Empirical Investigation." *Benefits Quarterly* 21:1. https://www.proquest.com/docview/194917543?sourcetype=Scholarly%20Journals.

Brumley, James. 2025. "Here's Last Year's Average 401(k) Contribution." Yahoo Finance. https://finance.yahoo.com/news/heres-last-years-average-401-133000844.html.

Bunn, Daniel, Sean Bray, and Joost Haddinga. 2023. "Insights into the Tax Systems of Scandinavian Countries." Tax Foundation. https://taxfoundation.org/blog/scandinavian-social-programs-taxes-2023/#.

Burkhauser, Richard V., and John A. Turner. 1978. "A Time Series Analysis on Social Security and its Effect on the Market Work of Men at Younger Ages," *Journal of Political Economy* 86 (August 1978): 701-715.

Burtless, Gary. 2016. "The Growing Life-Expectancy Gap Between Rich and Poor."

Brookings Institution. https://www.brookings.edu/articles/the-growing-life-expectancy-gap-between-rich-and-poor/.

Butler, Stuart. 2016. "It's Time to End Social Security for the Rich." Brookings Institution. https://www.brookings.edu/articles/its-time-to-end-social-security-for-the-rich/.

Bystry, Dawn. 2021. "How to Get Your New Baby's Social Security Number." https://blog.ssa.gov/how-to-get-your-new-babys-social-security-number/.

Works Cited

Bystry, Dawn. 2023. "Social Security's Commitment to the LGBQI+ Community." Social Security Administration. (In 2025, this blog was deleted from the Social Security Administration's website.)

Cagnassola, Mary Ellen. 2023. "Lawmakers Want to Boost Social Security Payments by Changing the Way COLA Is Calculated." *Money.* https://money.com/social-security-cola-cpi-e/.

Capitalize. 2023. "The True Cost of Forgotten 401(k) Accounts (2023)." https://www.hicapitalize.com/wp-content/uploads/2023/06/The-true-cost-of-forgotten-401k-accounts-2023.pdf.

Canada Pension Plan Investments. 2024. "2024 CEO Letter." https://www.cppinvestments.com/insight-institute/2024-ceo-letter/.

Caplan, Zoe, and Megan Rabe. 2023. "The Older Population: 2020." 2020 Census Briefs. https://www2.census.gov/library/publications/decennial/2020/census-briefs/c2020br-07.pdf.

Capretta, James C. 2006. "Building Automatic Solvency into U.S. Social Security: Insights from Sweden and Germany." Brookings Institution. https://www.brookings.edu/articles/building-automatic-solvency-into-u-s-social-security-insights-from-sweden-and-germany/.

Carbonaro, Giulia. 2024. "Social Security Reform Splits Young Americans and Boomers." *Newsweek.* https://www.newsweek.com/young-americans-boomers-clash-social-security-reform-1873646.

Case, Anne, and Angus Deaton. 2021. "Life Expectancy in Adulthood Is Falling for Those Without a BA Degree, But as Educational Gaps Have Widened, Racial Gaps Have Narrowed." PNAS. https://www.pnas.org/doi/10.1073/pnas.2024777118#fig01.

Cassidy, Bill. 2025. "Cassidy, Collins, Colleagues Reintroduce Legislation to Help Americans Better Plan for Retirement." https://www.cassidy.senate.gov/newsroom/press-releases/cassidy-collins-colleagues-reintroduce-legislation-to-help-americans-better-plan-for-retirement/.

Center on Budget and Policy Priorities. 2024a. "Chart Book: Tracking the Recovery from the Pandemic Recession." https://www.cbpp.org/research/economy/tracking-the-recovery-from-the-pandemic-recession.

Center on Budget and Policy Priorities. 2024b. "Policy Basics: Top Ten Facts about Social Security." https://www.cbpp.org/research/social-security/top-ten-facts-about-social-security.

Center on Budget and Policy Priorities. 2025. "Policy Basics: Where Do Our Federal Tax Dollars Go?" https://www.cbpp.org/research/federal-budget/where-do-our-federal-tax-dollars-go.

Cerullo, Megan. 2024. "The U.S. Minted 1,000 New Millionaires Each Day Last Year UBS Reports." Moneywatch, CBS News. https://www.cbsnews.com/news/1000-new-millionaires-created-each-day-2024-ubs-report/.

Charles Schwab. 2023. "Tracking Down a Lost 401(k)." https://www.schwab.com/learn/story/tracking-down-lost-401k.

Chen, Anqi, Alicia H. Munnell, and Nilufer Gok. 2025. "How Much Have Social Security Claiming Ages Increased?" Center for Retirement Research at Boston College. https://crr.bc.edu/how-much-have-social-security-claiming-ages-increased/.

Chen, Tianhong, Gerard Hughes, and John A. Turner. 2016. "Longevity Insurance Benefits for Social Security: International Experience." *Benefits Quarterly* 32(2): 43-53.

Chen, Tianhong, and John A. Turner. 2015. "Longevity Insurance Annuities: China Adopts a Benefit Innovation from the Past." *International Social Security Review*, 68(2): 27-41. https://www.researchgate.net/profile/Tianhong-Chen/publication/287841258_Longevity_insurance_annuities_China_adopts_a_benefit_innovation_from_the_past/links/567a0dd308ae40c0e27dfa46/Longevity-insurance-annuities-China-adopts-a-benefit-innovation-from-the-past.pdf.

Chen, Tianhong, John A. Turner, and Serena E. McCarthy. 2025. "Social Security Reforms Toward Sustainability in China." Unpublished paper.

Chen, Tingyun, John-Jacques Hallaert, Haonan Qu, Maximilien Queyranne, Alexander Pitt, Alaina Rhee, Anna Shabunina, Jérôme Vandenbussche, and Irene Yackovlev. 2018. "Inequality and Poverty Across Generations in the European Union." Staff Discussion Notes. International Monetary Fund. https://www.imf.org/en/Publications/Staff-Discussion-Notes/Issues/2018/01/23/Inequality-and-Poverty-across-Generations-in-the-European-Union-45137.

Chen, Yung-Ping. 1981. "The Growth of Fringe Benefits: Implications for Social Security." *Monthly Labor Review*, November. https://www.bls.gov/opub/mlr/1981/11/art1full.pdf.

Chen, Yung-Ping, and John A. Turner. 2007. "Raising the Retirement Age in OECD Countries." In *Work Options for Older Americans*, edited by Teresa Ghilarducci and John Turner, Sloan Foundation, pp. 359-369.

China, Chrystal R., and Michael Goodwin. 2025. "What Is COBOL?" IBM. https://www.ibm.com/think/topics/cobol.

Christian, Rachel. 2023. "Using Generative Artificial Intelligence as a Financial Tool." Bankrate. https://www.bankrate.com/investing/artificial-intelligence-as-financial-tool/.

Citizens Advice (UK). 2025. "State Pension." https://www.citizensadvice.org.uk/debt-and-money/pensions/types-of-pension/state-.

Citizens Information Board (Ireland). 2025. "Voluntary Social Insurance Contributions." https://www.citizensinformation.ie/en/social-welfare/irish-social-welfare-system/social-insurance-prsi/voluntary-prsi-contributions/.

Cohen, Wilbur J., and Robert J. Myers. 1950. "1950 Social Security Amendments." *Social Security Bulletin*, October. https://www.ssa.gov/history/1950amend.html.

Cohn, D'Vera, Gretchen Livingston, and Wendy Wang. 2014. "After Decades of Decline, A Rise in Stay-At-Home Mothers." Pew Research Center. https://www.pewresearch.org/social-trends/2014/04/08/after-decades-of-decline-a-rise-in-stay-at-home-mothers/.

Collinson, Catherine, and Heidi Cho. 2024. "Retiree Life in the Post-Pandemic Economy." Transamerica Center for Retirement Studies. https://www.transamericainstitute.org/docs/research/retirees/retiree-life-post-pandemic-economy-survey-report-2024.pdf?sfvrsn=e99c5ab5_9.

Committee for a Responsible Federal Budget. 2012. "Blahous: The End of Social Security Self-Financing." https://www.crfb.org/blogs/blahous-end-social-security-self-financing.

Committee for a Responsible Federal Budget. 2014. "General Revenue and the Social Security Trust Funds." https://www.crfb.org/blogs/general-revenue-social-security-trust-funds.

Committee for a Responsible Federal Budget. 2016a. "How Much Waste, Fraud, and Abuse Is There in Social Security?" https://www.crfb.org/press-releases/fact-sheet-how-much-waste-fraud-and-abuse-there-social-security.

Committee for a Responsible Federal Budget. 2016b. "Nine Social Security Myths You Shouldn't Believe." http://crfb.org/document/nine-social-security-myths-you-shouldnt-believe.

Committee for a Responsible Federal Budget. 2023a. "Principles for Social Security Reform." https://www.crfb.org/papers/principles-social-security-reform.

Committee for a Responsible Federal Budget. 2023b. "Social Security Reform Can Boost Incomes, Grow the Economy." https://www.crfb.org/blogs/social-security-reform-can-boost-incomes-grow-economy.

Committee for a Responsible Federal Budget. 2024. "$16,500 Cut Awaits Retirees if Social Security Isn't Reformed."

https://www.crfb.org/blogs/16500-cut-awaits-retirees-if-social-security-isnt-reformed?ftag=YHF4eb9d17.

Committee for a Responsible Federal Budget. 2025. "OBBBA Would Accelerate Social Security & Medicare Insolvency." https://www.crfb.org/blogs/obbba-would-accelerate-social-security-medicare-insolvency#:~:text=We%20estimate%20the%20One%20Big%20Beautiful%20Bill,Medicare%20insolvency%20by%20a%20year%2C%20to%202032.&text=The%20bill%20does%20not%20include%20any%20significant,large%20changes%20to%20Medicare%20and%20cut%20waste.

Communicable Disease Center. 1951. "Death Rates from Selected Causes." https://www.cdc.gov/nchs/data/dvs/mx194049.pdf.

Congress.gov. 2023a. "H.R. 281 – Bipartisan Social Security Commission Act of 2023." https://www.congress.gov/bill/118th-congress/house-bill/281.

Congress.gov. 2023b. "S.1211 - Social Security Caregiver Credit Act of 2023." https://www.congress.gov/bill/118th-congress/senate-bill/1211/.

Congressional Budget Office. 2018. "Budget Options: ax All Pass-Through Business Owners Under SECA and Impose a Material Participation Standard." https://www.cbo.gov/budget-options/2018/54808.

Congressional Budget Office. 2020. "Increase the Payroll Tax Rate for Social Security." *Options for Reducing the Deficit: 2021 to 2030*. Staff of the Joint Committee on Taxation. https://www.cbo.gov/budget-options/56861.

Congressional Budget Office. 2021. "The Distribution of Major Tax Expenditures in 2019." https://www.cbo.gov/publication/57585.

Congressional Budget Office. 2023. "CBO's 2023 Long-Term Projections for Social Security." June. https://www.cbo.gov/publication/59340.

Congressional Budget Office. 2024. "Raising the Full Retirement Age for Social Security." https://www.cbo.gov/system/files/2024-09/60516-Full-Retirement-Age.pdf.

Congressional Research Service. 2018. "The Interaction Between Medicare Premiums and Social Security COLAs." https://crsreports.congress.gov/product/pdf/R/R45324/2.

Congressional Research Service. 2022a. "Social Security: Potential Changes in Computation Years." https://crsreports.congress.gov/product/pdf/R/R47330.

Congressional Research Service. 2022b. "The Social Security Retirement Age." https://crsreports.congress.gov/product/pdf/R/R44670/14.

Congressional Research Service. 2023. "Social Security Trust Fund Investment Practices." https://crsreports.congress.gov/product/pdf/IF/IF10564.

Congressional Research Service. 2024a. "A Hypothetical Social Security Cost-of-Living Adjustment Based on the Research Consumer Price Index for the Elderly." https://crsreports.congress.gov/product/pdf/IF/IF12675.

Congressional Research Service. 2024b. "Social Security Benefit Taxation Highlights." https://crsreports.congress.gov/product/pdf/IF/IF11397.

Congressional Research Service. 2025. "Social Security: Cost-of-Living-Adjustments." https://crsreports.congress.gov/product/pdf/RS/94-803.

Coy, Peter. 2023. "How to Deal with the Coming Social Security Shortfall." *The New York Times.* https://www.nytimes.com/2023/07/03/opinion/fix-social-security.html.

D'Amato, Jon. 2023. "Protect Your Retirement Funds from State Seizure." *Forbes.* https://www.forbes.com/sites/forbesfinancecouncil/2023/05/17/protect-your-retirement-funds-from-state-seizure/.

Daugherty, Greg. 2024. "How the Ultrawealthy Have Exploited Roth IRAs." *Investopedia*. https://www.investopedia.com/ultrawealthy-exploit-roth-ira-5219797.

Davies, Paul S., and Zhe Li. 2022. "The Widow(er)'s Limit Provision." Congressional Research Service. https://crsreports.congress.gov/product/pdf/IF/IF12091.

Debt Reduction Task Force. 2010. "Restoring America's Future: Reviving the Economy, Cutting Spending and Debt, and Creating a Simple, Pro-Growth Tax System." Washington, DC: Bipartisan Policy Center (November). https://bipartisanpolicy.org/report/restoring-americas-future/.

DePaulo, Bella. 2017. "Social Security Massively Favors Married and Previously Married People." Unmarried Equality. https://www.unmarried.org/featured/social-security-massively-favors-married-and-previously-married-people/.

DeSilver, Drew. 2013. "Global Inequality: How the U.S. Compares." Pew Research Center. https://www.pewresearch.org/short-reads/2013/12/19/global-inequality-how-the-u-s-compares/.

de Tavernier, Wouter, and Hervé Boulhol. 2021. "Automatic Adjustment Mechanisms in Pension Systems." Chapter 2 in Pensions at a Glance 2021: OECD and G20 Indicators. Organisation for Economic Co-operation and Development. https://www.oecd-ilibrary.org/automatic-adjustment-mechanisms-in-pension-systems_d9c5d58d-en.pdf?itemId=%2Fcontent%2Fcomponent%2Fd9c5d58d-en&mimeType=pdf.

Diamond, Peter A., and Peter R. Orszag. 2004. *Saving Social Security: A Balanced Approach*. Brookings Institution Press.

Dono, Linda. 2025. "The Basics of Social Security Retirement Benefits." AARP. https://www.aarp.org/social-security/retirement/basics/.

Durante, Alex. 2024a. 'How Has the Payroll Tax Base Changed Over Time." Tax Foundation. https://taxfoundation.org/blog/how-the-payroll-tax-base-has-changed-over-time/.

Durante, Alex. 2024b. "Social Security: Lessons for Reform." Tax Foundation.

https://taxfoundation.org/research/all/federal/social-security-reform-options/.

Dushi, Irena, Leora Freiberg, and Anthony Webb. 2021. "Is the Adjustment of Social Security Benefits Actuarially Fair, and If So, for Whom?" Ann Arbor, MI. University of Michigan Retirement and Disability Research Center (MRDRC) Working Paper; MRDRC WP 2021-421. https://mrdrc.isr.umich.edu/publications/papers/pdf/wp421.pdf.

DWC. 2019. "What Is the Form 8955-SSA and What Does It Do?" https://www.dwc401k.com/blog/what-is-form-8955-ssa-what-does-it-do.

Eagan, John 2023. "Study: Vast Majority of Single Americans Feel Burden of 'Singles Tax'." *Forbes*. https://www.nasdaq.com/articles/study:-vast-majority-of-single-americans-feel-burden-of-singles-tax.

Eckstein, Griffin. 2025. "Maine Social Security 'Snafu' a Mistake, Trump Administration Says." MSN. https://www.msn.com/en-us/news/us/maine-social-security-snafu-a-mistake-trump-administration-says/ar-AA1AsHK7.

Economic Opportunity Institute. 2000. "Pension Privatization in Britain: A Boon to the Finance Industry, a Boondoggle to Workers." https://www.opportunityinstitute.org/research/post/pension-privatization-in-britain-a-boon-to-the-finance-industry-a-boondoggle-to-workers/.

Edleson, Harriet. 2021. "Have You Claimed Social Security and Then Gone Back to Work? You May Face the 'Earnings Test.'" MarketWatch. https://www.marketwatch.com/story/

have-you-claimed-social-security-and-then-gone-back-to-work-make-sure-you-do-this-right-away-11618341225.

Elliott, Justin, Patricia Callahan, and James Bandler. 2021a. "Lord of the Roths: How Tech Mogul Peter Thiel Turned a Retirement Account for the Middle Class Into a $5 Billion Tax-Free Piggy Bank." ProPublica. https://www.propublica.org/article/lord-of-the-roths-how-tech-mogul-peter-thiel-turned-a-retirement-account-for-the-middle-class-into-a-5-billion-dollar-tax-free-piggy-bank.

Elliott, Justin, Patricia Callahan, and James Bandler. 2021b. "The Number of People with IRAs Worth $5 Million or More Has Tripled, Congress Says." ProPublica. https://www.propublica.org/article/the-number-of-people-with-iras-worth-5-million-or-more-has-tripled-congress-says.

Elliott, Justin, Patricia Callahan, and James Bandler. 2021c. "The Ultrawealthy Have Hijacked Roth IRAs. The Senate Finance Chair Is Eyeing a Crackdown." ProPublica. https://www.propublica.org/article/the-ultrawealthy-have-hijacked-roth-iras-the-senate-finance-chair-is-eyeing-a-crackdown.

Employee Benefits Security Administration, US Department of Labor. 2024a. "Abandoned Plan Search." https://www.askebsa.dol.gov/AbandonedPlanSearch/.

Employee Benefits Security Administration. 2024b. "US Department of Labor Announces Proposed Information Collection to Build Online Search Tool to Help Find 'Lost' Retirement Savings." News Release. https://www.dol.gov/newsroom/releases/ebsa/ebsa20240415.

Epstein, Lita. 2024. "How Much Are Taxes on an IRA Withdrawal?" Investopedia. https://www.investopedia.com/articles/personal-finance/021015/how-much-are-taxes-ira-withdrawal.asp.

Fabino, Alexander. 2023. "New Social Security Plan Would Increase Taxes for These Americans." *Newsweek.* https://www.newsweek.com/social-security-reform-2100-act-taxes-over-400k-earners-1842497.

Fagin, Barry. 2024. "Please Cut My Social Security Benefits." *The Gazette.* https://gazette.com/opinion/column-please-cut-my-social-security-benefits/article_ed0a23d0-3ebc-11ef-be4a-abdc7aa86a29.html.

Family Caregiver Alliance. 2015. "Women and Caregiving: Facts and Figures." National Center on Caregiving at Family Caregiver Alliance. https://www.caregiver.org/resource/women-and-caregiving-facts-and-figures/.

Farmer, Liz. 2021. "Looking for That Lost Retirement Account? Why It's Easier to Find an IRA Than a 401(k)." *Forbes.* https://www.forbes.com/sites/lizfarmer/2021/09/13/looking-for-that-lost-retirement-account-why-its-easier-to-find-an-ira-than-a-401k/.

Favreault, Melissa M., Frank J. Sammartino, and C. Eugene Steuerle (eds.). 2002a. *Social Security and the Family: Addressing Unmet Needs in an Underfunded System.* The Urban Institute Press.

Favreault, Melissa M., Frank J. Sammartino, and C. Eugene Steuerle. 2002b. "Social Security Benefits for Spouses and Survivors: Options for Change." In *Social Security and the Family: Addressing Unmet Needs in an Underfunded System.* The Urban Institute Press.

Flanagan, Tammy. 2024. "What You Need to Know about the Social Security Earnings Test." *Government Executive.* https://www.govexec.com/pay-benefits/2024/01/what-you-need-know-about-social-security-earnings-test/393399/.

Folley, Aris, and Ashleigh Fields. 2025. "Senators Pitch $1.5 Trillion Investment Fund for Social Security: What to Know." *The Hill.* https://thehill.com/business/budget/5439992-bipartisan-senate-social-security-plan/.

Works Cited

Fortune 360 Group. 2024. "Social Security: The Elephant in the Room." https://www.fortune360group.com/resource-center/retirement/social-security-the-elephant-in-the-room.

Friedman, Milton. 1999. "The Biggest Ponzi Scheme on Earth." Hoover Institution. https://www.hoover.org/research/biggest-ponzi-scheme-earth.

Fritzberg, Suzanna, and Ksenia Shadrina. 2024. "Spotlighting Women's Retirement Security." US Department of the Treasury. https://home.treasury.gov/news/featured-stories/spotlighting-womens-retirement-security.

Fry, Richard, and Kim Parker. 2021. "Rising Share of U.S. Adults are Living Without a Spouse or Partner." Pew Research Center. https://www.pewresearch.org/social-trends/2021/10/05/rising-share-of-u-s-adults-are-living-without-a-spouse-or-partner/.

Fundsback. 2025. "Why Pay Voluntary Pension Contributions in Germany?" https://fundsback.org/voluntary-pension-contribution-germany/.

Gaehde, Nick. 2022. "Illiteracy is Costing America—Here's Why." *USA Today.* https://www.usatoday.com/story/sponsor-story/lexia-learning2022/2022/03/02/illiteracy-costing-america-heres-why/6848450001/.

Gallup. 2024a. "Increasingly Polarized Populace." *Front Page,* August 27 (email).

Gallup. 2024b. "Social Security." In Depth: Topics A to Z. https://news.gallup.com/poll/1693/social-security.aspx.

GEHA (Government Employees Health Association). 2024. "New for 2025: G.E.H.A. Prescription Drug Plan." https://www.geha.com/en/plans/prescriptions/prescription-drug-plan.

Georgetown University. 2023. "Young Adults and Workplace Wellness." https://businessforimpact.georgetown.edu/wp-content/uploads/2023/06/Final-Young-Adult-Report-.pdf.

Ghilarducci, Teresa, Anthony Webb, and Michael Papadopoulos. 2018. "Catch-Up Contributions: An Innovative Policy Proposal for Social Security." Schwartz Center for Economic Policy Analysis and Department of Economics, The New School for Social Research, Policy Note Series. https://www.economicpolicyresearch.org/images/docs/research/retirement_security/Catch-Up_Contributions.pdf.

Gibson, Carl. 2025. "'Devastating': Trump Admin Marks Thousands Legally 'Dead' to Stop Them from Making Money." MSN. https://www.msn.com/en-us/news/politics/devastating-trump-admin-marks-thousands-legally-dead-to-stop-them-from-making-money/ar-AA1CHyLM?ocid=entnewsntp&pc=LCTS&cvid=b3ab070cae2c430392b59b3d1e5accbf&ei=13.

Gibson, Kate. 2025. "Social Security Approves Bill to Expand Social Security to Millions of Americans." Money Watch. CBS News. https://www.cbsnews.com/news/social-security-fairness-act-senate-vote-passed/.

Gillespie, Lane. 2025. "Survey: 72% Worried They Won't See Social Security Benefits Upon Retirement Age." Bankrate. https://www.cpapracticeadvisor.com/2024/11/26/72-percent-worried-they-wont-see-social-security-benefits-upon-retirement-age/152567/#.

Gillion, Colin, John Turner, Clive Bailey, and Denis Latulippe (eds.). 2000. *Social Security Pensions: Development and Reform.* Geneva, Switzerland, International Labor Office, 2000.

Goda, Gopi Shah, Shanthi Ramnath, John B. Shoven, and Sita Nataraj Slavov. 2018. "The Financial Feasibility of Delaying Social Security: Evidence from Administrative Tax Data." *Journal of Pension Economics & Finance* 17(4): 419-436.

Godbout, Ted. 2018. "Knowledge Gap on Social Security May Lead to False Sense of Security." American Society of Pension Professionals and Actuaries (ASPPA). https://www.asppa.org/news/browse-topics/knowledge-gap-social-security-may-lead-false-sense-security.

Godbout, Ted. 2025. "Lifetime Income: Why Many Participants Prefer an In-Plan Solution." National Association of Plan Advisors. https://www.napa-net.org/news/2025/4/lifetime-income-why-many-participants-prefer-an-in-plan-solution/.

Gokhale, Jagadeesh. 2010. *Social Security: A Fresh Look at Policy Alternatives.* University of Chicago Press.

Goodwin, Doris Kearns. 1995. *No Ordinary Time: Franklin and Eleanor Roosevelt: The Home Front in World War II.* New York: Simon & Schuster.

Goss, Sherri. 2009. "Why Is Social Security So Hard to Understand?" FedSmith. https://www.fedsmith.com/2009/12/10/why-social-security-so-hard-understand/.

Goss, Stephen C. 2024. "Social Security: Examining Solvency and Impacts to the Federal Budget." Testimony before the House Budget Committee, June 13. https://www.ssa.gov/OACT/testimony/HouseBudget_20240613.pdf.

Government Accountability Office. 2001. "Social Security: Issues in Evaluating Reform Proposals." Statement of Barbara D. Bovbjerg, Director, Education, Workforce, and Income Security Issues to the Special Committee on Aging, US Senate. GAO-02-288T. https://www.gao.gov/assets/gao-02-288t.pdf.

Government Accountability Office. 2009. "Tax Gap: Actions Needed to Address Noncompliance with S Corporation Tax Rules." GAO-10-195. https://www.gao.gov/assets/gao-10-195.pdf.

Government Accountability Office. 2014a. "401(k) Plans: Greater Protections Needed for Forced Transfers and

Inactive Accounts." GAO-15-73. Report to Congressional Requesters. https://www.gao.gov/assets/gao-15-73.pdf.

Government Accountability Office. 2014b. "Individual Retirement Accounts: IRS Could Bolster Enforcement on Multimillion Dollar Accounts, but More Direction from Congress Is Needed." GAO-15-16. October. https://www.gao.gov/assets/d1516.pdf.

Government Accountability Office. 2015. "Social Security's Future: Answers to Key Questions." GAO-16-75SP. https://www.gao.gov/assets/gao-16-75sp.pdf.

Government Accountability Office. 2017. "Older Workers: Phased Retirement Programs, Although Uncommon, Provide Flexibility for Workers and Employers." GAO-17-536. https://www.gao.gov/assets/gao-17-536.pdf.

Government Accountability Office. 2019a. "Older Workers: Other Countries' Experiences with Phased Retirement." https://www.gao.gov/assets/gao-19-16.pdf.

Government Accountability Office. 2019b. "Retirement Accounts: Federal Action Needed to Clarify Tax Treatment of Unclaimed 401(k) Plan Savings Transferred to States." https://www.gao.gov/products/gao-19-88.

Government Accountability Office. 2023a. "Older Workers: Retirement Account Disparities Have Increased by Income and Persisted by Race Over Time." GAO-23-105342. https://www.gao.gov/assets/gao-23-105342.pdf.

Government Accountability Office. 2023b. "Social Security Series Part 1: The Dilemma." GAO-23-106667. https://www.gao.gov/assets/830/820379.pdf.

Government Accountability Office. 2023c. "Social Security Series Part 2: Criteria for Evaluating Reform Proposals." GAO-24-106778. https://www.gao.gov/assets/d24106778.pdf.

Government Accountability Office. 2024a. "Social Security Series Part 3: Options for Reform." GAO-24-107240. https://www.gao.gov/assets/gao-24-107240.pdf.

Government Accountability Office. 2024b. "Work Hours and Health." https://www.gao.gov/products/gao-24-106772.

Government of Canada. 2023a. "Canada Pension Plan Amounts and the Consumer Price Index." https://www.canada.ca/en/services/benefits/publicpensions/cpp/cpp-benefit/after-apply/consumer-price-index.html.

Government of Canada. 2023b. "Canada Pension Plan Enhancement." https://www.canada.ca/en/services/benefits/publicpensions/cpp/cpp-enhancement.html.

Government of Canada. 2024a. "Canada Pension Plan." https://www.canada.ca/en/services/benefits/publicpensions/cpp.html.

Government of Canada. 2024b. "CPP Retirement Pension: Do You Qualify." https://www.canada.ca/en/services/benefits/publicpensions/cpp/cpp-benefit/eligibility.html.

Government of Canada. 2024c. "CPP Retirement Pension: How Much You Could Receive." https://www.canada.ca/en/services/benefits/publicpensions/cpp/cpp-benefit/amount.html.

Government of Canada. 2024d. "Old Age Security." https://www.canada.ca/en/services/benefits/publicpensions/cpp/old-age-security.html.

Government of Canada. 2024e. "Old Age Security: Do You Qualify" https://www.canada.ca/en/services/benefits/publicpensions/cpp/old-age-security/eligibility.html.

Government of Canada. 2024f. "Old Age Security Payment Amounts." https://www.canada.ca/en/services/benefits/publicpensions/cpp/old-age-security/payments.html.

Government of Canada. 2024g. "Old Age Security Pension Recovery Tax." https://www.canada.ca/en/services/benefits/publicpensions/cpp/old-age-security/recovery-tax.html.

Government of Canada. 2024h. "Working While Receiving a Pension." https://www.canada.ca/en/financial-consumer-agency/services/retirement-planning/working-collecting-pension.html.

Government of Canada. 2025a. "Determine if a Benefit Is Taxable." https://www.canada.ca/en/revenue-agency/services/tax/businesses/topics/payroll/benefits-allowances/benefits-allowances-chart.html.

Government of Canada. 2025b. 'When to Start Your Retirement Pension." https://www.canada.ca/en/services/benefits/publicpensions/cpp/cpp-benefit/when-start.html.

Government of Québec. 2024. "Québec Pension Plan." https://www.quebec.ca/en/employment/plan-manage-career/plan-retirement/quebec-pension-plan.

Gov.UK. 2025. "Voluntary National Insurance." https://www.gov.uk/voluntary-national-insurance-contributions.

Grassley, Chuck. 2024. "Saving Social Security Shouldn't Be Political Kryptonite: Ronald Reagan and Tip O'Neill Showed Us How." https://www.grassley.senate.gov/blog/saving-social-security-shouldnt-be-political-kryptonite-ronald-reagan-and-tip-oneill-showed-us-how.

Green, John. 2025. *Everything is Tuberculosis: The History and Persistence of Our Deadliest Infection*. Penguin Random House.

Green, Ken. 2021. "UK Uber Drivers Are Now Classified as Workers." Union Track Blog. https://uniontrack.com/blog/uk-uber-drivers-are-now-classified-as-workers#:~:text=On%20February%202019%2C%202020%2C%20Uber,and%20Laura%20Batchelor%20at%20CNBC.

Greszler, Rachel. 2025. "Ending the Retirement Earnings Test: A Pro-Growth Proposal to Cut Social Security Taxes and

Improve Program Solvency." The Heritage Foundation. https://www.heritage.org/budget-and-spending/report/ending-the-retirement-earnings-test-pro-growth-proposal-cut-social.

Hadass, Yael, Marion Labouré, Sally Shen, and John A. Turner. 2020. "New Approaches to Communicating to Workers About Pensions." Products, Tools, and Strategies That Address Retirement Risks – Essay Collection. Society of Actuaries, 2020. https://www.soa.org/globalassets/assets/files/resources/research-report/2020/products-tools-strategies-retirement-essays.pdf.

Hallez, Emile. 2021. "Unclaimed Retirement Accounts a Big Problem for Most States." *Investment News*. https://www.investmentnews.com/industry-news/news/unclaimed-retirement-accounts-a-big-problem-for-most-states-202284.

Haltzel, Laura. 2023. "Social Security's Trust Funds Should Stop Paying the Bill for Fringe Benefits." The Century Foundation. https://tcf.org/content/commentary/social-securitys-trust-funds-should-stop-paying-the-bill-for-fringe-benefits/.

Hannon, Kerry. 2024. "Millennials Likely to Feel Biggest Burden of Fixing Social Security, Report Finds." Yahoo Finance. https://finance.yahoo.com/news/millennials-likely-to-feel-biggest-burden-of-fixing-social-security-report-finds-090039636.html.

Hansen, Randy. 2022. "After My Felony Conviction, I Lost My Social Security Benefits." The Prison Journalism Project. https://prisonjournalismproject.org/2022/07/28/lost-social-security-after-felony-conviction/.

Hahn, Joseph. 2024. "Retirement and Estate Planning for Unmarried Couples." J.P. Morgan Wealth Management. https://www.jpmorgan.com/insights/wealth-planning/trusts-and-estates/retirement-and-estate-planning-for-unmarried-couples.

Hayes, Adam. 2024. "Bernie Madoff: Who He Was, And How His Ponzi Scheme Worked." Investopedia. https://www.investopedia.com/terms/b/bernard-madoff.asp.

Heilman, Greg. 2025. "Raising Retirement Age to 69? Republican Committee Unveils New Proposal for Social Security Reform." AS. https://en.as.com/latest_news/raising-retirement-age-to-69-republican-committee-unveils-new-proposal-for-social-security-reform-n/.

Hertel-Fernandez, Alexander. 2009. "Against False Choices: True Intergenerational Equity in Social Insurance." National Academy of Social Insurance. https://www.nasi.org/wp-content/uploads/2009/11/Alexander_Hertel-Fernandez.pdf.

Higham, Aliss. 2025. "Baby Boomers 'Worried' About Social Security Benefit Changes." *Newsweek*. https://www.newsweek.com/baby-boomers-worried-social-security-benefit-changes-2051379.

Hobson, Frank, Steven Kennedy, and Andrew Mackley. 2022. "An Introduction to Social Security in the UK." Research Briefing. UK Parliament. House of Commons Library. https://researchbriefings.files.parliament.uk/documents/CBP-9535/CBP-9535.pdf.

Horowitz, Juliana Menasce, Nikki Graf, and Gretchen Livingston. 2019. "The Landscape of Marriage and Cohabitation in the U.S." Pew Research Center. https://www.pewresearch.org/social-trends/2019/11/06/the-landscape-of-marriage-and-cohabitation-in-the-u-s/.

Hoskins, Dalmer D. 2010. "U.S. Social Security at 75 Years: An International Perspective." *Social Security Bulletin* 70(3): 79-87. https://www.ssa.gov/policy/docs/ssb/v70n3/v70n3p79.pdf.

Hussein, Fatima. 2025. "Social Security Head Steps Down over DOGE Access of Recipient Information, AP Sources Say." APNews. https://apnews.com/article/social-security-elon-musk-doge-164c91f8477d5e7833af7f6de4bbde57.

Works Cited

Huston, Barry F. 2021. "Social Security Long-Range Projections: Why 75 Years?" Congressional Research Service. https://crsreports.congress.gov/product/pdf/IF/IF11851.

Huston, Barry F. 2023. "Social Security: Future Financial Status and Accuracy of Projections." Congressional Research Service. https://crsreports.congress.gov/product/pdf/R/R47650/3.

Huston, Barry F., and Katelin P. Isaacs. 2025. "Social Security's Projected Shortfall: The Role of Demographic Factors." Congressional Research Service. https://www.congress.gov/crs-product/R48557.

Ianzito, Christina. 2025. "AARP Backs Efforts to Improve SSA's Assistance for Identity Fraud Participants." https://www.aarp.org/politics-society/advocacy/info-2025/improving-service-identity-theft-victims.html?cmp=EMC-ADV-20250626-2100208&encparam=V%2bQF01MLHHegaCqZSoiBnMwni1YaHtetNt2oMeUEieM%d.

Institute for Health Metrics and Evaluation. 2025. "U.S. College Graduates Live an Average of 11 Years Longer Than Those Who Never Finish High School." https://www.healthdata.org/news-events/newsroom/news-releases/us-college-graduates-live-average-11-years-longer-those-who.

Internal Revenue Service. 2024a. "401(k) Limit Increases to $23,000 for 2024, IRA Limit Rises to $7,000." https://www.irs.gov/newsroom/401k-limit-increases-to-23000-for-2024-ira-limit-rises-to-7000.

Internal Revenue Service. 2024b. "Family Employees." https://www.irs.gov/businesses/small-businesses-self-employed/family-employees.

Internal Revenue Service. 2024c. "FAQs Regarding Form 8955-SSA." https://www.irs.gov/retirement-plans/faqs-regarding-form-8955-ssa.

Internal Revenue Service. 2024d. "Instructions for Form 8955-SSA." https://www.irs.gov/pub/irs-pdf/i8955ssa.pdf.

Internal Revenue Service. 2024e. "IRA FAQs - Distributions (Withdrawals)." https://www.irs.gov/retirement-plans/retirement-plans-faqs-regarding-iras-distributions-withdrawals.

Internal Revenue Service. 2024f. "Issue Snapshot - 401(k) Plan Catch-up Contribution Eligibility." https://www.irs.gov/retirement-plans/401k-plan-catch-up-contribution-eligibility.

Internal Revenue Service. 2024g. "Retirement Plan FAQs Regarding Contributions—Are Retirement Plan Contributions Subject to Withholding for FICA, Medicare or Federal Income Tax?" https://www.irs.gov/retirement-plans/retirement-plan-faqs-regarding-contributions-are-retirement-plan-contributions-subject-to-withholding-for-fica-medicare-or-federal-income-tax.

Internal Revenue Service. 2024h. "Retirement Topics: Catch-up Contributions." https://www.irs.gov/retirement-plans/plan-participant-employee/retirement-topics-catch-up-contributions.

Internal Revenue Service. 2024i. "Saver's Credit Can Help Low- and Moderate-Income Taxpayers to Save More in 2024." https://www.irs.gov/newsroom/savers-credit-can-help-low-and-moderate-income-——taxpayers-to-save-more-in-2024.

Internal Revenue Service. 2024j. "Student Exception to FICA Tax." https://www.irs.gov/charities-non-profits/student-exception-to-fica-tax.

Internal Revenue Service. 2024k. "Taxable and Nontaxable Income." https://www.irs.gov/pub/irs-pdf/p525.pdf.

Internal Revenue Service. 2025a. "Employer's Supplemental Tax Guide." https://www.irs.gov/pub/irs-pdf/p15a.pdf.

Internal Revenue Service. 2025b. "Publication 15 (2025), (Circular E), Employer's Tax Guide." https://www.irs.gov/publications/p15.

Internal Revenue Service. 2025c "Qualified Small Business Payroll Tax Credit for Increasing Research Activities." https://www.irs.

gov/businesses/small-businesses-self-employed/qualified-small-business-payroll-tax-dredit-for-increasing-research-activities.

Internal Revenue Service. 2025d. "Retirement Plan and IRA Required Minimum Distributions FAQs." https://www.irs.gov/retirement-plans/retirement-plan-and-ira-required-minimum-distributions-faqs.

Internal Revenue Service. 2025e. "Retirement Plan FAQs Regarding Contributions - Are Retirement Plan Contributions Subject to Withholding for FICA, Medicare or Federal Income Tax?" https://www.irs.gov/retirement-plans/retirement-plan-faqs-regarding-contributions-are-retirement-plan-contributions-subject-to-withholding-for-fica-medicare-or-federal-income-tax.

Internal Revenue Service. 2025f. Self-Employment Tax (Social Security and Medicare Taxes.) https://www.irs.gov/businesses/small-businesses-self-employed/self-employment-tax-social-security-and-medicare-taxes.

Investing.com. 2024. "United States 10-Year Bond Yield." https://www.investing.com/rates-bonds/u.s.-10-year-bond-yield-historical-data.

Investment Company Institute. 2024a. "Quarterly Retirement Market Data." https://www.ici.org/research/stats/retirement.

Investment Company Institute. 2024b. "The Role of IRAs in US Households' Saving for Retirement, 2023." *ICI Research Perspective*. 30 (1). February. https://www.ici.org/system/files/2024-02/per30-01.pdf.

Investopedia Team. 2024. "Canada Pension Plan (CPP) vs. U.S. Social Security." Retirement Planning. https://www.investopedia.com/ask/answers/102714/what-are-differences-between-canada-pension-plans-cpp-and-social-security-benefits.asp.

IRA Financial Group. 2023. "Romney vs. Thiel—Who is the King of the Self-Directed IRA?" *IRA Financial Blog*. https://www.irafinancialgroup.com/learn-more/self-directed-ira/romney-vs-thiel-who-is-the-king-of-the-self-directed-ira/.

Irish Government. 2024. "State Pension (Contributory)." Department of Social Protection. https://www.gov.ie/en/service/e6f908-state-pension-contributory/.

Isaacs, Katelin P. 2017. "Social Security: Revisiting Benefits for Spouses and Survivors."

Ivanova, Irina. 2023. "Wages Surged for Lowest-Paid Americans After the Pandemic." CBS News. https://www.cbsnews.com/news/wages-surged-lowest-paid-americans-pandemic-covid-19/.

Iwry, J. Mark, and John A. Turner. 2009. "Automatic Annuitization: New Behavioral Strategies for Expanding Lifetime Income in 401(k)s." In *Automatic: Changing the Way America Saves*, edited by William G. Gale, J. Mark Iwry, David John, and Lina Walker. Brookings Institution Press.

Jacobs, Sabrina. 2023. "Voters Strongly Oppose Raising the Retirement Age." Data for Progress. https://www.dataforprogress.org/blog/2023/4/17/voters-strongly-oppose-raising-the-retirement-age.

Jarrett, B.J. 2025. "Will Remarrying Affect My Social Security Benefits?" Social Security Administration. https://blog.ssa.gov/will-remarrying-affect-my-social-security-benefits/.

Jay, Marley, and Rob Wile. 2024. "How a Government Shutdown Could Affect Social Security Payments." NBC News, December 18. https://www.msn.com/en-us/news/politics/how-a-government-shutdown-could-affect-social-security-payments/ar-AA1wb9UR?ocid=BingNewsSerp&apiversion=v2&noservercache=1&domshim=1&renderwebcomponents=1&wcseo=1&batchservertelemetry=1&noservertelemetry=1.

Johnson, Richard W., and Karen E. Smith. 2023. "Limitations on Social Security Benefits for Black Retirees: Exploring Structural Racism's Impact." Research Report. Urban Institute. https://www.urban.org/research/publication/limitations-social-security-benefits-black-retirees.

Johnson, Richard W., and Karen E. Smith. 2024. "If Social Security Runs Out of Money, Poverty among Older Adults and People with Disabilities Will Soar." Urban Institute. https://www.urban.org/urban-wire/if-social-security-runs-out-money-poverty-among-older-adults-and-people-disabilities.

Jones, Jeffrey M. 2023. "Americans More Upbeat About Future Social Security Benefits." https://news.gallup.com/poll/546890/americans-upbeat-future-social-security-benefits.aspx.

Kenney, Rachel, and Chantel Boyens. 2023. "Three Ways Social Security Could Become More Equitable and Sustainable." Urban Institute. https://www.urban.org/urban-wire/three-ways-social-security-could-become-more-equitable-and-sustainable.

Kent, Ana Hernández. 2024. "The State of U.S. Wealth." St. Louis Fed's Institute for Economic Equity. https://www.stlouisfed.org/institute-for-economic-equity/the-state-of-us-wealth-inequality.

Kintzel, Dale, and John A. Turner. 2020. "Provision of Longevity Insurance Annuities." *Financial Analysts Journal* 76 (4): 119-133.

Koba, Mark. 2014. "How the Gingrich-Edwards Tax Loophole Works." https://www.cnbc.com/2014/03/05/cnbc-explains-the-gingrich-edwards-tax-loophole.html.

Kochanek, Kenneth D., Sherry L. Murphy, Jiaquan Xu, and Elizabeth Arias. 2024. "Mortality in the United States, 2022." Centers for Disease Control and Prevention (CDC). National Center for Health Statistics. NCHS Data Brief No. 492, March. https://www.cdc.gov/nchs/products/databriefs/db492.htm.

Konish, Lorie. 2023a. "Social Security Rule for Beneficiaries Who Keep Working Is 'Poorly Understood,' Report Finds." CNBC. https://www.cnbc.com/2023/12/20/why-social-security-retirement-earnings-test-is-poorly-understood.html.

Konish, Lorie. 2023b. "With Social Security Trust Funds 'Rapidly Heading to Zero,' Some Ask Whether the Money Should Be Invested in Equities." CNBC. https://www.cnbc.com/2023/10/05/as-social-security-faces-shortfall-some-propose-investing-in-stocks.html#:~:text=How%20government%20retirement%20funds%20use,over%20the%20past%2010%20years.

Konish, Lorie. 2024. "As Republicans Propose to Raise the Social Security Retirement Age, Here's How Benefits May Change." CNBC. https://www.cnbc.com/2024/03/22/how-social-security-benefits-may-change-under-republican-democrat-proposals.html.

Kotlikoff, Laurence. 2012. "Thomas Jefferson Is Rolling in His Grave—A Rant on Social Security's Complexity." *Forbes*. https://www.forbes.com/sites/kotlikoff/2012/08/06/thomas-jefferson-is-rolling-in-his-grave-a-rant-on-social-securitys-complexity/.

KPMG. 2024. "Time to Reform the SFT on Pension Funds." KPMG in Ireland > Insights. https://kpmg.com/ie/en/home/insights/2024/02/pension-tax-reform-needed.html.

Kritzer, Barbara E., and Barbara A. Smith. 2016. "Public Pension Statements in Selected Countries: A Comparison." *Social Security Bulletin* 76(1): 27-56. https://www.ssa.gov/policy/docs/ssb/v76n1/v76n1p27.pdf.

Kuttner, Robert. 2023. "Fake Generational Warfare." The American Prospect. https://prospect.org/blogs-and-newsletters/tap/2023-12-20-fake-generational-warfare-social-security/.

Lakeford, Kimberly, and Donna Levalley. 2025. "Delay Social Security Benefits—Even by a Month—to Boost Your Check." *Kiplinger*. https://www.kiplinger.com/article/retirement/t051-c001-s003-boost-social-security-benefit-when-you-delay.html.

Latulippe, Denis, and John A. Turner. 2019. "Social Security Retirement Policy in Canada and the United States: Different Reforms, Different Outcomes." *Canadian Public Policy* 45(4): 393-402.

Leibenluft, Jacob, Devin O'Connor, and Kathleen Romig. 2025. "Trump Administration, DOGE Activities Risk SSA Operations and Security of Personal Data." Center on Budget and Policy Priorities. https://www.cbpp.org/research/social-security/trump-administration-doge-activities-risk-ssa-operations-and-security-of.

Leigh, Wilhelmina A., and Melissa R. Wells. 2013. "Solvency and Adequacy for the Social Security System: Perspectives of African Americans and White Americans." Joint Center for Political and Economic Studies. https://jointcenter.org/wp-content/uploads/2021/02/Solvency-and-Adequacy-for-the-Social-Security-System-1.pdf.

Levalley, Donna. 2025. "47 Local Social Security Offices to Close After Doge Cuts." *Kiplinger.* https://www.kiplinger.com/retirement/social-security/social-security-offices-close-after-doge-cuts.

Levin, Yuval. 2023. "What Old and Young Americans Owe One Another." *The New York Times*, March 11. https://www.nytimes.com/2023/03/11/opinion/social-security-medicare-intergenerational-compact.html.

Li, Zhe. 2020. "Social Security Retirement Earnings Test (RET): Earnings Exemption for COVID-19-Related Work Response." Congressional Research Service. https://crsreports.congress.gov/product/pdf/IN/IN11352.

Li, Zhe. 2022. "Poverty Among the Population Aged 65 and Older." Congressional Research Service. https://sgp.fas.org/crs/misc/R45791.pdf.

Li, Zhe. 2024. "Social Security Coverage of State and Local Government Employees." Congressional Research Service.

CRS Report Prepared for Members and Committees of Congress. https://sgp.fas.org/crs/misc/R46961.pdf.

Liebman, Jeffrey B., and Erzo F.P. Luttmer. 2012. "The Perception of Social Security Incentives for Labor Supply and Retirement: The Median Voter Knows More than You'd Think." *Tax Policy and the Economy* 26(1): 1-42. https://www.journals.uchicago.edu/doi/pdf/10.1086/665501.

Lightman, David. 2023. "Calling Social Security? Brace for Long Waits as Phone Line Struggles. What's the Hold Time?" *The Sacramento Bee,* December 19. https://www.sacbee.com/news/politics-government/article283093808.html.

Liu, Lillian. 1999. "Retirement Income Security in the United Kingdom." *Social Security Bulletin* 62(1): 23-46. https://www.ssa.gov/policy/docs/ssb/v62n1/v62n1p23.pdf.

Longo, Tracey. 2024. "Social Security to End 'Clawback Cruelty' On Benefit Overpayments." *Financial Advisor.* https://www.famag.com/news/social-security-to-end--clawback-cruelty--on-.

Loo, Jaden. 2024. "Marriage: More Than a Century of Change, 1900-2022." Bowling Green State University. https://www.bgsu.edu/ncfmr/resources/data/family-profiles/FP-24-10.html.

Loo, Jaden, and Susan L. Brown. 2024. "Marital Status Distribution of U.S. Adults Aged 65 and Older, 1990-2022." National Center for Family and Marriage Research. https://www.bgsu.edu/ncfmr/resources/data/family-profiles/marital-status-distribution-of-u-s--adults-aged-65-and-older--19.html.

Lopez, Ashley, and McLaughlin, Jenna. 2025. "The Social Security Administration Says It Plans to Cut Some 7,000 jobs." NPR. https://www.npr.org/2025/02/28/nx-s1-5296986/trump-worker-cuts-social-security-administrationbenefit-overpayments-77387.html.

Luhby, Tami. 2025. "Social Security Targets Tech Team for Cuts at a Time when Systems Are under Strain." CNN. https://www.cnn.com/2025/04/04/politics/social-security-tech-team-layoffs.

Mancini, Jeannine. 2024. "Can You Guess How Many Retire with A $5 Million Nest Egg?" Yahoo Finance. https://finance.yahoo.com/newsi/guess-many-retire-5-million-170011124.html.

Männis, Marten. 2020. "Uber Drivers Considered Employees in France, Court Rules." European Company Lawyer's Association. https://inhouse-legal.eu/public-policy-regulations/uber-france/.

Margenau, Tom. 2022. *Social Security: 100 Myths and 100 Facts.* Creators Publishing.

Markowitz, Andy. 2018. "Can I Collect Spousal Benefits and Wait Until I Am 70 to Collect My Own Social Security?" AARP. https://www.aarp.org/retirement/social-security/questions-answers/spousal-benefits-until-70.html.

Markowitz, Andy. 2024a. "Are the Last Boomers Ready for Retirement?" AARP. https://www.aarp.org/retirement/planning-for-retirement/info-2024/peak-boomer-readiness.html.

Markowitz, Andy. 2024b. "If I Wait Until 70 to Claim Social Security, Will My Spouse Get a Bigger Benefit as Well?" AARP. https://www.aarp.org/social-security/faq/maximizing-spousal-benefit/.

Markowitz, Andy. 2025. "7 Things That Can Lower Your Monthly Social Security Payments." AARP. https://www.aarp.org/retirement/social-security/info-2022/deductions-from-benefits-payments.html.

Martin, Patricia P., and Kintzel, Dale. 2016. "A Comparison of Free Online Tools for Individuals Deciding When to Claim Social Security Benefits." *Social Security Administration Research and Statistics Notes.* https://www.ssa.gov/policy/docs/rsnotes/rsn2016-03.html.

Masala, Francesco. 2024. "National Insurance Contributions: An Introduction." Research Briefing. UK Parliament. House of Commons Library. https://researchbriefings.files.parliament.uk/documents/SN04517/SN04517.pdf.

MassMutual. 2024. "Nearly 80% of Near Retirees Failed or Barely Passed a Basic Social Security Quiz from MassMutual." Press Release. https://www.massmutual.com/about-us/news-and-press-releases/press-releases/2024/02/nearly-80-of-near-retirees-failed-or-barely-passed.

McDade, Zachary J. 2014. "Social Security Is Not a Ponzi Scheme." Urban Institute. https://www.urban.org/urban-wire/social-security-not-ponzi-scheme.

McKenna, Kristin. 2024. "The Growing Appeal of Semi-Retirement." *Forbes*. https://www.forbes.com/sites/kristinmckenna/2024/04/08/the-growing-appeal-of-semi-retirement/.

McIsaac, Chris. 2024. "Taxing the Rich Is No Silver Bullet for Saving Social Security." The Hill. https://thehill.com/opinion/4785332-biden-social-security-tax-proposal/.

McNabb, Jennifer, David Timmins, Jae Song, and Carolyn Puckett. 2009. "Use of Administrative Data at the Social Security Administration." *Social Security Bulletin* 69(1). https://www.ssa.gov/policy/docs/ssb/v69n1/v69n1p75.html#:~:text=Data%20Sharing%20Authority%20and%20Procedures&text=SSA%20policy%20is%20to%20share,individuals%20and%20for%20certain%20purposes.

Mechanic, Michael. 2021. "America Is Spending a Fortune to Help Rich People Retire in Luxury." *Mother Jones*. https://www.motherjones.com/politics/2021/09/america-spends-fortune-rich-retire-luxury-401k-iras-roth-subsidies-wealth-inequality/.

Medina, Lauren, Shannon Sabo, and Jonathan Vespa. 2020. "Living Longer: Historical and Projected Life Expectancy in the United

States, 1960-2060." US Census Bureau. https://www.census.gov/content/dam/Census/library/publications/2020/demo/p25-1145.pdf.

Mercer. 2025. "Changes to the Standard Fund Threshold." https://www.mercer.com/en-ie/insights/pensions/new-standard-fund-threshold-limits-in-ireland/.

Merriam-Webster. 2025. "Full." https://www.merriam-webster.com/dictionary/full.

Miller, Brett. 2022. "Sanders Bill Targets Rich to Expand Social Security, Extend Solvency." https://www.sanders.senate.gov/sanders-bill-targets-rich-to-expand-social-security-extend-solvency/.

Mishel, Lawrence, Elise Gould, and Josh Bivens. 2015. "Wage Stagnation in Nine Charts." Economic Policy Institute. https://www.epi.org/publication/charting-wage-stagnation/.

Mitchell, Olivia S., Robert J. Myers, and Howard Young (eds.). 1999. *Prospects for Social Security Reform*. University of Pennsylvania Press.

Moeller, Phillip. 2016. "Beware of Being Automatically Enrolled in a Medicare Plan You Don't Want." PBS. https://www.pbs.org/newshour/economy/beware-of-being-automatically-enrolled-in-a-medicare-plan-you-dont-want.

Monk, Courtney, John A. Turner, and Natalia A. Zhivan. 2010. "Adjusting Social Security for Increasing Life Expectancy: Effects on Progressivity." Center for Retirement Research at Boston College WP 2010-9. http://crr.bc.edu/wp-content/uploads/2010/08/wp2010-9-508.pdf.

Moskovska, Andriana. 2024. "33 Startling Wrongful Conviction Statistics (2024 Update)." The High Court. https://thehighcourt.co/wrongful-convictions-statistics/.

Muller, Leslie A., and John A. Turner. 2022. "Sample Selection Bias due to Differential Mortality: A Supplementary Measure of Old-Age

Poverty." *Journal of Aging & Social Policy* 34(3): 496-514. https://www.tandfonline.com/doi/abs/10.1080/08959420.2021.1926196.

Munnell, Alicia H. 2019. "Social Security's Earnings Test Is Too Complicated – And It Discourages Work." Center for Retirement Research at Boston College. https://crr.bc.edu/social-securitys-earnings-test-is-too-complicated-and-it-discourages-work/.

Munnell, Alicia H. 2022. "Social Security's Retirement Age Is 70." Center for Retirement Research at Boston College. https://crr.bc.edu/social-securitys-retirement-age-is-70/.

Munnell, Alicia H. 2023a. "Any Social Security Legislative Package Should Include an Automatic Adjustment Mechanism." Center for Retirement Research at Boston College. https://crr.bc.edu/any-social-security-legislative-package-should-include-an-automatic-adjustment-mechanism/.

Munnell, Alicia H. 2023b. "This Is a Good Time to Rethink How Social Security Should Be Financed." Center for Retirement Research at Boston College. https://crr.bc.edu/this-is-a-good-time-to-rethink-how-social-security-should-be-financed/.

Munnell, Alicia H. 2024a. "Canada's Pension Plan Falls Short of Indexed Benchmark." Center for Retirement Research at Boston College. https://crr.bc.edu/canada-pension-plan-fall-short-of-indexed-benchmark/.

Munnell, Alicia H. 2024b. "Social Security's 75 Year Deficit Is Not Surprising." Center for Retirement Research at Boston College. https://crr.bc.edu/social-securitys-75-year-deficit-is-not-surprising/.

Munnell, Alicia H. 2024c. "Social Security's COLA: Let's Not Mess with the Index." Center for Retirement Research at Boston College. https://crr.bc.edu/social-securitys-cola-lets-not-mess-with-the-index/.

Munnell, Alicia H. 2024d. "To Fix Social Security, Raising the Wage Base Should be Part of the Solution." Center for Retirement

Research at Boston College. https://crr.bc.edu/to-fix-social-security-increasing-the-wage-base-should-be-part-of-the-solution/.

Munnell, Alicia H., and Steven A. Sass. 2006. *Social Security and the Stock Market: How the Pursuit of Market Magic Shapes the System*. Upjohn Institute.

National Academy of Social Insurance (NASI). 2013. "Public Opinions on Social Security." https://www.nasi.org/learn/social-security/public-opinions-on-social-security/.

National Commission on Fiscal Responsibility and Reform. 2010. "The Moment of Truth." Report of the National Commission on Fiscal Responsibility and Reform. https://www.ssa.gov/history/reports/ObamaFiscal/TheMomentofTruth12_1_2010.pdf.

National Institute on Retirement Security. 2020. "New Report: 40% of Older Americans Rely Solely on Social Security for Retirement Income." Press Release. https://www.nirsonline.org/2020/01/new-report-40-of-older-americans-rely-solely-on-social-security-for-retirement-income/.

National Institute on Retirement Security. 2024. "87 Percent of Americans Want Action Now to Address Social Security Funding Shortfall." Press Release. https://www.nirsonline.org/2024/07/87-percent-of-americans-want-action-now-to-address-social-security-funding-shortfall/.

The National Registry of Exonerations. 2024. "2023 Annual Report." This is a project of the University of California Irvine Newkirk Center for Science & Society, University of Michigan Law School, and Michigan State University College of Law. https://www.law.umich.edu/special/exoneration/Documents/2023%20Annual%20Report.pdf.

National Volunteer Fire Council. 2025. "Volunteer Fire Service Fact Sheet." https://www.nvfc.org/wp-content/uploads/2024/03/fire-service-fact-sheet-updated-032024.pdf.

Nationwide. 2024. "More Than Three in Four U.S. Adults Believe the Social Security System Needs to Change." https://news.nationwide.com/adults-believe-social-security-system-needs-to-change/.

Nationwide Retirement Institute. 2021. "Understanding the Social Security Widow Benefit." https://www.fa-mag.com/userfiles/ads_2021/Nationwide_Feb_Sept_2021/NFM-13670AO.5_Understanding_the_SS_Widow_Benefit.pdf.

Nationwide Retirement Institute. 2023. "The Nationwide Retirement Institute® 2023 Social Security Survey." https://nationwidefinancial.com/media/pdf/NFM-23094AO.pdf.

Nationwide Retirement Institute. 2024. "The Nationwide Retirement Institute® 2024 Social Security Survey." https://nationwidefinancial.com/media/pdf/NFM-24093AO.pdf.

Nazarro, Miranda. 2023. "2 in 5 Young Adults Surveyed Say Marriage an Outdated Tradition." The Hill. https://thehill.com/changing-america/respect/equality/4107946-2-in-5-young-adults-surveyed-say-marriage-an-outdated-tradition/.

Nelson, William J., Jr. 1985. "Employment Coverage Under the Social Security Program, 1935-1984." *Social Security Bulletin* 48(4): 33-39. https://www.ssa.gov/policy/docs/ssb/v48n4/v48n4p33.pdf.

Newkirk, Kaitlin, and Sarah Webber. 2024. "Taxation of Influencers: Gifts with Strings Attached?" *Journal of Accountancy*. https://www.journalofaccountancy.com/issues/2024/sep/taxation-of-influencers-gifts-with-strings-attached.html.

OASDI Trustees. 2024. "The 2023 Annual Report of the Board of Trustees of the Federal Old-Age and Survivors Insurance and Federal Disability Insurance Trust Funds." https://www.ssa.gov/oact/TR/2023/tr2023.pdf.

Ochieng, Nancy, Juliette Cubanski, Tricia Neuman, and Anthony Damico. 2024. "How Many Older Adults

Live in Poverty?" KFF. https://www.kff.org/medicare/issue-brief/how-many-older-adults-live-in-poverty/.

Office of the Chief Actuary, Social Security Administration. 2023. "Summary of Provisions That Would Change the Social Security Program." https://www.ssa.gov/oact/solvency/provisions_tr2023/summary.pdf.

Office of the Chief Actuary, Social Security Administration. 2024. "Letter to the Honorable Peter Welch." https://www.ssa.gov/OACT/solvency/PWelch_20240925.pdf.

Olsen, Anya, and Kathleen Romig. 2013. "Modeling Behavioral Responses to Eliminating the Retirement Earnings Test." *Social Security Bulletin* 73(1): 39-58. https://www.ssa.gov/policy/docs/ssb/v73n1/v73n1p39.pdf.

Olsen, Kelly A., and Don Hoffmeyer. 2001/2002. "Social Security's Special Minimum Benefit." *Social Security Bulletin* 64(2): 1-15. https://www.ssa.gov/policy/docs/ssb/v64n2/v64n2p1.pdf.

Organisation for Economic Cooperation and Development. 2015. *Pensions at a Glance: OECD and G20 Indicators.* Paris: OECD Publishing. https://www.oecd-ilibrary.org/social-issues-migration-health/pensions-at-a-glance-2015_pension_glance-2015-en.

Organisation for Economic Cooperation and Development. 2021. *Pensions at a Glance 2021.* OECD iLibrary. https://www.oecd-ilibrary.org/eligibility-and-indexation-for-first-tier-benefits_79b569c0-en.pdf?itemId=%2Fcontent%2Fcomponent%2F79b569c0-en&mimeType=pdf.

Parker, Tim. 2024a. "How Is Your 401(k) Taxed in Retirement?" Investopedia. https://www.investopedia.com/articles/personal-finance/061915/how-your-401k-taxed-when-you-retire.asp.

Parker, Tim. 2024b. "What Is the Average Retirement Savings by Age?" Investopedia. https://www.investopedia.com/articles/personal-finance/011216/average-retirement-savings-age-2016.asp.

Pecorin, Allison. 2024. "Senate to Vote on Expanding Social Security Payments for Some Teachers, Firefighters." ABC News. https://abc7.com/post/senate-vote-expanding-social-security-payments-teachers-firefighters/15671556/.

Penner, Rudolph G. 2016. "The Reliability of Long-Term Budget Projections." Chapter 3 in *Fixing Fiscal Myopia: Why and How We Should Emphasize the Long Term in Federal Budgeting.* https://www.urban.org/sites/default/files/publication/86211/2001010-the-reliability-of-long-term-budget-projections_3.pdf.

Perron, Rebecca. 2023. "Social Security Has Widespread Support, Needs Funding Solutions." AARP. https://www.aarp.org/pri/topics/work-finances-retirement/social-security/social-security-legislative-activity.html.

Peter G. Peterson Foundation. 2022. "Social Security Reform: Options to Raise Revenues." https://www.pgpf.org/blog/2022/11/social-security-reform-options-to-raise-revenues.

Peter G. Peterson Foundation. 2023a. "New Survey: 9-in-10 Voters Call for Bipartisan Fiscal Commission as New Speaker Takes Helm." https://www.pgpf.org/press-release/2023/10/fci-press-release.

Peter G. Peterson Foundation. 2023b. "Should We Eliminate the Social Security Tax Cap?" https://www.pgpf.org/article/should-we-eliminate-the-social-security-tax-cap-here-are-the-pros-and-cons/.

Peter G. Peterson Foundation. 2025a. "Lawmakers Are Running Out of Time to Fix Social Security." https://www.pgpf.org/article/lawmakers-are-running-out-of-time-to-fix-social-security/.

Peter G. Peterson Foundation. 2025b. "The Ration of Workers to Social Security Beneficiaries Is at a Low and Projected to Decline Further." https://www.pgpf.org/article/the-ratio-of-workers-to-social-security-beneficiaries-is-at-a-low-and-projected-to-decline-further/.

Pethokoukus, James. 2025. "A Fascinating (And Demoralizing) Bit of 'What If' Economic History." American Economic Institute. https://www.aei.org/economics/a-fascinating-and-demoralizing-bit-of-what-if-economic-history/.

Pew Research Center. 2009. "Growing Old in America: Expectations vs. Reality." https://www.pewresearch.org/social-trends/2009/06/29/growing-old-in-america-expectations-vs-reality/.

Pew Research Center. 2019. "Views on Retirement, Social Security, and Long-Term Care." https://www.pewresearch.org/social-trends/2019/03/21/retirement-social-security-and-long-term-care/.

Picchi, Aimee. 2025. "Social Security to Reduce Overpayment Clawbacks to 50%, Down from 100%." CBS News. https://www.cbsnews.com/news/social-security-overpayment-clawback-change-50-percent-doge/?ftag=CNM-00-10aac3a.

Portalatin-Perez, Lizbeth. 2025. "You May Be Eligible for Social Security and SSI Benefits." Social Security Administration. https://blog.ssa.gov/you-may-be-eligible-for-ssi-and-social-security-benefits/#:~:text=About%202.5%20million%20adults%20and,no%20income%20and%20few%20resources.

Porter, T.J. 2024. "What Impact Will an S Corp Have on Your Future Social Security Benefits?" https://www.collective.com/blog/s-corp-social-security.

Primus, Wendell, Tara Watson, and Jack A. Smalligan. 2025. "Fixing Social Security: Blueprint for a Bipartisan Solution." Brookings. https://www.brookings.edu/wp-content/uploads/2026/02/20240211_CHP_Primus_FixingSS_Final.pdf.

Program for Public Consultation. 2024. "In Swing States Majorities of Republicans and Democrats Agree on Measures to Eliminate Most of the Social Security Shortfall." *The Swing Six*

Issue Surveys. School of Public Policy, University of Maryland. https://publicconsultation.org/swing-six-ss/social-security/.

Rajnes, David, and John A. Turner. 2014. "Social Security and Pension Trends Around the World." Chapter 2 in *Social Security and Pension Reform: International Perspectives*, Marek Szczepański and John A. Turner, eds. Kalamazoo, MI: W.E. Upjohn Institute for Employment Research, pp. 13-38. http://dx.doi.org/10.17848/9780880994705.ch1, https://citeseerx.ist.psu.edu/document?repid=rep1&type=pdf&doi=e5e9497c862520eaac586206832e32cd16b1287c.

Ritz, Ben, and Nate Morris. 2025. "Reform that Rewards Work: A New Vision for Strengthening Social Security's Intergenerational Compact." Progressive Policy Institute. https://www.progressivepolicy.org/reform-that-rewards-work-2025/.

Roberts, Karen. 2024. "Top 9 Reasons to Make 401(k) Catch-Up Contributions." Bankrate. https://www.bankrate.com/retirement/top-reasons-to-make-401k-catch-up-contributions/.

Robeznicks, Andis. 2023. "How Medicare's Budget-Neutrality Rule is Slanted Against Doctors." American Medical Association. https://www.ama-assn.org/practice-management/payment-delivery-models/how-medicare-s-budget-neutrality-rule-slanted-against.

Robinson, Steve. 2023. "History and Future of the Social Security Trust Fund: Part III." The Concord Coalition. https://www.concordcoalition.org/wp-content/uploads/2023/08/History-and-Future-of-the-Social-Security-Trust-Fund_-Part-III.pdf.

Romig, Kathleen. 2023a. "Raising Social Security's Retirement Age Would Cut Benefits for All New Retirees." Center on Budget and Policy Priorities. https://www.cbpp.org/research/social-security/raising-social-securitys-retirement-age-would-cut-benefits-for-all-new.

Romig, Kathleen. 2023b. "What the 2023 Trustees' Report Shows about Social Security." Center on Budget and Policy

Priorities. https://www.cbpp.org/research/social-security/what-the-2023-trustees-report-shows-about-social-security.

Romig, Kathleen. 2025. "Setting the Record Straight on Social Security." Center on Budget and Policy Priorities. https://www.cbpp.org/blog/setting-the-record-straight-on-social-security.

Romig, Kathleen, and Devin O'Connor. 2025. "Reassignment Won't Fix the Largest-Ever Social Security Staffing Cut." Center on Budget and Policy Priorities. https://www.cbpp.org/research/social-security/reassignment-wont-fix-the-largest-ever-social-security-staffing-cut.

Rosanes, Mark. 2024. "What Happens to a Remarried Widow's Social Security Benefits?" *InvestmentNews*. https://www.investmentnews.com/guides/what-happens-to-a-remarried-widows-social-security-benefits/258157.

Royal, James. 2024. "When Do Most Americans Take Social Security?" Bankrate. https://www.bankrate.com/retirement/when-do-most-americans-take-social-security/.

Royal, James. 2025. "Social Security Spousal Benefits: Here's How Much Spouses Can Get." Bankrate. https://www.bankrate.com/retirement/social-security-spousal-benefits/.

Rubin, April. 2023. "Life Expectancy Gap in America Widens Depending on College Education." Axios. https://www.axios.com/2023/10/16/life-expectancy-educated-adults-mortality-rate.

Ruffing, Kathy, and Paul N. Van Der Water. 2011. "Bowles-Simpson Social Security Proposal Not a Good Starting Point for Reforms." Center on Budget and Policy Proposals. https://www.cbpp.org/research/bowles-simpson-social-security-proposal-not-a-good-starting-point-for-reforms.

Rutgers University. 2025. "Student Worker Tax Exemptions." https://finance.rutgers.edu/student-abc/tax-information/student-worker-tax-exemptions.

Sammartino, Frank. 2017. "Taxation of Pass-Through Businesses." Tax Policy Center. Urban Institute & Brookings Institution. https://taxpolicycenter.org/sites/default/files/publication/138171/2001133-taxation-of-pass-through-businesses_1.pdf.

Sanders, Bernard. 2024. "The Right to a Secure Retirement." https://berniesanders.com/issues/expand-social-security/.

Sanders, Linley. 2023. "How Americans Evaluate Social Security, Medicare, and Six Other Entitlement Programs." YouGov. https://today.yougov.com/politics/articles/45187-americans-evaluate-social-security-medicare-poll.

Saxegaard, Elif C. Arbatli, Csaba Feher, Jack J. Ree, Ikuo Saito, and Mauricio Soto. 2016. "Automatic Adjustment Mechanisms in Asian Pension Systems?" (No. 2016/242). International Monetary Fund. https://www.imf.org/en/Publications/WP/Issues/2016/12/31/Automatic-Adjustment-Mechanisms-in-Asian-Pension-Systems-44460.

Schneider, Lisa, Arie Kapteyn, Matthew Greenwald, and Olivia S. Mitchell. 2010. "How Much Do People Know About Social Security?" Financial Literacy Center. https://pensionresearchcouncil.wharton.upenn.edu/wp-content/uploads/2015/11/HowMuchDoPeopleKnow.pdf.

Schulz, Matt. 2025. "2025 Credit Card Debt Statistics." Lendingtree. https://www.lendingtree.com/credit-cards/study/credit-card-debt-statistics/.

Schreur, Elliot, and Benjamin Veghte. 2018. "Social Security and Independent Contractors: Challenges and Opportunities." National Academy of Social Insurance. https://www.nasi.org/research/social-security/social-security-and-independent-contractors-challenges-and-opportunities/.

S Corp. 2025. "The History and Challenges of America's Dominant Business Structure" https://s-corp.org/our%20history/.

Seitz, Amanda, and Hannah Fingerhut. 2023. "Most Oppose Social Security, Medicare Cuts: AP-NORC Poll." https://apnews.com/article/social-security-medicare-cuts-ap-poll-biden-.

Shanton, Karen L., and Jacob R. Strauss. 2025. "Congressional Commissions: Overview and Considerations for Congress." https://www.congress.gov/crs-product/R40076.

Shenkman, Rick. 2005. "When Did Social Security Become the Third Rail of American Politics?" History News Network (HNN). https://www.historynewsnetwork.org/article/when-did-social-security-become-the-third-rail-of-.

Shoven, John B., and Sita Nataraj Slavov. 2014. "Does It Pay to Delay Social Security?" *Journal of Pension Economics & Finance* 13(2): 121-144.

Shu, Suzanne and John W. Payne. 2023. "Social Security and Claiming Intentions: Psychological Ownership, Loss Aversion, and Information Displays." NBER Working Paper No. 31499. https://www.nber.org/system/files/working_papers/w31499/w31499.pdf.

Slavov, Sita. 2023. "Two Decades of Social Security Claiming." Working Paper No. 30843. National Bureau of Economic Research.

Slavov, Sita N., and Alan D. Viard. 2021a. "Letter: Social Security Earnings Test Isn't Really a Tax." American Enterprise Institute. https://www.aei.org/articles/letter-social-security-earnings-test-isnt-really-a-tax/.

Slavov, Sita N., and Alan D. Viard. 2021b. "Misperceptions about the Social Security Earnings Test Need to Be Corrected." American Enterprise Institute. https://www.aei.org/op-eds/misperceptions-about-the-social-security-earnings-test-need-to-be-corrected/.

Smith, Karen E., Richard W. Johnson, and Melissa M. Favreault. 2020. "Five Democratic Approaches to Social Security Reform: Estimated Impact of Plans from the 2020 Presidential

Campaign." Research Report. Urban Institute. https://www.urban.org/sites/default/files/publication/103050/five-democratic-approaches-to-social-security-reform-estimated-impact-of-plans-from-the-2020-presidential-campaign_0.pdf.

Social Security Administration. 2013a. "Benefits for Spouses." https://www.ssa.gov/oacts/quickcalc/spouse.html.

Social Security Administration. 2013b. "Marriage Trends and the Effects on Women's Benefits."

Social Security Administration. 2018a. "Social Security Programs Throughout the World: Europe, 2018." https://www.ssa.gov/policy/docs/progdesc/ssptw/2018-2019/europe/germany.pdf.

Social Security Administration. 2018b. "Social Security When You Are Self-Employed." https://blog.ssa.gov/social-security-when-you-are-self-employed/.

Social Security Administration. 2019. "Social Security Programs Throughout the World: The Americas, 2019." https://www.ssa.gov/policy/docs/progdesc/ssptw/2018-2019/americas/guide.html.

Social Security Administration. 2020. "Japan Approves Social Security Reform Package." *International Update,* June. https://www.ssa.gov/policy/docs/progdesc/intl_update/2020-06/index.html.

Social Security Administration. 2021a. "5 Things Every Woman Should Know about Social Security." Publication No. 05-10044. https://www.ssa.gov/pubs/EN-05-10044.pdf.

Social Security Administration. 2021b. "Special Minimum Benefit." https://www.ssa.gov/policy/docs/program-explainers/special-minimum.html.

Social Security Administration. 2022a. "Can Noncitizens Receive Social Security Benefits or Supplemental Security (SSI)?" https://www.ssa.gov/faqs/en/questions/KA-02447.html.

Works Cited

Social Security Administration. 2022b. "If You're a Farm Worker." https://www.ssa.gov/pubs/EN-05-10074.pdf.

Social Security Administration. 2022c. "Survivors Benefits for Same-Sex Spouses and Partners." https://www.ssa.gov/pubs/EN-17-019.pdf.

Social Security Administration. 2022d. "What Is Enumeration at Birth and How Does It Work?" https://www.ssa.gov/faqs/en/questions/KA-10041.html#:~:text=The%20Enumeration%20at%20Birth%20(EAB,for%20Children%20for%20more%20information.

Social Security Administration. 2022e. "Will Unemployment Benefits Affect My Social Security Benefits?" https://www.ssa.gov/faqs/en/questions/KA-01933.html.

Social Security Administration. 2023a. "American Indians and Alaska Natives." https://www.ssa.gov/people/aian/.

Social Security Administration. 2023b. "Retirement Benefits." https://www.ssa.gov/pubs/EN-05-10035.pdf.

Social Security Administration. 2023c. "What Prisoners Need to Know." Publication Number 05-10133. https://www.ssa.gov/pubs/EN-05-10133.pdf.

Social Security Administration. 2023d. "Will Social Security Be There for Me?" https://www.ssa.gov/pubs/marketing/fact-sheets/will-social-security-be-there-for-me.pdf.

Social Security Administration. 2024a. "Automatic Determinations in Recent Years." https://www.ssa.gov/oact/cola/autoAdj.html.

Social Security Administration. 2024b. "Beneficiary Projection: Women & Dual Entitlement, 2025-2095." https://www.ssa.gov/policy/docs/projections/populations/women-dual-2025.html.

Social Security Administration. 2024c. "Contribution and Benefit Base." https://www.ssa.gov/oact/cola/cbb.html.

Social Security Administration. 2024d. "Cost-of-Living Adjustment (COLA) Information for 2024." https://www.ssa.gov/cola/.

Social Security Administration. 2024e. "Detailed Single Year Tables." Long Range Solvency Projections. https://www.ssa.gov/oact/solvency/provisions/tables/table_run147.html.

Social Security Administration. 2024f. "Donations to the Social Security Trust Funds." https://www.ssa.gov/agency/donations.html.

Social Security Administration. 2024g. "Exempt Amounts Under the Earnings Test." https://www.ssa.gov/oact/cola/rtea.html.

Social Security Administration. 2024i. "Formula for Maximum Family Benefit." https://www-origin.ssa.gov/oact/COLA/familymax.html.

Social Security Administration. 2024i. "How Work Affects Your Benefits." https://www.ssa.gov/pubs/EN-05-10069.pdf.

Social Security Administration. 2024j. "How You Earn Credits." https://www.ssa.gov/pubs/EN-05-10072.pdf.

Social Security Administration. 2024k. "If You Are Self-Employed." https://www.ssa.gov/pubs/EN-05-10022.pdf.

Social Security Administration. 2024l. "Latest Cost-of-Living Adjustment." https://www.ssa.gov/oact/cola/latestCOLA.html.

Social Security Administration. 2024m. "Life Expectancy for Social Security." Social Security History. https://www.ssa.gov/history/lifeexpect.html.

Social Security Administration. 2024n. "Military Service and Social Security." https://www.ssa.gov/pubs/EN-05-10017.pdf.

Social Security Administration. 2024o. "Office of the Chief Actuary's Estimates of Individual Changes Modifying Social Security." https://www.ssa.gov/OACT/solvency/provisions/index.html.

Works Cited

Social Security Administration. 2024p. "Office of the Chief Actuary's Estimates of Proposals to Change the Social Security Program or the SSI Program." https://www.ssa.gov/oact/solvency/index.html.

Social Security Administration. 2024q. "Primary Insurance Amount." https://www.ssa.gov/oact/COLA/piaformula.html.

Social Security Administration. 2024r. "PROPOSAL: Eliminate the Retirement Earnings Test." Office of Research, Evaluation, and Statistics. Policy Option Projections. https://www.ssa.gov/policy/docs/projections/policy-options/eliminate-ret.pdf.

Social Security Administration. 2024s. "PROPOSAL: Reduce Spousal Benefits from 50% to 33% of the Worker's Primary Insurance Amount." Office of Research, Evaluation, and Statistics. Policy Option Projections. https://www.ssa.gov/policy/docs/projections/policy-options/reduce-spousal-benefits.pdf.

Social Security Administration. 2024t. "Proposals Affecting Trust Fund Solvency." Actuarial Publications. https://www.ssa.gov/oact/solvency/.

Social Security Administration. 2024u. "Provisions Affecting Retirement Age." Long-Range Solvency Provisions. Office of the Chief Actuary. https://www.ssa.gov/oact/solvency/provisions/retireage.html.

Social Security Administration. 2024v. "Receiving Benefits While Working." Benefits Planner. https://www.ssa.gov/benefits/retirement/planner/whileworking.html.

Social Security Administration. 2024w. "Repay Overpaid Social Security Benefits." https://www.ssa.gov/manage-benefits/repay-overpaid-benefits.

Social Security Administration. 2024x. "Retirement Earnings Test Calculator." https://www.ssa.gov/oact/cola/RTeffect.html.

Social Security Administration. 2024y. "Social Security Benefit Amounts." https://www.ssa.gov/oact/cola/Benefits.html.

Social Security Administration. 2024z. "Social Security Credits." https://www.ssa.gov/benefits/retirement/planner/credits.html.

Social Security Administration. 2024aa. "Summary Measures and Graphs." Long Range Solvency Projections. Office of the Chief Actuary. https://www.ssa.gov/oact/solvency/provisions/charts/chart_run147.html.

Social Security Administration. 2024bb. "Summary of Provisions That Would Change the Social Security Program." Office of the Chief Actuary. https://www.ssa.gov/oact/solvency/provisions/summary.pdf.

Social Security Administration. 2024cc. "Survivors Benefits." Publication Number 05-10084. https://www.ssa.gov/pubs/EN-05-10084.pdf.

Social Security Administration. 2024dd. "Taxable Maximum Earners." Population Profiles. https://www.ssa.gov/policy/docs/population-profiles/tax-max-earners.html.

Social Security Administration. 2024ee. "Understanding Supplemental Security Income SSI Income—2024 Edition." https://www.ssa.gov/ssi/text-income-ussi.htm.

Social Security Administration. 2024ff. "What Is the Maximum Social Security Retirement Benefit Payable?" https://faq.ssa.gov/en-US/Topic/article/KA-01897.

Social Security Administration. 2024gg. "What You Need to Know When You Get Retirement or Survivors Benefits." https://www.ssa.gov/pubs/EN-05-10077.pdf.

Social Security Administration. 2024hh. "Workers with Maximum-Taxable Earnings." https://www.ssa.gov/oact/cola/examplemax.html.

Social Security Administration. 2025a. "Benefit Calculators." https://www.ssa.gov/benefits/calculators/.

Social Security Administration. 2025b. "Create Your Personal *my* Social Security Account Today." https://www.ssa.gov/myaccount/?gad_sourc e=1&gclid=Cj0KCQiA4rK8BhD7ARIsAFe5LXLjyqihj-G324Ww-nT q4o9x4TMYhHfYNyfihTpVqro4qSHhxnQsZy0aAncTEALw_wcB.

Social Security Administration.2025c. "Definition: Deductions." https://www.ssa.gov/help/myCYB_deductions.html.

Social Security Administration. 2025d. "Effective Interest Rates." https://www.ssa.gov/oact/progdata/effectiveRates.html.

Social Security Administration. 2025e. "Eligibility for Social Security in Retirement." https://www.ssa.gov/retirement/eligibility.

Social Security Administration. 2025f. "Form SSA-2 | Information You Need to Apply for Spouse's or Divorced Spouse's Benefits." https://www.ssa.gov/forms/ssa-2.html.

Social Security Administration. 2025g. "Form SSA-10: Information You Need to Apply for Widow's, Widower's, or Surviving Divorced Spouse's Benefits." https://www.ssa.gov/forms/ssa-10.html.

Social Security Administration. 2025h. "Online Social Security Handbook." https://www.ssa.gov/ OP_Home/handbook/handbook.html.

Social Security Administration. 2025i. "Social Security Administrative Expenses." https://www.ssa.gov/oact/STATS/admin.html.

Social Security Administration. 2025j. "Social Security Applauds Passage of Legislation Providing Historic Tax Relief for Seniors." https://blog.ssa.gov/social-security-applauds-passage-of-legislation-providing-historic-tax-relief-for-seniors/.

Social Security Administration. 2025k. "Social Security Credits." https://www.ssa.gov/benefits/retirement/planner/credits.html.

Social Security Administration. 2025l. "Social Security Is Improving Our National 800 Number and Reducing Call Wait Times." https://blog.ssa.gov/social-security-is-improving-our-national-800-number-and-reducing-call-wait-times/?utm_medium=email&utm_source=govdelivery.

Social Security Administration. 202ml. "Social Security's Statement on President Trump's Memorandum, "Preventing Illegal Aliens from Obtaining Social Security Act Benefits." https://blog.ssa.gov/social-security-statement-on-president-trumps-memorandum-preventing-illegal-aliens-from-obtaining-social-security-act-benefits/?utm_medium=email&utm_source=govdelivery.

Social Security Administration. 2025n. "Special Issue Securities." https://www.ssa.gov/oact/progdata/specialissues.html.

Social Security Administration. 2025o. "SSI Federal Payment Amounts for 2025." https://www.ssa.gov/oact/cola/SSI.html.

Social Security Administration. 2025p. "Taxation of Social Security Benefits." https://www.ssa.gov/oact/progdata/taxbenefits.html.

Social Security Administration. 2025q. "What You Could Get from Survivor Benefits." https://www.ssa.gov/survivor/amount.

Social Security Administration. 2025r. "Who Can Get Survivor Benefits." https://www.ssa.gov/survivor/eligibility.

Social Security Administration, Office of the Chief Actuary. 2025a. "Benefit Reduction for Early Retirement." https://www.ssa.gov/oact/quickcalc/earlyretire.html.

Social Security Administration, Office of the Chief Actuary. 2025b. "Benefits for Spouses." https://www.ssa.gov/oact/quickcalc/spouse.html.

Social Security Administration, Office of the Chief Actuary. 2025c. "Early or Late Retirement." https://www.ssa.gov/oact/quickcalc/early_late.html.

Social Security Administration, Office of the Chief Actuary. 2025d. "Estimates of the Financial Effects on Social Security of Potential Legislation to Improve the Solvency of the Social Security Trust Funds, requested by Representative Steny Hoyer and Wendell Primus." Office of the Chief Actuary's Estimates of Proposals to Change the Social Security Program or the SSI Program. https://www.ssa.gov/oact/solvency/HoyerPrimus_20250103.pdf.

Social Security Administration, Office of the Inspector General. 2024. "Audit Report: The Social Security Administration's Enforcement of the Earnings Test." https://oig.ssa.gov/assets/uploads/a-08-21-51049.pdf.

Social Security Administration, Office of the Inspector General. 2025. "Overpayments Assessed in Fiscal Years 2020 Through 2023." https://oig.ssa.gov/assets/uploads/062405.pdf.

Social Security Administration, Press Office. 2025a. "Social Security Announces Workforce and Organization Plans." https://www.ssa.gov/news/press/releases/2025/#2025-02-28.

Social Security Administration, Press Office. 2025b. "Social Security to Reinstate Overpayment Recovery Rate." https://www.ssa.gov/news/press/releases/2025/?utm_medium=email&utm_source=govdelivery#2025-03-07-a.

Social Security Administration, Research, Statistics, & Policy Analysis. 2024. "Government Pension Offset." https://www.ssa.gov/policy/docs/program-explainers/government-pension-offset.html.

Social Security Advisory Board. 2023. "Retirement Trajectories and Social Security's Retirement Earnings Test." Research Portfolio on Retirement. https://s3-us-gov-west-1.amazonaws.com/cg-778536a2-e58c-44f1-9173-29749804ec54/uploads/2023/12/Retirement-Trajectories-and-the-Retirement-Earnings-Test.pdf.

Social Security and Medicare Boards of Trustees. 2024. "Status of the Social Security and Medicare Programs: A Summary of the 2024 Annual Reports." https://www.ssa.gov/oact/trsum/.

Spector, Nicole. 2025. "41 States That Won't Tax Social Security Benefits in 2025." MSN. https://www.msn.com/en-us/money/retirement/41-states-that-won-t-tax-social-security-benefits-in-2025/arAA1mNYKT?ocid=entnewsntp&pc=LCTS&cvid=09d40a03f5874e08c0f54301e668d594&ei=37.

Sprick, Emerson. 2024a. "The Retirement Plan Access Gap: Why It Exists, What States Are Doing About It, and Principles for Decisive Federal Action." Bipartisan Policy Center. https://bipartisanpolicy.org/report/retirement-plan-access-gap/.

Sprick, Emerson. 2024b. "Social Security Claiming Age: Importance, Claiming Behavior, and Trends." Bipartisan Policy Center. https://bipartisanpolicy.org/blog/social-security-claiming-age-importance-claiming-behavior-and-trends/.

Springstead, Glenn R., Kevin Whitman, and Dave Shoffner. 2014. "Proposed Revisions to the Special Minimum Benefit for Low Lifetime Earners." Office of Retirement and Disability Policy. https://www.ssa.gov/policy/docs/policybriefs/pb2014-01.html.

Staff Reports. 2024. "Grieving Husband Asks About His Survivor Benefits." *Brown County Democrat*. https://bcdemocrat.com/2024/07/02/grieving-husband-asks-about-his-survivor-benefits/.

Steuerle, C. Eugene. 2015. "Recent Social Security Reform Doesn't Fix Unfair Spousal Benefits." Urban Institute. https://www.urban.org/urban-wire/recent-social-security-reform-doesnt-fix-unfair-spousal-benefits.

Steuerle, C. Eugene. 2025. "Fixing the Programs of a Broken Government." *The Government We Deserve*.

https://governmentwedeserve.substack.com/p/fixing-the-programs-of-a-broken-government.

Steuerle, C. Eugene, and Jon M. Bakija. 1994. *Retooling Social Security for the 21st Century*. The Urban Institute Press. https://citeseerx.ist.psu.edu/document?repid=rep1&type=pdf&doi=9c2be9106a0de77c3acd7155e1a8853f72c4ef1a.

Steuerle, Eugene, and Glenn Kramon. 2024. "Younger Americans Can't Keep Funding Boomers and Beyond." *The New York Times*. September 1. https://www.nytimes.com/2024/09/01/opinion/boomers-youth-social-security-medicare.html.

Stevenson, Bryan. 2014. *Just Mercy: A Story of Justice and Redemption*. Random House.

Sun, Wei, Teresa Ghilarducci, Michael Papadopoulos, and Anthony Webb. 2019. "The Impact of a Social Security Proposal for 'Catch-Up' Contributions." Schwartz Center for Economic Policy Analysis and Department of Economics, The New School for Social Research, Working Paper Series 2019-3. https://www.economicpolicyresearch.org/images/docs/research/retirement_security/Catch-up_for_couples_2019_WP_final.pdf.

Tamborini, Christopher R., and Kevin Whitman. 2007. "Women, Marriage, and Social Security Benefits Revisited." Office of Retirement and Disability Policy. Social Security Administration. https://www.ssa.gov/policy/docs/ssb/v67n4/v67n4p1.html.

Taylor, Kelley R. 2025. "Social Security Email About 'Big, Beautiful Bill' Tax Changes Sparks Confusion." *Kiplinger*. https://www.kiplinger.com/taxes/social-security-email-on-big-beautiful-bill-tax-changes-sparks-confusion?utm_term.

Thaler, Richard H., and Cass R. Sunstein. 2009. *Nudge: Improving Decisions About Health, Wealth, and Happiness*. Penguin Random House.

Thompson, Lawrence H., and Adam Carasso. 2002. "Social Security and the Treatment of Families: How Does the United States Compare with Other Developed Countries?" In Melissa M. Favreault, Frank J. Sammartino, and C. Eugene Steuerle (eds.), *Social Security and the Family: Addressing Unmet Needs in an Underfunded System.* The Urban Institute Press.

Thorpe, Robert. 2025. "Social Security Taxes to Change Under New Bill: Here's Who's Impacted." *Newsweek.* https://www.newsweek.com/social-security-taxes-change-under-new-bill-impacting-millions-retirees-2027449.

Thrift Savings Plan. 2024a. "Expenses and Fees." https://www.tsp.gov/tsp-basics/expenses-and-fees/.

Thrift Savings Plan. 2024b "G Fund." https://www.tsp.gov/funds-individual/g-fund/?tab=fees.

Totenberg, Nina, and Anunli Ononye. 2025. "Supreme Court Grants DOGE Access to Confidential Social Security Records." NPR. https://www.npr.org/2025/06/06/nx-s1-5422283/supreme-court-doge-social-security-records.

Toth, Albert. 2024. "What is the Triple Lock Plus – and What Could It Mean for Pensions?" *The Independent.* https://www.independent.co.uk/news/uk/home-news/triple-lock-plus-state-pension-tax-explained-b2556986.html.

TreasuryDirect. 2025. "Treasury Bonds." https://treasurydirect.gov/marketable-securities/treasury-bonds/.

Tucker, Jasmine V., Virginia P. Reno, and Thomas N. Bethell. 2013. "Strengthening Social Security: What Do Americans Want?" National Academy of Social Insurance. https://www.nasi.org/wp-content/uploads/2013/03/What_Do_Americans_Want.pdf.

TurboTax. 2024a. "At What Income Does a Minor Have to File an Income Tax Return?" https://turbotax.intuit.

com/tax-tips/family/at-what-income-does-a-minor-have-to-file-an-income-tax-return/L6HOdGp6i.

TurboTax. 2024b. "How an S-Corp Can Reduce Your Self-Employment Taxes." https://turbotax.intuit.com/tax-tips/small-business-taxes/how-an-s-corp-can-reduce-your-self-employment-taxes/L4abUcaRn.

Turner, John A. 1984. "Population Age Structure and the Size of Social Security." *Southern Economic Journal* 50(4): 1131-1146. https://www.jstor.org/stable/1058439.

Turner, John A. 2006a. "12 Myths About Individual Accounts for Social Security Reform." Upjohn Institute. https://research.upjohn.org/cgi/viewcontent.cgi?article=1113&context=empl_research.

Turner, John A. 2006b. *Individual Accounts for Social Security Reform: International Perspectives on the U.S. Debate*, Kalamazoo, MI: W.E. Upjohn Institute for Employment Research.

Turner, John A. 2010. "Political Risk with Automatic Adjustment Mechanisms for Social Security: Is 'Automatic' Really Automatic?" The International Social Security Association (ISSA). 6th International Policy and Research Conference on Social Security. https://www.issa.int/sites/default/files/external-references/files/2Turner-paper-1--57408.pdf.

Turner, John A. 2013. "Providing Longevity Insurance Annuities: A Comparison of the Private Sector Versus Social Security." *The Journal of Retirement* 1(2): 125-131. https://www.pm-research.com/content/iijretire/1/2/125.abstract?implicit-login=true.

Turner, John A. 2016a. "Longevity Insurance Benefits for Social Security." Pension Section News, Society of Actuaries, May. Issue 89: 20-23. https://www.soa.org/globalassets/assets/library/newsletters/pension-section-news/2016/may/psn-2016-05-iss89-turner.pdf.

Turner, John A. 2016b. *Sustaining Social Security in an Era of Population Aging.* WE Upjohn Institute. https://research.upjohn.org/cgi/viewcontent.cgi?article=1257&context=up_press.

Turner, John A. 2017. "Social Security Policy Procrastination: A Behavioral Economics Response." *Journal of Retirement* 5(1): 32-47. http://www.actuaries.org/CANCUN2017/Papers/3.%20Turner_Paper.pdf.

Turner, John A. 2019. "Top-Up Contributions to Social Security." *The Journal of Retirement* 7(2): 42-50. https://jor.pm-research.com/node/2186.

Turner, John A. 2022. "Pension Policies." Chapter 26 in *International Handbook of Population Policies,* edited by John May. Springer, 2022, pp. 571-594. https://www.aacademica.org/jorge.paz/146.pdf#page=581.

Turner, John A. 2024. "Proactively Addressing the Missing Pensioner Problem." *New York University Journal of Employee Benefits and Executive Compensation.*

Turner, John A. 2025. "Pension Tax Breaks for the Wealthy: Assessing ERISA at 50." *Benefits Quarterly* 41(2): 30-38. https://www.iscebs.org/home/education---resources/benefits-quarterly.

Turner, John A., Richard Fullmer, and Jonathan Barry Forman. 2021. "Tontines and Collective Annuities: Lessons from an International Survey." *New York University Review of Employee Benefits and Executive Compensation*, 2021, Chapter 4.

Turner, John A., and David D. McCarthy. 2013. "Longevity Insurance Annuities in 401(k) Plans and IRAs." *Benefits Quarterly* 29(1): 58-62. https://www.researchgate.net/profile/John-Turner-26/publication/353444821_longevity_insurance_annuities_in_401k_plans_and_iras/links/60fd489d169a1a0103b640c3/longevity-insurance-annuities-in-401k-plans-and-iras.pdf.

Turner, John A., David D. McCarthy, and Norman P. Stein. 2014. "Defined Contribution Plans with Very Large Individual Account Balances." *The Journal of Retirement* 1(3). https://researchdiscovery.drexel.edu/esploro/outputs/journalArticle/Defined-Contribution-Plans-with-Very-Large/991021867173804721.

Turner, John A., David D. McCarthy, and Norman P. Stein. 2016. "Pension Tax Subsidies for the Super Rich." *Benefits Quarterly* 32(3). https://openurl.ebsco.com/EPDB.

Turner, John A., David D. McCarthy, and Norman P. Stein. 2025. "Pension Tax Breaks for the Wealthy Assessing ERISA at 50." *Benefits Quarterly* 41(2): 30-38.

Turner, John A., and Dana M. Muir. 2014. "Financial Literacy, Education and Advice." In *Social Security and Pension Reform: International Perspectives*, edited by Marek Szczepański and John A. Turner. Kalamazoo, Michigan; W.E. Upjohn Institute, pp. 299-324.

Turner, John A., and David Rajnes. 2021. "Workers' Expectations about Their Future Social Security Benefits: How Realistic Are They?" *Social Security Bulletin* 81(1). https://www.ssa.gov/policy/docs/ssb/v81n4/v81n4p1.html.

Turner, John A., Gerard Hughes, Agnieszka Chłoń-Domińczak, and David M. Rajnes. 2016. "Improving Pension Income and Reducing Poverty at Advanced Older Ages: Ireland and Poland as Models."

Turner, John A., Gerard Hughes, Agnieszka Chłoń-Domińczak, and David M. Rajnes. 2017. "Longevity Insurance Annuities: Potential Role in Social Insurance." *Journal of Insurance, Financial Markets, & Consumer Protection* 2(3): 3-21. https://ru.rf.gov.pl/wp-content/uploads/2017/10/zeszt25_net.pdf.

Turner, John A., and Jonathan Wood. 2023. "Using Pension Coverage to Encourage Job Tenure: Pensions for Volunteer Firefighters." *Benefits Quarterly* 39(1): 52-59.

Turner, John A., Saisai Zhang, Gerard Hughes, and David M. Rajnes. 2019. "Irrational Expectations, Future Social Security Benefits, and Life Cycle Planning." *Journal of Retirement* 6(3): 60-68.

UK Government. 2024a. "Over 80 Pension: Overview." https://www.gov.uk/over-80-pension.

UK Government. 2024b. "Rates and Thresholds for Employers 2023 to 2024." https://www.gov.uk/guidance/rates-and-thresholds-for-employers-2023-to-2024#tax-thresholds-rates-and-codes.

UK Government. 2025a. "Delay (Defer) Your State Pension." https://www.gov.uk/deferring-state-pension/what-you-get.

UK Government. 2025b. "National Insurance and Tax After State Pension Age." https://www.gov.uk/tax-national-insurance-after-state-pension-age/stopping-paying-national-insurance.

UK Government. 2025c. "Voluntary National Insurance." https://www.gov.uk/voluntary-national-insurance-contributions.

UK Parliament. 2024. "Direct Taxes: Rates and Allowances 2023/24." https://commonslibrary.parliament.uk/research-briefings/cbp-9754/.

Umpierrez, Amanda. 2024. "Small Businesses Still Avoid Offering Retirement Plans." 401k Specialist. https://401kspecialistmag.com/small-businesses-still-avoid-offering-retirement-plans/.

UnitedHealthcare. 2025. "How to Enroll in Medicare." https://www.uhc.com/medicare/medicare-education/how-to-enroll-in-medicare.html#:~:text=You'll%20be%20automatically%20enrolled%20in%20Medicare%20Part,because%20of%20a%20disability%20or%20medical%20condition.

Universities Academic Pension Plan (UAPP). 2024. "Year's Maximum Pensionable Earnings Under CPP for 2024 Increases to $68,500 from $66,600 in 2023." https://uapp.

ca/years-maximum-pensionable-earnings-under-cpp-for-2024-increases-to-68500-from-66600-in-2023/#.

Urban, Carly, and J. Michael Collins. 2023. "Under-Claiming of Survivors' Benefits Among Non-Elderly Adults." Retirement and Disability Research Center, University of Wisconsin-Madison. https://rdrc.wisc.edu/files/working-papers/WI23-Q3_Report_Urban-Collins_9.24.pdf.

Urban Institute. 2010. "The Future of Social Security: Solvency, Work, Adequacy, and Equity." https://www.urban.org/sites/default/files/publication/29336/412253-The-Future-of-Social-Security-Solvency-Work-Adequacy-and-Equity.PDF.

USA.gov. 2023. "Report the Death of a Social Security or Medicare Beneficiary." https://www.usa.gov/social-security-report-a-death.

US Bureau of Labor Statistics. 2023a. "73 Percent of Civilian Workers Had Access to Retirement Benefits in 2023." https://www.bls.gov/opub/ted/2023/73-percent-of-civilian-workers-had-access-to-retirement-benefits-in-2023.htm.

US Bureau of Labor Statistics. 2023b. "Celebrating National Family Caregivers Month with BLS Data." https://www.bls.gov/blog/2023/celebrating-national-family-caregivers-month-with-bls-data.htm.

US Bureau of Labor Statistics. 2023c. "Contingent and Alternative Employment Arrangements- July 2023." https://www.bls.gov/news.release/pdf/conemp.pdf.

US Bureau of Labor Statistics. 2023d. "Women in the Labor Force: A Data Book." https://www.bls.gov/opub/reports/womens-databook/2022/.

US Bureau of Labor Statistics. 2024a. "Employee Tenure in 2014." https://www.bls.gov/news.release/pdf/tenure.pdf.

US Bureau of Labor Statistics. 2024b. "Employer Costs for Employee Compensation Summary." https://www.bls.gov/news.release/ecec.nr0.htm#:~:text=Total%20employer%20compensation%20costs%20for%20private%20industry,and%20accounted%20for%20the%20remaining%2029.6%20percent.

US Bureau of Labor Statistics. 2024c. "R-CPI-E Homepage." https://www.bls.gov/cpi/research-series/r-cpi-e-home.htm.

US Bureau of Labor Statistics. 2025. "AI Impacts in BLS Employment Projections." https://www.bls.gov/opub/ted/2025/ai-impacts-in-bls-employment-projections.htm.

US Census Bureau. 2022. "Measuring America: How the U.S. Census Bureau Measures Poverty." Library Census Infographics & Visualizations.

US Census Bureau. 2024. "Income in the United States: 2023." https://www.census.gov/library/publications/2024/demo/p60-282.html.

US Centers for Disease Control and Prevention. 2024. "TB Incidence and Mortality." https://www.cdc.gov/tb-surveillance-report-2023/tables/table-1.html.

US Department of Labor. 2025. "Misclassification of Employees as Independent Contractors Under the Fair Labor Standards Act." Wage and Hours Division. https://www.dol.gov/agencies/whd/flsa/misclassification#:~:text=Misclassification%20occurs%20when%20an%20employer%20treats%20a,which%20they%20are%20entitled%20under%20the%20law.

US General Services Administration. 2024. "Technology Modernization Fund Announces Investments Upgrading Customer Experiences in Housing and Social Security Services." https://www.gsa.gov/about-us/newsroom/news-releases/technology-modernization-fund-announces-investments-upgrading-customer-experienc-10222024.

Van Bramer, James. 2025. "Social Security Trust Funds Now on Pace to Deplete by 2034." PlanSponsor. https://www.plansponsor.com/social-security-trust-funds-now-on-pace-to-deplete-by-2034/?utm_source=newsletter&utm_medium=email&utm_campaign=Newsdash&oly_enc_id=1138G9741701F5V.

Vernon, Steve. 2024. "What Would Raising Social Security's Retirement Age Mean for Retirees?" *Forbes*. https://www.forbes.com/sites/stevevernon/2024/03/08/raising-retirement-age/.

Waldron, Hilary. 2012. "The Sensitivity of Proposed Social Security Benefit Formula Changes to Lifetime Earnings Definitions." *Social Security Bulletin* 72(2). https://www.ssa.gov/policy/docs/ssb/v72n2/v72n2p1.pdf.

Walker, Elisa. 2025. "Social Security at 90: Policy Options for Strengthening the Program's Finances and Avoiding Automatic Benefit Cuts." National Academy of Social Insurance." https://www.nasi.org/wp-content/uploads/2025/06/Social-Security-at-90-Policy-Options-for-Strengthening-the-Programs-Finances-and-Avoiding-Automatic-Benefit-Cuts.pdf.

Walker, Elisa A., Virginia P. Reno, and Thomas N. Bethell. 2014. "Americans Make Hard Choices on Social Security: A Survey with Trade-Off Analysis." National Academy of Social Insurance. https://democrats-waysandmeans.house.gov/sites/evo-subsites/democrats-waysandmeans.house.gov/files/documents/Rep.%20Larson%20-%20National%20Academicy%20on%20Social%20Insurance%20Survey.pdf.

Warshawsky, Mark J. 2016. "Modernizing Social Security." *National Affairs* 29: 83-96.

Warshawsky, Mark J. 2021. "It Is Time to Update the Adjustment Factors for Age in Social Security Retirement Benefits." AEI Economics Working Paper, No. 2021-12. https://www.econstor.eu/bitstream/10419/280642/1/aei-ewp2021-12.pdf.

Warshawsky, Mark J. 2022. "Reforming Social Security." American Enterprise Institute. https://www.aei.org/articles/reforming-social-security/.

Warshawsky, Mark J. 2024. "Social Security's Financial Reality Is Worse Than Reported." American Enterprise Institute. https://www.aei.org/economics/social-securitys-financial-reality-is-worse-than-reported/.

Weaver, R. Kent. 2001. "Whether Social Security Funds Should Be Invested Collectively or Through a System of Individual Accounts." Brookings Institution. https://www.brookings.edu/articles/whether-social-security-funds-should-be-invested-collectively-or-through-a-system-of-individual-accounts/.

West, Darrell M. 2025. "Why Social Security Disinformation is Dangerous." Brookings, https://www.brookings.edu/articles/why-social-security-disinformation-is-dangerous/.

Index

A
actuarial factors, 157, 159, 161–63, 165, 229
age discrimination, 113
America Association of Retired Persons (AARP), 42–43, 94, 123, 167, 179
American Enterprise Institute, 180
American Medical Association, 68
annuities, 167, 170
artificial intelligence, 29
Australia, 178
automatic adjustment mechanisms (AAMs), 53–57, 217
average indexed monthly earnings (AIME), 114–116, 119, 183, 224

B
baby boom generation, 10, 25, 44
Bain Capital, 205
behavioral economics, 50
Belgium, 71, 103, 118
benefit reductions, 15, 86–89, 164
Biden, President Joseph, 67
Big Beautiful Bill Act, 15, 67

Bipartisan Policy Center, 86–87, 174
birth rates, 10, 50, 56
Boston College, 179
Bowles-Simpson National Commission, 44
budget neutrality, 68
budget reconciliation procedures, 64
Byrd Rule, 64

C
cafeteria plans, 76–77, 220
Canada, 56, 63, 75, 80, 90, 103, 110, 182, 202
Canada Pension Plan (CPP), 56, 90, 202
caregivers, 36–37, 146–147
Cassidy, Senator Bill, 110, 202
catch-up contributions, 167–68, 171
Center on Budget and Policy Priorities, 42, 61, 108
Chicago Police Department, 138
children, 22, 132–133, 226
China, 133
civil unions, 127, 183
clawbacks, 85, 89–95, 221, 278
cohabiting couples, 120, 127
Cole, Representative Tom, 65
college graduates, 58

compensatory benefits, 86, 140
Congressional Budget Act, 64, 67, 218
Congressional Budget Office, 75, 100
Congressional Research Service, 48
consumers, 46–47
contract workers, 78–81, 220
contribution years, 70–71, 218
cost-of-living adjustment (COLA), 46–47, 57, 96, 217
Covid-19 pandemic, 26, 62, 171
Coy, Peter, 61
credit card debt, 199
cybersecurity, 133–135, 200

D

defined contribution plans, 12, 78, 188, 200, 205
demographics, 9–12, 30, 49, 55
    population aging, 11, 33–34, 48, 215, 235–237, 239
Department of Government Efficiency (DOGE), 145
disabilities, 122, 132, 193
disability benefits, 127
disability insurance, 23, 62, 179, 194
Disability Insurance Trust Fund, 173
divorce, 121–122, 165, 224
    rates of, 12, 117

E

earnings credits, 147, 170–171
earnings test, 28, 85–94, 221
eligibility age, 121, 187
    for spousal and survivors' benefits, 119–122, 224
    Supplemental Security Income, 194, 232
emergency medical technicians (EMTs), 147
Employee Benefits Security Administration (EBSA), 200
equity, intergenerational, 25, 30, 34–35
ERISA pension law, 19, 36
escheatment laws, 198
European countries, 63, 182

F

Fair Labor Standards Act, 79
farmers, 81, 200
federal government employees, 212
Federal Reserve, 206, 208
financial advisors, 98–99, 123
financial literacy, 20, 22, 29, 31, 50, 85, 107
firefighters, 49, 147–148, 228, 286
flexible spending accounts (FSAs), 75, 77
freedom, 9, 139, 171
freelancers, 70
Friedman, Milton, 21

fringe benefits, 74–77, 219
full-time workweek, 102

G
Germany, 55, 63, 70–71, 92, 103, 178, 188
Government Accountability Office (GAO), 24, 28, 83, 198, 200
government bonds, 47, 202–203
government databases, 146, 227–228
Government Employees Health Association (GEHA), 192
government jobs, 67, 141–142
Government Pension Offset law, 142–143
Grassley, Senator Charles, 13, 135
Great Resignation, 199

H
health insurance, 25, 75–76, 192, 194
  employer-provided, 75
health savings accounts (HSAs), 75, 77
hospitals, 132–133, 226
Hoyer, Representative Steny, 83

I
identity theft, 133, 135, 226
immigration, 10, 50, 62, 69, 143
incarceration, 138, 140–141, 227
  exonerations of wrongfully convicted, 138–140
  family members, 140–141, 227
  wrongful convictions, 137–140, 227
income tax, federal, 13, 73–74, 76, 153, 169, 195, 209, 219
individual retirement accounts (IRAs), 204–206, 208
inequality, 11, 18, 26–27, 30, 109, 213
  and life expectancy, 30, 58
inflation, 25, 46–47, 57, 155, 185, 231
Internal Revenue Service, 80, 220
Ireland, 70, 178, 188, 206
Italy, 55–56, 103

J
Japan, 57, 103, 174, 178

K
Kaine, Senator Tim, 202

L
labor force participation, 55–56, 113, 143
  women, 12, 119
life expectancy, 10, 24, 36, 45, 56, 58, 100–105, 160, 164, 177–178, 187
  averages, 12, 27, 108, 161, 163

cohort measure, 178
and education levels, 26, 58
and wealth inequality, 27, 30, 160, 194
life insurance, 75, 77
local government employees, 48–49
longevity insurance, 185, 187–89, 214, 231

M
Madoff, Bernie, 21
marriage rates, 12, 30, 117, 119
means-tested benefits, 193
means-tested companion program, 145
Medicaid, 191
Medicare, 68, 71, 73, 77, 82–83, 126, 145, 210
   payroll tax, 82
   prohibiting automatic enrollment, 191–192, 232
Medicare Hospital Insurance Trust Fund, 16, 194
mental health, 69
midwives, 133, 226
military, 148, 203, 212, 228
military spouses, 228
millennials, 26, 44, 93
minimum wage, 79, 139
minorities, 26, 86
mobile health care units, 132
mobile service units, 131–132, 226

mortality rates, 50, 178, 186
Musk, Elon, 21

N
National Registry of Exonerations, 138–140
Netherlands, 103
normal retirement age (NRA), 108, 160, 164, 214

O
Obama, President Barack, 44
Old-Age and Survivors Insurance (OASI), 15, 58, 119, 177, 179, 189, 211
old-age dependency ratio, 10, 34, 48–50, 55, 215, 236–240
online benefit calculators, 98
Organization for Economic Cooperation and Development (OECD), 55

P
parents, 12, 22, 33, 38, 72–73, 132–133, 226
   same-sex, 12
payroll tax ceiling, 25, 72, 78, 219–220
payroll taxes, 39, 44, 58, 84, 152, 220
payroll tax rate, 19, 34, 44, 47, 57, 171, 215, 217, 236, 238–240
pensions, federal government, 142

Index

Peter G. Peterson Foundation, 42, 49, 65, 77, 220
physicians, 68, 81–82
police officers, 49, 147–148, 228
Ponzi scheme, 21–22
population growth, 55
poverty, 23, 51, 139, 186
    rates of, 23, 35, 186
primary insurance amount (PIA), 107, 111, 114–16, 124, 214, 223, 225
Primus, Wendell, 83, 299
Prison Journalism Project, 140
prison population, 139
privacy laws, 200
public health, 10

Q

Quebec Pension Plan (QPP), 90

R

racism, 139
ratio of beneficiaries to workers, 10–11, 34, 48, 236–237
Reagan, President Ronald, 66
Republican Study Committee, 101
required minimum distributions (RMDs), 174
retirees, financial situations of, 167, 186, 208
retirement
    delaying benefits, 98, 101, 108, 110–111, 157, 159–163, 165–166, 174, 181, 229
    early, 29, 58, 97, 103, 160, 163, 229
    phased, 92–93
    savings, 20, 167, 213, 220
retirement accounts, unclaimed, 198–200
Ribble, Representative Reid, 188
robo advisors, 29, 99, 222
Romney, Mitt, 204–205
Roosevelt
    Eleanor, 9
    President Franklin, 9, 33, 177, 186
Roth IRAs, 77, 204, 207
    use of by ultrawealthy, 204, 207–208

S

same-sex couples, 127, 225
Sanders, Senator Bernie, 48, 59, 239
savings habits, 18, 31
S corporations, 82–83
Self-Employed Contributions Act (SECA), 82, 84, 220
self-employed workers, 47, 77–81, 151–153, 169–171, 228
self-employment, 71, 84, 169
Senate Finance Committee, 207
shadow prices, 49, 237

Simpson-Bowles Commission, 49, 155
small businesses, 78, 152, 171
Small Business Tax Credit, 152, 228
social media influencers, 81
Social Security
  administrative costs, 90–91, 93, 211–212, 221, 234
  automatic adjustments, 56–57
  calculating benefits, 111, 113
  Caregiver Credit Act, 146
  catch-up contributions, 169, 171
  communications, 111, 214
  complexity of, 22, 29, 87–88, 124
  cost of delaying reforms, 13, 53
  covered earnings, 69–71, 112–113, 115, 154–155, 218, 229
  critics of, 21, 107
  customer service, 98, 129–131, 135, 226
  death benefits, 95
  disinformation, 20–21
  earnings test, 85–88, 90–92, 221
  effectiveness of, 18
  field offices, 130, 132
  financial condition of, 15, 39, 60–61, 69, 197
  fraudulent claims, 133
  full retirement age, 45, 99, 222
  general revenue funding, 212, 234
  historical data, 48, 239
  history of, 12
  information technology of, 133, 135, 226
  low-income beneficiaries, 102, 153, 193, 213, 228–229
  overpayments, 88–89, 92, 94
  policy inertia, 17, 54
  preferences for reform, 50
  privatization of, 31
  records protections, 143, 146, 227–228
  reform process, 53–67, 215, 217
  replacement rate, 115, 184–85, 214, 224, 231, 238
  solvency projections, 16, 23, 59, 61, 63, 67
  spousal and survivors' benefits, 93, 117–118, 120–127, 141–142, 147, 181–183, 225, 227, 231
  as the "third rail," 12–13, 17, 20, 50
  trust fund depletion, 15, 57, 59, 197, 212, 217, 236
  underserved areas, 132, 226
  understaffing of, 130

Index

voluntary contributions, 70, 169, 171
Social Security Act, 9, 20, 37, 60, 70, 144, 146, 177, 188, 227
Social Security Expansion Act, 59
Social Security Fairness Act, 18, 67, 141–143, 154
Spain, 103, 178
student debt, 35
students, 72–73, 219
super contributions, 171–173, 230
Supplemental Poverty Measure (SPM), 186
Supplemental Security Income (SSI), 145, 193–194, 232
Supreme Court, 145
Sweden, 55, 103

T
tax subsidies, 20, 205
    for high-income workers, 31, 205, 214
temporary benefit withholding, 87
Thrift Savings Plan, 203
tontine, 188
Trump, President Donald, 67, 130, 145, 177
tuberculosis, 9

U
Uber, 79–80
UK National Insurance Fund (NIF), 211
unemployment, 169
unemployment insurance, 195, 232
UnitedHealthcare, 191–192
United Kingdom, 90, 103, 118, 168, 187–188, 210–211
Urban Institute, 16, 21
US Bureau of Labor Statistics, 74, 79, 99
US Treasury Department, 152–153

V
Video Service Delivery Centers (VSDCs), 131

W
wages, average, 25, 118
Wall Street, 36
Warren, Senator Elizabeth, 59
widowers, 120–121
women, 36–37, 41, 101, 117, 119–120, 178, 181
workers
    disaster relief, 147
    high-earning, 180, 183–184, 231
    low-wage, 31, 113, 151, 153, 155, 224
workforce development, 133
World Bank, 107
Wyden, Senator Ron, 146, 207